# THE
# RIGHT
# MAN

# THE RIGHT MAN

*The Suprise Presidency of*
*George W. Bush*

## DAVID FRUM

Weidenfeld & Nicolson

LONDON

First published in Great Britain in 2003 by
Weidnfeld & Nicolson

First published in USA in 2003 by Random House, Inc.,
New York, and simultaneously in
Canada by Random House of Canada Limited, Toronto

A CIP catalogue record for this book is available
from the British Library

ISBN 0 297 84732 5

Printed in Great Britain by
Clays Ltd, St Ives plc

Weidenfeld & Nicolson

The Orion Publishing Group Ltd
Orion House
5 Upper Saint Martin's Lane
London
WC2H 9EA

*To Murray Frum—*
*my father and my friend*

# CONTENTS

# THE
# RIGHT
# MAN

# 1

## INTO THE MESS

M ISSED YOU AT Bible study."
Those were, quite literally, the very first words I
heard spoken inside the Bush White House. I had just stepped
through the side door to the West Wing—not the front door you
see on television, the one the marine guard in red-striped pants
opens for congressmen and ambassadors, but the staff door,
which is one floor down and a little to the side. I had been invited into the West Wing to have breakfast in the mess with
Michael Gerson, George W. Bush's chief speechwriter and the
principal author of the inaugural address Bush had delivered
just five days before. The reproach about missing Bible study
was directed to Gerson, not to me. Even so, it made me twitch.
It had been a month since Gerson had asked me to consider
joining the new administration's speechwriting staff. Today we
were to discuss the proposition in earnest over breakfast in the
White House mess. The news that this was a White House

where attendance at Bible study was, if not compulsory, not quite *uncompulsory,* either, was disconcerting to a non-Christian like me.

My appointment that morning had been scheduled for 8:10. Not 8:00, not 8:15, but 8:10—my first introduction to the White House habit of parceling the day into five-minute increments. I already knew enough about the new administration to know that I had better arrive exactly on time.

The mess is a windowless suite of wood-paneled rooms decorated with nautical prints and old brass shipfittings. As Gerson spoke about the job, I found myself fingering the blue-bordered paper menu, trying not to gawk at the room as if I were Gerson's third cousin from Des Moines. I had to keep my attention focused on the business at hand: explaining to him the reasons why I believed I was unsuited to the job he was offering me.

I had no connection to the Bush campaign or the Bush family. I had no experience in government and little of political campaigns. I had never written a speech for anyone other than myself. And I had been only a moderately enthusiastic supporter of George W. Bush. True, I had preferred Bush to John McCain in the primaries; the whole point of the McCain campaign had seemed to be to vex and annoy conservative Republicans like me. But like many even within the Republican party, I was not excited by Bush. No, it was worse than that: I strongly doubted that he was the right man for the job.

Although people who met Bush individually or in small groups claimed to be highly impressed by him, on television he did not look like a man ready to be president. The late-night comedians and Bush's Democratic opponents had an easy explanation for Bush's awkwardness: stupidity. David Letterman offered these top ten headlines from a George W. Bush presidency: PRESIDENT FAILS IN SHOE-TYING BID and AMERICA HELD HOSTAGE: DAY 16 OF PRESIDENT'S HEAD STUCK IN BANISTER. Jay Leno called Bush-Cheney the "Wizard of Oz ticket": "One needs a heart, the other needs a brain." *Saturday Night Live* depicted Bush as a party-hearty frat boy interested only in "huntin' and executin'," who responded to tough debate questions with a good-natured "Pass." *Slate* magazine published a daily digest of Bush's verbal gaffes; former Clinton aide Paul Begala used one of those gaffes for the title of his anti-Bush book: *"Is Our Children Learning?"*

Bush cheerfully replied that his critics "misunderestimated" him, and Bush's supporters explained that their man's stumbles and malapropisms were signs of nervousness, not ignorance. That was not a whole lot more encouraging: For a president, nerves are even more indispensable than brains. It is important that a president be in command of his words. It is essential that he be in command of himself.

My fellow conservatives did not worry that the candidate was too dumb; they worried that his campaign was too clever. Bush had borrowed a maneuver from Dick Morris: He ran almost as hard against his own party as he did against the other. In the space of a single week in October 1999, Bush accused congressional Republicans of "balancing the budget on the backs of the poor" and complained in a major address in New York City that too often "my party has painted an image of America slouching toward Gomorrah"—*Slouching Towards Gomorrah* being the title of a recent best-selling book by conservative hero Robert Bork.

Bush described himself as a "compassionate conservative,"

which sounded less like a philosophy than a marketing slogan: Love conservatism but hate arguing about abortion? Try our new *compassionate conservatism*—great ideological taste, now with less controversy. Conservatives disliked the "compassionate conservative" label in the same way that people on the Left would dislike it if a Democratic candidate for president called himself a "patriotic liberal."

In August, I traveled up to Philadelphia to hear Bush speak to the Republican national convention. I was filing three reports a day for three different newspapers, and I think I witnessed every event, media event, and pseudoevent over the convention's four-day span. It was pretty disheartening. The same metal detectors that inspected for bombs and guns seemed also to have been calibrated to block out ideas—not merely conservative ideas, but *any* ideas. Instead, the delegates heard from a professional wrestler, watched a pep rally by inner-city schoolchildren, and listened in prime time to the testimony of a woman who had lost a sister to breast cancer. In the evenings, the convention showcased minorities, women, and heartwarming anecdotes, all seemingly intended to prove that Newt Gingrich's GOP had been remade into as soft a box of caramels as ever melted inside a glove compartment.

By the time Bush himself came to the rostrum to speak, I was as ready to scoff as any of the cynical journalists in the press boxes. When he finished, I was wobbled. The speech was not only very good, it was very smart—and not smart in the disturbing way that the campaign had been smart, but smart in an interesting way, even a promising way.

Bush's first challenge was to explain why voters should vote against incumbents after eight years of prosperity. The Democrats had lost in 1984 and 1988 by denying that the prosperity of the 1980s was real. Bush avoided that mistake. He acknowledged the prosperity—and then changed the subject to the moral failings of the people who had presided over it. "For eight years, the Clinton/Gore administration has coasted through prosperity. And the path of least resistance is always downhill. But America's way is the rising road."

Bush found a way to identify with his baby boom generation without boasting or condemning. "My generation tested limits—and our country, in some ways, is better for it. Women are now treated more equally. Racial progress has been steady, if still too slow. We are learning to protect the natural world around us. We will continue this progress, and we will not turn back. At times, we lost our way. But we are coming home." Conservatives had attacked the baby boomers for producing Bill Clinton; Bush sorrowfully reproached Clinton for betraying the boomers. "Our current president embodied the potential of a generation. So many talents. So much charm. Such great skill. But, in the end, to what end? So much promise, to no great purpose."

Then Bush did something truly ingenious. He took his greatest personal vulnerability—his reputation for wildness—and used it to cancel his party's greatest vulnerability—its image as a claque of moralistic Church Ladies. "I believe in a God who calls us, not to judge our neighbors, but to love them. I believe in grace, because I have seen it; in peace, because I have felt it; in forgiveness, because I have needed it."

Altogether, a superb performance. But was it wholly convincing? Everyone knew Bush hadn't written his words. Whose voice were we really hearing?

The 2000 election was the messiest and most nerve-racking in 125 years. Bush's reinvention of the Republican Party did not quite work. He lost the popular vote by half a million ballots and had to be carried over the finish line by the U.S. Supreme Court. To put that in perspective, remember that we call the 2000 election "the closest in history" only because Bush was declared the winner in the end. If the recount had gone the other way—if Gore had somehow found the five-hundred-plus votes he needed to carry Florida—Gore's margin over Bush would actually have been larger than Kennedy's over Nixon in 1960.

In the elections of the nineteenth century, at least three presidents received fewer votes than their main opponent.* But it has been a long time since it last happened, and in the meantime, the country's attitudes toward voting and democracy have changed dramatically. Bush arrived in office politically crippled.

On one of my first trips with Bush after I joined his staff, I fell into conversation with a local Republican activist, a woman in her early forties who had quit a high-powered job to stay home with her children. Somehow she had failed to obtain a ticket to the event at which Bush was speaking. I was able to persuade the Secret Service to let her through. "Thank you," she said, "I wanted so badly to see my president." She had summed up Bush's dilemma in two words. To half the country, he was "*my* president." To the other half, he was not the president at all.

The lines that divided those two halves from each other were not mainly lines of race. (Although Bush lost the black vote overwhelmingly, he won a smaller share of the white vote

---

* John Quincy Adams in 1824, Rutherford B. Hayes in 1876, and Benjamin Harrison in 1888.

than his father did in 1988.) Nor were they lines of class. (The large majority of Americans who described themselves to exit pollsters as "middle class" divided their votes between Bush and Gore almost exactly equally.) They were lines defined by family status and religious observance. Bush beat Gore by fifteen points among married people with children and by seventeen points among people who attend church every week. Gore beat Bush by nineteen points among women who work outside the home and by twenty-nine points among people who never attend church at all.

Bush's strongest supporters were not the richest Americans—in fact, Americans who described themselves as "upper class" voted for Gore over Bush. Bush's strongest supporters were the people most outraged by Clinton's misconduct. One of the questions the exit pollsters asked in 2000 was, "What is the most important thing to consider when you decide who to vote for?" One-quarter of all voters listed "honesty" as the most important thing. They voted 80 percent for Bush.

Bush's base liked his tax-cut plan. They supported him on missile defense, on Social Security reform, on faith-based charities, even (if less enthusiastically) on education. But what they most wanted from him was something much simpler: They wanted him not to be Clinton. In other words, Bush had come into office with half the country thinking him little better than some Paraguayan colonel who seized the presidential palace and the other half pretty much indifferent to everything in his program except the promise to lay off the interns. That was not much of a mandate to govern.

So now, in this new year, he would have to begin all over again: He would have to win the political majority that had eluded him in November. Then he would have to find something important and worthwhile to do with that majority. It was difficult to be optimistic about his chances.

But I wasn't a bookmaker. I was a journalist, and I was being offered an up-front view of the biggest story America has to tell. I had so often walked along Pennsylvania Avenue and looked inward at the old mansion, glowing cool and opal by night, refulgent with reflected sunlight in the day. Everybody in the world wants to know what goes on in there. So did I. An English historian once described government as "the endless adventure." Bush's adventure might succeed. I hoped so. But succeed or fail, it would be worth witnessing. My faith in Bush was not deep. But my curiosity was.

Besides, what was the alternative? Gerson challenged me directly: Conservatives had been losing political battles for a dozen years. Was I really content to heckle from the sidelines as they lost again? Gerson knew that as a journalist I had published articles critical of Bush. Yet Bush was willing to take a chance on me—would I refuse to take a chance on Bush?

The ceiling in the mess is very low, not even eight feet. You can feel the weight of the West Wing above your head, and with it the weight of American memory. The tape recorders that had wrecked the Nixon presidency had whirred away just a few feet from where I was sitting now. Over yonder was the colonnade where President Kennedy had paced during the terrifying hours of the Cuban missile crisis. Lincoln had walked here, too, when the White House stables stood where the Executive Office Building now stands and the West Wing itself was just a path leading to the telegraph offices in the War Department on the other side of Seventeenth Street. George Washington had watched the mansion rise, had chosen the contrasting round and peaked pediments of the mansion's windows, had perhaps touched the walls that every staffer touched whenever he or she thought nobody was looking.

Yes, I was ready to join the adventure myself. I had been looking in from the outside for a very long time. If only for a little while, I would like to look out from the inside. Besides, it wouldn't kill me to know my Bible better.

# 2

# THE UN-CLINTON

ON THE MORNING of January 30, 2001, I donned a dark
suit and sober necktie and drove downtown to begin my
first day of work in the Bush administration. Hundreds of other
eager staffers did exactly the same thing. We parked in the
White House parking lots, answered our White House telephones, printed out documents on White House stationery . . .
everything that real White House employees do. But when we
turned on our television sets—and almost every White House
office has a television in it—we viewed a parallel universe, where
ex-president Bill Clinton remained America's top news maker.

On inauguration weekend, Americans had learned that
Clinton's final official act as president had been to pardon
wealthy felons under circumstances most politely described as
fishy. Americans learned that Hillary Clinton had requested and
received hundreds of thousands of dollars of gifts from rich
friends for her new houses in New York and Washington. And

they learned that the Clintons had loaded hundreds of pieces of White House furniture into their moving trucks.

For Bush, this final storm of Clinton scandal was a very favorable wind out of port. The instant the scandal story broke, Bush's approval rating gusted up to 60 percent, and there it hovered for the rest of the winter and through the spring. It was no longer only a religious minority who hungered for an un-Clinton as president; the whole country seemed to have had enough. As I passed the open doorway of the Oval Office one weekend afternoon, a guard pointed out the famous *Resolute* desk, the desk used by Presidents Kennedy, Reagan, Clinton, and now Bush.

"I think it's nailed to the floor," he said.

"Really?"

"Must be. That's why it's still here."

Well, if the country wanted an un-Clinton administration, they had hired the right team.

Was Clinton famously unpunctual? Bush was always on time.

Had Clinton liked to wander into the Oval Office in his sports clothes? Bush required jackets and ties at all times, even weekends.

Did Clinton's wife aspire to be co-president? Bush's wife moved the First Lady's office back from the West Wing to the East Wing and eschewed any role at all in the making of public policy.

Were the Clintons morally slack? Bush opened every cabinet meeting with a prayer and scorned the petty untruths of the politician. In mid-March 2001, Bush signed a leftover Clinton-era order releasing billions of federal dollars to pay for the restoration of the Florida Everglades. The plan was for him to fly into Florida to take a bow. He took the flight all right—but not the bow. "Today I signed an Everglades agreement with the state of Florida. It's legislation that passed prior to my time." On another trip, this time to West Virginia, he referred to his campaign book, *A Charge to Keep,* as "the book I wrote." He caught himself with a chuckle. "Well, they say I wrote it." He insisted on accuracy to the point of pedantry. If his schedule called for him to record a radio address in Washington to be broadcast during a visit to California the following day, nothing could induce him to say, "Today, I am in California." He would look up from the script with exasperation. "But I'm not in California."

Nor would he make the little gestures politicians make to establish a connection with their audiences. Clinton would assure farmers that he had studied farming and tell Jews that he wished he could shoulder a rifle for Israel. When Bush visited Connecticut in April 2001, he refused to mention that he had been born in the state, or that he had attended college there, or that his grandfather had represented Connecticut in the U.S. Senate. We learned not to insert idle compliments like "I'm happy to be here with you" into his speeches: If he was not happy to be here with you, he would not pretend that he was.

A few weeks after I joined the White House, I read a memoir by Clinton's chief speechwriter, Michael Waldman. Waldman described late-night editing sessions in the Roosevelt Room, the big meeting room on the main floor of the West Wing. By midnight, he recalled, the long conference table would be covered with pizza boxes and capsized French fries. Pizza! At midnight! In the Roosevelt Room! In the Bush White House, the idea would have been as incredible as spitting on the carpet.

I once asked George Stephanopoulos whether it was true, as I'd heard, that the Clinton staff did not rise when Clinton entered the room. He looked embarrassed and said, "Well, we had a lot of trouble at the beginning adjusting to the idea that Clinton really was the president." No such trouble for the Bushies. The Bush staff rose to their feet with a snap that would have impressed a Prussian field marshal. When Bush was in a kidding mood, he would direct the staff like an orchestra conductor: He would press his hands palms down to direct them to sit and then, when they had taken their seats, raise his hands palms up to order them to rise again. Only then would they get the final palms-down. Even in the informality of Air Force One, the staff would leap up whenever Bush stepped into view. He learned to bark, "Sit!" at the very instant he entered the rear staff cabins so as to spare the staff from springing up as they sat at tables covered with papers, books, and lunch.

Nobody ever referred to the president as "Bush," not even in private conversation, and certainly never as "POTUS," the ironically pompous acronym for "president of the United States" that the Clinton people had liked to use. Bush was "the president" on the phone, "the president" in e-mails, "the president" in meetings, "the president" when kidding around in the corridors.

The Bush White House was the last place in America where a man could feel a little underdressed if he came to work in a brown suit. Men wore blue or gray suits on weekdays—and for the first three months after September 11, Saturday counted as a weekday. Women could wear brighter colors—but never higher than the knee.

The Bush team lived clean. With the sole exception of Deputy Chief of Staff Josh Bolten's occasional excursions with the actress Bo Derek, the only time the personal lives of Bush staffers made the newspapers was when one of them announced an engagement or the birth of a child. I counted only a single senior Bush staffer who smoked; I never heard of—much less saw—any of them having even one drink too many. I know of at least one case where a qualified person was denied a job, and not a high-level job, either, because she had flunked the Bush administration's unwritten "no marijuana after college" rule.

The Bushies did not curse, either. Early in my White House stint, somebody asked me at a meeting whether I was sure of something. I said I was. He pressed me: "Are you *sure?*" Irritated, I replied emphatically: "Yes, I am damn sure." The temperature in the room suddenly seemed to drop about a dozen degrees. There was a prolonged silence as I tried to figure out my mistake. I got it. "Er—I mean, yes indeed, I am quite sure."

The White House is governed by so many rules—and so many of them are irrational, if not actively crazy—that it is almost impossible for a human being to obey them all. For instance: White House staff must list every foreign trip they have taken over the past fifteen years, including dates of departure, dates of return, and every country visited in between. The rule was instituted in the days when most Americans could probably count on one hand the number of times in their whole lives that they left the country, but it has endured into the era of the $299 weekend fare to Paris.

"This is madness!" I complained to the ethics advisers.

"It's the law," they would reply grimly—and I would hear in their voices the unspoken second half of the sentence: *and we're going to live up to its every last absurdity . . . not like those other guys!*

My new colleagues wanted very badly to do the right thing. I suppose all new White Houses feel that way. But there was an unusual intensity about the moral fervor of the Bush White House. Because of the weakness of our political position, we were not in much of a position to do good. All the more important, then, that we *be good.*

Goodness had been one of the main themes of the campaign speeches of George W. Bush. He often observed that if the government could ever write a law that could make people love their neighbors, he would be glad to sign it. This was, when you think about it, an odd thing for a Republican president to say. If Congress had sent Ronald Reagan a law obliging people to love their neighbors, he would have vetoed it as an impertinent infringement of personal liberty, and unconstitutional besides.

But Bush came from and spoke for a very different culture from that of the individualistic Ronald Reagan: the culture of modern Evangelicalism. To understand the Bush White House, you must understand its predominant creed. It was a kindly faith, practical and unmystical. It had absorbed a surprising amount of the culture of the nonevangelical world around it: feminism, country-rock music, psychotherapy, even permissive child rearing. I was again and again surprised to discover that I, a not especially observant Jew, was a much stricter parent than my evangelical colleagues. Secular people often imagine the devout, and especially the evangelically devout, as censorious personalities, keen to forbid and to punish. But the evangelicals in the Bush White House were its gentlest souls, the most patient, the least argumentative. They were numerous enough to set the tone of the White House, and the result was an office in which I seldom heard a voice raised in anger—and never witnessed a single one of those finger-jabbing confrontations you see in movies about the White House. The television show *The West Wing* might as well have been set aboard a Klingon starship for all it resembled life inside the Bush White House.

I did my best to live up to the upright and hygienic local norms. I was assigned to the strangest office I will probably ever occupy in my life: a room on the first floor of the Executive Office Building, about twelve feet wide, twenty feet long—and twenty feet high. Wedged against the short wall opposite my desk was a once elegant pink sofa, flocked with embroidered roses, that had probably graced the White House family quarters sometime around 1970—and had since gradually bumped its way down the hierarchy, like Black Beauty in the children's story, until it had come to rest here. The first time I sat on the sofa, I detonated a mushroom cloud of dust and insect fragments that hovered about my head for a quarter of a minute. The rest of the place was not much more hygienic: The phones were greasy to the touch, the carpet was spotted with dried chewing gum, and the surface of my desk was sticky with ancient coffee and soda spills. My wife was so horrified by her first visit to the place that she arrived the following weekend with disinfectant, vacuum cleaner, and scouring pads. The two of us cleaned up after eight years of Clinton-Gore in the most literal possible way.

Because ten days elapsed between the inaugural and my first

day on the job, I can't corroborate or refute the stories of vandalism in the final hours of the Clinton administration. The stories circulated inside the White House, but the damage always seemed to have been witnessed by a friend of the person telling the story, seldom by the person telling the story himself. The General Accounting Office investigation found that more than $10,000 worth of damage was done during the transition, but in a relatively small number of offices. I suspect that the rumors gained credence inside the White House because of the surprising shabbiness and dirt of much of the Executive Office Building. Years before, some kindhearted soul had awarded the contract for cleaning the building to a local home for the mentally impaired. The cleaners certainly meant well, but they seldom managed to do more than empty the wastebaskets every second or third day and pass a vacuum over the three or four square feet of carpet in the center of each room. Walk for the first time into an office that has received that amount of cleaning over eight years of hard use, and you would probably think it had been vandalized, too.

We in the new administration were determined to keep our White House clean, both literally and metaphorically. You would not find any of the doubtful characters that had filled the Clinton White House in *our* halls. We would have no private detectives, no blond presidential cousins mysteriously on the payroll, no barroom bouncers who liked to paw through other people's FBI files, no court intellectuals who doubled as rumor-mongers and conspiracy theorists.

Yet sometimes I found myself wondering whether there was not a danger of overdoing this solid and sensible business. There were days when my colleagues reminded me of the sort of girl my grandmother's friends encouraged me to take out in my dating days: "What's she like?"

"She's nice."

"Nice—and what else?"

"Just nice. What else do you want?"

If you looked around the Bush cabinet table, for example, you saw a number of very able, solid, and reliable people—but only one, Donald Rumsfeld, whose mind could truly be said to sparkle. And if you looked more narrowly at the White House staff, there was again a dearth of really high-powered brains. One seldom heard an unexpected thought in the Bush White House or met someone who possessed unusual knowledge. Aside from the witty and ingenious Mitch Daniels at the Office of Management and Budget and of course Karl Rove, who played the unusual dual role of political guru and leading intellectual, conspicuous intelligence seemed actively unwelcome in the Bush White House. Bush had brought no David Watkins, no Harold Ickes, no Susan Thomases, no Web Hubbell, to Washington with him, and everybody appreciated that. But Clinton had also hired Robert Rubin, Larry Summers, Joseph Stiglitz, Ira Magaziner, and Les Aspin—eccentrics, some of them, perhaps, but also powerful intelligences, open to new ideas. The country could trust the Bush administration not to cheat and not to lie. But could the administration cope with an unprecedented crisis or a wholly novel problem? That might be rather dicier.

I understood the reasons for the bias toward the ordinary. In the White House of the first President Bush ("Bush 41," as he was called by veterans of that administration), the most conspicuously brilliant person had been Budget Director Richard Darman. Darman had also been the most manipulative and destructive person in the White House, and in the end his corrosive intellect had been deployed against Bush 41 himself. Only a month before the 1992 presidential election, *The Washington Post* published a four-part series by Bob Woodward full of quotes from unnamed Bush insiders to the effect that Bush had never believed in his "read my lips" pledge not to raise taxes. The story could not have been more damaging had James Carville written it. Its principal source was widely believed to be Darman himself. And the lesson the younger Bush took from that experience was: No new Darmans.

The man in charge of enforcing the "no new Darmans" rule was Chief of Staff Andy Card. Card had served as deputy to Bush 41's first chief of staff, John Sununu. If Darman had been the most devious member of that administration, Sununu had been the most tyrannical. He may well have been the most tyrannical chief of staff in any White House ever. Sununu was famous for his rages, his curses, and his threats against anyone who defied or even disagreed with him.

Card, by astonishing contrast, was the nicest of all the administration's nice guys: a cheerful, stocky man with a nice wife and a nice family and the appealing accent of the Massachusetts north shore. Just as certain Christians govern their conduct by the shorthand code WWJD ("What would Jesus do?"), Card seemed constantly to be asking WWJSD ("What would John Sununu do?")—so that he could then do precisely the opposite. Sununu had insisted on being addressed as "Governor" (in deference to his service as governor of New Hampshire); Card got agitated whenever anybody addressed him as anything other than plain "Andy." Sununu bellowed orders; Card prefaced his instructions with a tactful formula like "I wonder whether it would not be a good idea to . . ." Sununu was notorious for sealing himself off from his underlings; Card made a point of lunching almost every day at the big staff table in the mess, where anybody could sit down next to him and talk about whatever was on his or her mind as Card sipped his frugal bowl of tomato soup. Occasionally, Card would decide that the air in the mess was getting too rarefied, and on those days he would stroll over to the cafeteria in the Executive Office Building, take a tray, and walk with his soup over to a table of secretaries and junior aides.

Card set the administration's pleasant tone—and enforced its code of unspotted loyalty. He had got his start in national politics when he'd volunteered as the elder George Bush's driver during the 1980 New Hampshire Republican primary. Asked once by a reporter whether the younger Bush spoke more effectively from a TelePrompTer or in more informal circumstances, Card replied, "The president is magnificent in all settings." I called Card's standard of conduct "Bushido"—a pun on the Japanese word for the code of the samurai.

A few weeks after Inauguration Day, Card summoned the newly sworn-in special assistants to the president for the first in a series of lectures on Bushido. White House titles can be very confusing. The eighty or so top staffers are divided into three castes: assistants to the president, deputy assistants, and special assistants. Once upon a time, special assistant was a very grand rank indeed. Today, special assistant is to assistant as the Special

Olympics are to the Olympics. I was special assistant to the president for economic speechwriting, a fine illustration of the Washington rule that the more important the job, the shorter the title.

Card opened his talk with a story. His own White House service had begun almost exactly twenty years ago to the week. Soon after that, he had attended his first meeting in the Roosevelt Room. He was greeted at the door by a secretary, who asked him like an usher at a wedding, "Baker side or Meese side?" When he walked farther into the room, he saw that it wasn't like a wedding at all—more like the negotiating table at Panmunjom, with the South Reaganeans on one side behind their little flags and bottles of mineral water and the North Reaganeans on the other.

This, Card pleaded, must never happen here. "You are not Karl's people or Karen's people," referring to the two most powerful of all the presidential aides, Karl Rove and Karen Hughes. "You are all the president's people."

There must be no bickering. "The president deserves to be served by the best and the brightest. He is in fact served by you. Therefore *you must be* the best and the brightest—and so must all your colleagues. And if you ever doubt that, you'd do best to keep your doubts to yourself."

Aides must resist the temptation to self-aggrandizement. "You've probably already noticed how the room goes quiet when you say you work at the White House. That would be a good moment for you to go quiet, too." Everyone should remember how entirely dispensable he or she was. "The average tenure of a chief of staff is about eighteen months. I will be here only so long as I help the president to do his job. And that's how long each of you will be here as well. I wouldn't count on vesting in the government's pension plan."

Card, in fact, survived much longer than the eighteen-month norm. He was a wonderful man to work for, save for one flaw: a rather excessive frugality about small sums of money. This cheeseparing seldom did the taxpayer much good—and it often did the administration considerable harm. A friend of mine was offered a job on the National Security Council with responsibility for overseeing policy toward several of the world's leading economic powers. The NSC proposed to pay him $57,000 a year, rather less than a good plumber can earn in the Washington area. My friend was willing to take a pay cut to serve his country—but not so steep a pay cut as that. The slot was filled instead by somebody sent over from the State Department, who earned a civil service salary twice as high as that which NSC offered my friend. Of course, the substitute reflected the institutional views of his department rather than the principles of the president, but on the other hand, his salary was not charged to the president's account. The Bush White House saved itself $57,000 at the cost of losing control over an important portion of its foreign policy.

Thanks to Mike Gerson, the speechwriters at least were protected from such petty economies. Not for a long time had a chief speechwriter wielded as much bureaucratic clout as Gerson did. Bush was not an articulate man, but unlike his father—who responded to his verbal infelicity by denigrating the importance of words—the younger Bush valued the skills he lacked. I think too that Bush admired Gerson's deep and animating religious faith. While Bush's Christianity often seemed at odds with his sharp and competitive character, Gerson's grew naturally out of his amiable personality. The president and the writer formed an unlikely bond. Gerson hated sports and loved poetry, and he was as anxious as Bush was confident. When a major speech came due, you would often see Gerson wandering through the presidential complex, squinting at a pad of paper covered with his wild, illegible scrawl, mumbling to himself, and making orator's gestures with his free hand as he walked. Rove once showed one of Gerson's pads to a reporter and said: "You know, when these go into the archives, future generations will be amazed that we let a crazy person this close to the president of the United States." Gerson chewed nervously on the ends of his black pens until they exploded and covered him, or the people near him, with ink. He ate his way through about a box a week. I once suggested to him that a diet of pencils might be healthier, or anyway less messy, but the habits of a lifetime are hard to break.

Bush spared Gerson—and most of those who worked with him—the ritual of presidential nicknaming. I was once an exception to this rule, and I did not wholly enjoy it. I had written some remarks Bush liked, and when he saw me in a corridor just after he delivered them, he lightly whacked my midriff with a roll of papers he was carrying and said, "Nice to see you, Davey me lad." Normally, Bush addressed his writers by their last names, British boarding school fashion. And that was how I was greeted when I first met him, about two weeks after I started at the White House. The writers were summoned into the Oval Office for a get-acquainted chat on a mid-February afternoon at four o'clock. Bush shook our hands as we filed in.

"Good afternoon, Mr. President," I said. "My name's David Frum. I'm new here."

He gave me a skeptical once-over and replied, "Welcome, Frum."

And we took our seats.

The Oval Office is a large room, more than thirty-five feet long, and it seems all the larger because it is so empty. At one end are the president's big desk and his leather chair; at the other, two armchairs and two small couches on either side of the famous fireplace. Some side chairs stand along the wall, in between the bookcases containing a few pieces of nineteenth-century porcelain and a couple of rows of untouched antique books. The presidential seal is carved into the hard plaster of the ceiling overhead. The room's size and emptiness create a faint, unnerving echo. The temperature of the room is surprisingly arctic: closer to sixty-five than seventy degrees, I would guess, in both summer and winter. The only relief for the eye from the overwhelming whiteness of the room is the bowl of fresh-cut roses on the low table between the couches.

Anyone who can be cool about his first visit to the Oval Office has lost so much body heat that rigor mortis is probably about to set in. Maybe that's why the temperature of the room is kept so frigid; if not, the president would spend his day looking at a procession of people with beads of sweat on their brows.

I certainly was not cool, but I managed to scratch some notes to keep my memory fresh. As I reread them now, I am startled at how much of what would happen over the next year is prefigured there: Bush's optimism about Russia and Vladimir Putin, his wariness of China, his focus on the danger presented by Iran, his determination to dig Saddam Hussein out of power in Iraq, his conviction that the country hungered for a revival of the ideals of duty and service. He spoke with a commanding self-assurance I had never seen in his public appearances, not even in the small-scale events I had attended over the previous three weeks. Where had that command come from? And where did it go when he left this room?

But then, a lot changed when he left this room. In here, Bush was a sharp exception to the White House code of niceness. He was tart, not sweet. He asked us all how we thought things were going so far. We replied with an enthusiastic round of compliments. He nodded grimly. As a governor, he said, he could walk into a store, buy a jug of milk, ask the clerk how he was doing—and get an honest answer. Now he was locked in a bubble, and whatever he did, he heard only, "Wonderful, Mr. President! Great speech, Mr. President! You knocked it out of the park, Mr. President!" No wonder, he commented ruefully, that Reagan used to spend two hours every day reading his mail.

Bush relaxed in his chair as he talked. Yet there was something taut about him even when he slumped. Bush's fiercest critics paid tribute to his likability, but in private, Bush was not the easy, genial man he was in public. Close up, one saw a man keeping a tight grip on himself. His best moment in his debates with Gore had been the knowing nod he flashed during debate three, when Gore crossed the stage to crowd him. Gore, a bigger man than Bush, was attempting to assert some kind of primal dominance. But any sportsman could see in that single glance of Bush's that if it came to a fight, the man to bet on was the fierce, wiry guy, not the lummox.

A friend of mind has a theory that the secret to Bush's character is his drinking, or rather his ex-drinking. "Every morning," my friend suggests, "Bush wakes up knowing one thing for absolute certain: Today is a day on which he will not have a drink. Everything else falls into place after that."

Yet this tightly controlled man did something very puzzling in that first meeting and again in many of the meetings that followed: He would let fall in the course of the conversation at least one jaw-droppingly candid remark—a brutally frank assessment of some foreign leader or an expression of doubt about some program to which he was publicly committed. If Bush were a less disciplined man, you might think he was careless. If he were more trusting, you might think he was showing his faith in his staff. But Bush is relentlessly disciplined and very slow to trust. Even when his mouth seems to be smiling at you, you can feel his eyes watching you. He never loses track of the time. Why would he lose track of his words?

The explanation, I gradually came to think, was that Bush was taking a calculated risk. Direct marketers will sometimes tuck a dollar bill into a questionnaire, knowing that once a person accepts a gift, odds are he will feel obliged to the giver. Bush was thrusting a gift upon us, the most precious gift a president can offer: a little piece of himself. By revealing himself to us, he bound us to him.

Bush knew how to create the loyalty he demanded. A friend of mine was a junior member of a staff team assigned an important project. The project fell badly behind schedule. Bush was furious and called the whole team to the Oval Office for a presidential chewing out. The lecture did not last long, only about a million years or so. As the crestfallen staffers rose to leave, Bush called out the name of my friend, who was the lowest-ranking, most vulnerable, and most abjectly miserable member of the team. "Stay back for a second! I have one more thing to say to *you.*" Then, when the door closed again, Bush said: "I want you to know that I don't blame you for what happened. I know the fault lies elsewhere." And then he asked after each of my friend's children by name. When he emerged from the Oval Office, my friend would have charged a machine gun for George W. Bush.

The grandfather clock in the Oval Office clicked five o'clock. Our time was up and we rose to go. Bush thanked us politely for our work for him, and we filed out of the chilly, ghostly room into the blue-carpeted halls of the West Wing and back to our desks.

In that hour, Bush had settled one thing in my mind: I could never again take seriously the theory that somebody else was running this administration—not Cheney, not Rove, not Card. Bush was leading all right—but where was he leading us all to?

Bush seemed utterly unperturbed by the weakness of his political position. He sketched a vision of the political future in which a win on taxes led to a win on education, which led to wins on missile defense and Social Security—a series of maneuvers as stately and smooth as the solution to a chess puzzle in the Sunday paper.

How could he be so calm and confident? Was he blind? Was he arrogant? Was he putting on a false front in order to reassure his followers? Three months later, he delivered a speech that suggested the true answer.

In May 2001, Bush gave the commencement address at Yale. When work began on the speech, Bush seemed uninterested in it. His feelings toward his old school were less than fond. When one of the writers working on the speech unearthed some curious bit of Yale history, Bush asked with surprise: "Did you go to Yale?"

The writer said no.

Bush replied, "Well, you didn't miss much."

Yet he ended up working harder on that Yale speech than any speech he gave that spring except the State of the Union. The longer he worked on it, the more sentimental he became—and the more candid. In the end, the speech evolved into the most self-revealing document of that first year.

"When I left here, I didn't have much in the way of a life plan. I knew some people who thought they did. But it turned out that we were all in for ups and downs, most of them unexpected. Life takes its own turns, makes its own demands, writes its own story. And along the way, we start to realize we are not the author."

And that was why Bush was so confident: not because he was arrogant, but because he believed that the future was held in stronger hands than his own.

# 3

# WARNING LIGHT

O THER THAN DIVINE providence, reasons for confidence were awfully sparse that spring. The economy was plunging into what the administration's own chief economic adviser, Lawrence Lindsey, privately predicted would be an extremely severe recession. The left-wing writer Christopher Hitchens had joked that the Clinton presidency would be remembered as a sexual moment between the Bushes. Very funny. But if the second Bush turned out to be as recessionary as the first, the laughter would turn bitter.

My first speechwriting assignment was to sound an alert on the impending recession. This was not an easy job for me. Adjusting to presidential speechwriting after a career in journalism is like switching to one of those huge graphite tennis rackets after learning the game on an old-fashioned wooden one: With all that extra power in your hand, you have to learn to hit the ball much more softly.

I erased draft after draft trying to find words that would send the right message, without triggering panic on the financial markets. But everything I tried, though it might read well on the page, sounded simply terrifying when I imagined it emerging from the president's mouth.

After four or five hours of struggle, I gave up and went home, hoping for inspiration in the morning. I had forgotten that the next day would be my turn to drive the five children in our car pool to their school in suburban Maryland. Instead of arriving at my desk early, I had to hustle the kids into my wife's minivan, turn the key, and . . . Damn! The yellow low-fuel indicator clicked on. The needle stood less than a millimeter above empty. There was no gas station on the route, and we were too late to make a detour. I drove the whole twenty-five miles from my house to the school and then to the office worrying that the van could stall at any second. It felt like . . . like . . . like . . . Hey: It felt the way the whole economy must feel to the president.

I arrived at my desk a little past nine, switched on the computer, and wrote: "A warning light is flashing on the dashboard of our economy."

Twenty-four hours later, I walked over into the Rose Garden to watch the president deliver my maiden speech. When he finished, I returned to my office and flicked on the cable news. Top story: "A warning light is flashing on the dashboard of our economy." That evening, I watched the network news broadcasts, and it was dashboard on CBS, dashboard on NBC, and dashboard on ABC. The dashboard warning was the top item in *The Wall Street Journal*'s news column and the lead sentence in *The New York Times*'s and *Washington Post*'s White House front pagers. That weekend, *Newsweek* bannered the warning light on the dashboard as the quote of the week. It was my first buzz from the presidential speechwriter's hookah, and it was pretty intoxicating.

But presidents cannot just complain about the economy. They are expected to *do* something about it. And the odds were not looking promising for Bush's proposed remedy: a big tax cut phased in over the next ten years.

Bush had proposed the tax cut back in 1999 to fix what then seemed the country's biggest economic problem: the huge budget surpluses gathering in the federal treasury. If that money stayed in Washington, sooner or later Congress would spend it. Bush liked to repeat a line he had heard from a grandmother in the Carnegie Library in Council Bluffs, Iowa: "I've learned that if you leave cookies out on a plate, they always get eaten." Now, with the economy spiraling downward, Bush attached a new purpose to his tax plan: averting or at least mitigating the impending recession.

But if the economic climate had changed, the political math had not: The public supported Bush's tax plan very tepidly, at best. While more Americans wanted a tax cut than not, less than 25 percent of Americans listed tax relief as the nation's top priority; more than three-quarters put either debt repayment or social spending first.* In early February, the Pew Research Center conducted a poll that asked Americans what they liked best about their new president. Only 7 percent of those surveyed mentioned Bush's tax cut, and only 14 percent mentioned *any* of

* ABC News/*Washington Post* Poll, February 21–25, 2001.

his policies. A plurality of those surveyed, 22 percent, cited some aspect of his character: his honesty and integrity, his calm and dignified demeanor, or his religious faith. Rather than adding to Bush's strength, the tax cut may have reinforced his greatest weakness—his image as a man excessively sympathetic to the rich and to big corporations.

But Bush had a plan for winning the tax battle. In fact, he had two.

Sports fan that he was, Bush had two basic strategies for getting bills through Congress: a ground game and a passing game. The ground game—the brutal pushing and shoving along the congressional line of scrimmage, the muddy state-by-state struggle for yardage—was the domain of his chief political aide, Karl Rove. The passing game—the general appeals to the big public, the politics of image and of symbolism—Bush assigned to his chief communications aide, Karen Hughes.

Karl and Karen, as everybody called them, were the two dominant personalities in the pre-9/11 White House. They could not have been more different from each other. Rove was a risk taker and an intellectual. Hughes loathed risk and abhorred ideas. Rove was a reader and a questioner—a curious man, always eager to learn. Hughes rarely read books and distrusted people who did—anything she did not already know she saw no point in knowing. A profile of Karen Hughes in *Esquire* magazine described a characteristic Rove-Hughes interaction: Hughes was about to depart on a two-day trip. "Karl Rove . . . has sent over four books on presidential power for Hughes to read on her trip. She flips through them—giant, ponderous books—skims them for a few seconds, tosses three on the floor in the corner, and halfheartedly shoves the fourth into her blue bag with the presidential seal. 'I don't know why he gives me these things,' she mutters. 'At this point, I think I have a pretty good idea of how power really operates.' "*

Rove was a lifelong politico, who had dropped out of college to manage campaigns and twenty-five years later returned to the University of Texas to simultaneously finish his B.A. and teach a class. Hughes was the daughter of an army officer; she began a degree at Southern Methodist University but also left before she finished, in her case for a career in local television journalism. It was from that line of work that Bush had plucked her eight years before.

Hughes was a tough, brusque personality, relentlessly disciplined. You could inject her full of sodium pentathol and shove bamboo shoots up her fingernails—and still all you would get from her was the talking point of the day. Rove was the White House's Mr. Congeniality. He ambled through the corridors like a small-town mayor, firing wisecracks, pausing sometimes to straighten somebody's necktie or grab somebody's shoulders. He had a legendarily idiosyncratic sense of humor, once entertaining a carload of aides on a long drive by singing out every highway sign as if it were a Bob Dylan lyric: "Slewwwwww roooooood a-hayyyyyyyd!" "DAYYYYN-jer-us currrrrrves!"

Rove had ideas that nobody else had—and that was his value to the president. Hughes had the same ideas that everybody else had—and that was hers.

The most important difference between them, though, was their approach to politics. Journalists sometimes tried to report the Rove-Hughes story as a revival of the old conservatives-vs.-

---

* Ron Suskind, "Mrs. Hughes Takes Her Leave," *Esquire,* July 2002, p. 105.

moderates battles of the Reagan days, with Rove filling in for Ed Meese and Hughes as the second coming of James Baker. That was wrong. Rove was not a down-the-line conservative: He was the White House's leading advocate of amnesty for illegal aliens and protection for embattled domestic steel producers, to name only two of his deviations from right-wing orthodoxy. Nor was Hughes a wishy-washy moderate: She was, for example, an ardent advocate of the faith-based programs that dismayed so many liberals in the media.

The difference between them was the way they imagined democracy worked. When Rove thought of the American electorate, he saw an enormous bag of toy magnets. Some of the magnets were white, and some were black or brown; some were rural, some were urban; some married, others single. No politician could ever hope to scoop up all the magnets in his hands. There were too many: If he tried to grab them all, he would end up with none. And picking up certain magnets inevitably repelled others—pick up the energy-producing magnet, for example, and the Hollywood liberal magnet jumped out of your hands. The job of a political strategist was to gather together the maximum feasible number of magnets. A truly great strategist, such as Rove's much admired Charles Dawes, the manager of William McKinley's landslide presidential campaign in 1896, brought together a huge number of magnets in surprising new combinations.

Hughes, on the other hand, perceived the American electorate as something like the television audience in the days before cable, an undifferentiated mass of people whose attention could all be held by a simple story with big themes: children, health, jobs, faith, patriotism. Hughes often reacted to Rove's cunning stratagems with the same irritated incredulity that a 1950s TV executive might have felt toward a producer who suggested canceling *I Love Lucy* in favor of some early version of *Seinfeld:* "I don't get it—and believe me, if I don't get it, the people at home won't get it."

Hughes's biggest "I told you so" over Rove was the worst blooper of the first year: the arsenic decision. Arsenic occurs naturally in some soils, from which it can leach into drinking water. The federal government sets standards for local water systems and for years had permitted arsenic levels of up to fifty parts per billion. Some environmentalists thought that this standard was too permissive, and in the 1990s they lobbied the Clinton Environmental Protection Agency to reduce it to a maximum of ten parts per billion. For eight years, Clinton refused. The health benefits from the new standard were pretty small, and the costs of the new standard to municipal water authorities were very high, especially in the Southwest, where natural arsenic is most abundant: The ten-parts-per-billion standard would add almost $300 a year to the average water bill in Albuquerque, New Mexico, for example. In January 2001, though, Clinton decided that a new arsenic standard would be a nice little bomb to leave behind for the incoming administration, and he issued the order at last. This legacy presented the Bush administration with a dilemma: Keep the order—and whack family budgets all over the Republican Southwest? Or reverse it—and endure vicious criticism in the national media? Rove pressed for reversal: Bush had come within a few hundred votes of carrying New Mexico in 2000, and the right decision on arsenic might carry the state in 2004. Hughes resisted. Arsenic was scary, arsenic in the water even scarier, and the wrath of the environmentalists scariest of all. Hughes proved to be right: The attempt to shift five electoral votes Bushward handed the national Democrats their most devastating anti-Bush message of 2001.

The two most important magnets in Rove's strategy were white evangelicals and middle-class Hispanics. Hughes's strategy, by contrast, was aimed at women all over the country. Hughes sought to convince women that George W. Bush was caring and compassionate, quite different from Newt Gingrich and the upsetting congressional Republicans. Hughes believed, as she frequently said, in "putting things in people terms." She forced every Bush speech through a drastic translation process. She barred the word *business;* businesses were always to be called "employers." The word *parents* was strictly forbidden: We were to say "moms and dads" instead. The phrase *tax cuts* was unacceptable—too drastic; instead we were to offer "tax relief," like a healing balm. Hughes disliked verbs. Verbs conveyed action, not feeling. If verbs could not be eliminated altogether, they could at least be made as nebulous as possible: "create," "act," and "keep in mind" were some of the less objectionable. Above all things, she hated the word *but,* a word that suggested harsh choices, conflict, even confrontation. A text for the president must never read: "We have done much, but we must do more." It should say instead, "We have done much, *and* we must do more."

Here is an example of Hughes's work at its most characteristic, from a January 2002 speech Bush delivered in Charleston,

West Virginia: "I'm worried about people being able to find jobs. My economic plan is based upon this word: jobs. I want to ask that question all around the country, what do we do to create work? There's a lot of good people who want to work, and we've got to help them find work. And so I'm asking Congress, when they come back, to keep in mind one word: jobs." This kind of talk might not impress the editors of *The Wall Street Journal,* but Hughes believed it resonated with anxious mothers across America.

Inside the White House and out, Washingtonians gossiped about the relative standing of Karen and Karl. Who was closer to the president? What did the two of them really think of each other? The answer was an impenetrable mystery. In the eighteen months that Rove and Hughes cohabited in the White House before Hughes returned to Texas for family reasons, and then afterward, they worked together with perfect self-discipline. No journalist ever got an anti-Rove quote from any of Hughes's people, not even on the deepest background; not one word critical of Hughes ever emanated from Rove's domain—a phenomenon absolutely unparalleled in the sixty-five years since Franklin Roosevelt invented the White House staff back in 1938. If Rove ever thought that Hughes was doing a less than splendid job, nobody except Mrs. Rove ever heard about it, if even she did; and the reverse was true for Hughes. Nor did the two seem to go in and out of favor, the way aides like George Stephanopoulos and Dick Morris did in the Clinton years, or Hamilton Jordan and Lloyd Cutler in Jimmy Carter's day. Bush seemed equally attached to each of them, but in entirely different ways. One longtime observer of the Bush operation described Bush's attitude to the pair in this way: "Bush reveres Karl; he depends on Karen." And they in turn loved him in their distinct own ways: Rove the way a great coach loves his best athlete; Hughes the way a mother bear loves her cub.

Hughes was the only person in the White House who could criticize Bush. She would tell him that he had done a poor job at a speech practice session or at a press conference, and he would react with none of the angry defensiveness that criticism from a less supportive person could provoke. It was somehow appropriate that Bush turned in the worst press conference of his presidency on the day Hughes departed the White House, July 8, 2002. And in turn, her praise mattered more to Bush than that of anyone else on staff.

One day, he did an especially good job at an event. The next day in the Oval Office, there was a gathering of those involved with the event, including Hughes. Bush pulled his reading glasses down his nose, looked straight at Hughes, and said mock scoldingly: "And who predicted it would go well?"

Hughes's face flushed prettily. "You did, sir."

He grunted with pride. "That's right." Then he grinned the way a child does when he pulls the blue ribbon out of his knapsack for his mother.

Hughes exercised more power in the White House than any woman since Edith Wilson, not excluding Nancy Reagan and Hillary Clinton. She controlled the entire presidential communication effort. Every press officer anywhere in the executive branch reported to her—from Victoria Clarke at Defense all the way down the kicking order to whatever poor soul was taking questions at the Department of Labor that week.

In the six weeks after I joined the White House, I became so fascinated by Bush's extraordinary intimacy with Hughes that I asked four different people who had worked with them in Texas whether they thought there was, or ever had been, something between them: if not a relationship, then perhaps an attraction. Every one of them was astonished by the idea—and not just the men, who can be obtuse about these things, but the women, too. My theory, for what little it is worth, is this: Bush had a much more strained relationship with his mother than is often acknowledged. Barbara Bush can be a difficult-to-please woman— and George W. Bush was a son it would often have been difficult to be pleased by. There's a famous story about him being introduced to Queen Elizabeth during his father's vice presidency and joking, "I'm the black sheep of the family." People who make jokes like that are not always joking. When it came time to marry, Bush sought out a woman as unlike his mother as possible: warm not stern, shy not assertive, domestic not political. When he ran for governor, he recruited Hughes—a woman very *like* his mother (she even looks much as Barbara Bush did in her mid-forties), but who offered him the unqualified admiration his mother never did. His wife was his mother antidote. His aide was his mother substitute.

Now, with his tax plan, Bush faced the first great battle of his presidency. To win it, he unleashed his two top aides, each to fight in his or her own distinctive way.

Rove's tax-cut ground game began not with a Gallup poll, but with a simple head count: Although the Senate was divided fifty-fifty between Republicans and Democrats, nineteen of those Democrats came from states that Bush had won, while only eleven Republicans came from states that Gore had won. This disparity created a large inherent advantage for Bush, and Rove pushed it to the limit.

From March through May, Bush campaigned through the thirty states that had voted for him. He flew to Omaha, Nebraska; Atlanta, Georgia; Council Bluffs, Iowa; Sioux Falls, South Dakota; Fargo, North Dakota; Tyler, Texas; and Lafayette, Louisiana. He went to towns where a steak dinner costs $8.99 and high school basketball makes the evening news; where the highways are lined with billboards calling motorists to Christ and the presidential suite is *two* side-by-side rooms in the local Embassy Suites. It's not glamorous being a red-state president.

Of all the thrills the presidency has to offer its employees, a ride on Air Force One is the absolute best. Air Force One is not a plane to ride if you have any tendency toward trouble with authority—because after you've flown on it, it is impossible to listen ever again to the safety instructions on commercial planes. Air Force One takes off like a rocket, roaring full throttle at a forty-five-degree angle, racing to cut to the minimum the number of seconds at which it is moving within reach of an assassin's surface-to-air missile. It descends just as fast and just as steeply, and for the same reasons. On the tarmac, it moves at about twenty miles an hour and hugs curves as tight as if it were a sports car, not a double-decked jumbo jet. And through it all . . . *nobody wears a seat belt. They don't even sit down.* People stand at the photocopying machine making copies through takeoff and landing, leaning against the thrust of the plane, their cheeks puckering slightly at the G-forces, but otherwise upright. And they all survive, perfectly unscathed. I think of that sometimes when I board a commercial flight and the flight attendant sternly orders me to sit back in my seat as the plane taxis from the terminal. . . .

I tagged along on the first overnight trip Bush took as president—a trip made much more pleasant for me by a fact that could easily have barred me from it altogether: my foreign citizenship. I was a Canadian citizen when I entered the White House. Surprisingly enough, there is no rule against noncitizens working for the president. The rules do, however, require that noncitizens be escorted at all times inside the White House complex. Eventually I received a special dispensation that allowed me to go about my business. But for close to a month I had to manage as best I could with an escort-at-all-times temporary pass. Every evening, my name would be entered into the security system for a visit the following day. Every morning, I would park in my assigned parking space, show my driver's license, and wait to be escorted into the complex by Krista Ritacco, Mike Gerson's infinitely patient assistant. Krista would walk me toward my office as if she were seeing me to my desk, then turn back to her own desk in the West Wing and leave me to make my own surreptitious way. Theoretically, I was not allowed to be alone anywhere in the complex, not even my own room. But before September 11, nobody looked very closely at badges. Nonetheless, from time to time, a uniformed guard would spot my telltale insignia as I walked to the bathroom or the library or the mess and demand to know where my escort was. Usually I could talk my way out of the situation—usually, but not always. One afternoon I was actually arrested.

"Where's your escort?"

"Sorry. I just stepped away to the washroom for a moment."

"Where are you going now?"

"Room 190."

"Whose office is that?"

"Mine."

This answer baffled the guard. "That is not possible. You are a foreign national. You come with me." He led me to some kind of security area near the boilers in the basement. I waited there for a quarter of an hour as he phoned around and—to his mounting amazement—established that I was indeed a staffer, that yes, I had an office, and that no, I was not regarded as a threat to the president or the presidency.

It was absolutely maddening. Something as simple as stepping out for coffee required me to ask a colleague to walk me back into the office. But my first Air Force One trip requited it all.

Our itinerary called for an overnight stay in North Little Rock, Arkansas. The motorcade disgorged the staff into the lobby of our hotel, where we were met by a brisk woman with a clipboard handing out keys and room numbers. I stepped out of the last van with my friend John Gardner, the deputy staff secretary. The woman consulted her clipboard mournfully. "I am so sorry!" she said to the two of us. "We didn't get word until late that you had been added to the roster. I don't have a room for you." Gardner rolled his eyes, but he at least had access to the staff room, a hotel room that functioned as a communications center for the trip but that underneath all the temporary gear still contained a bed and a bathroom. Where was I to go? North Little Rock does not abound in hotels, and anyway, once you step outside the security perimeter of a presidential trip, it can be difficult to reenter.

The woman stared at the pad a little longer and then brightened. "I'll tell you what: Colonel So-and-so has an extra bed in his room. We'll double you up with him."

I took the elevator to Colonel So-and-so's room and rapped on the door, which had been left slightly ajar. He didn't hear me, so I pushed it open, walked through his little living room, and rapped again on the door to his bedroom. Through the doorway I could see his brightly shined shoes and air force peaked cap perched on a small table. I stepped into the bedroom.

"Excuse me, Colonel," I said. "I'm sorry to intrude on you, but there's something of a room shortage, and I've been billeted with you. Would you mind very much if I slept over"—and I rotated toward the second bed, on which was perched what looked like an overstuffed black nylon computer bag with a thick antenna protruding out of it—"over . . . there." My voice dropped. "Over there," I realized abruptly, was the football, the computer containing the codes that control the launch of the nuclear forces of the United States. The colonel looked at me with incredulity.

"Are you nuts?" he demanded angrily. "You can't stay here. What the hell kind of clearance do you have, anyway?"

"No clearance at all, Colonel. Actually," I added, the light bulb over my head switching on, "as a matter of fact, I'm a foreign national."

"*What?!* Let me look into this." He picked up the phone

and jabbered commandingly into it. Ten minutes later, I had my own room.

On these Air Force One tours through red-state America, it did not much matter from Karl Rove's point of view exactly what Bush said. The idea was to drop the president into town, attract a bigger crowd than the wavering senator had ever seen in his or her life, and let the senator draw his or her own conclusions about the healthfulness of defying the president. But of course, the president had to say *something*—and what he said always came out of the playbook of Hughes's passing game.

The kickoff for her game was Bush's address to the joint session of Congress on February 27, 2001. This would be Bush's first nationally televised address since his inaugural five weeks before, and the speechwriters seized the challenge eagerly.

The writing shop was recognized as an exception to all the normal rules governing the Bush White House. We were allowed to shut our doors and hit the "Do Not Disturb" buttons on our telephones—behavior that would have provoked a scandal just about anywhere else. The excuse "I'm writing" covered a lot of derelictions. Our shop was also a refuge for eccentrics and eggheads.

Here was Matthew Scully, the most graceful writer in the building, an always good-humored but absolutely unyielding animal advocate. Scully would not eat meat, drink milk, or wear leather. In his office, he always kept large Ziploc bags of peanuts to feed to the squirrels on the White House lawn. I thought the animals accepted his treats with an unbecomingly haughty air, but their attitude did not bother Scully. Ungrateful squirrels, temperamental colleagues, irritable superiors: He greeted them all with the same imperturbable benevolence.

John McConnell was our virtuoso of the deadpan. McConnell was nominally the vice president's writer; he and Scully usually worked together. The two of them manufactured many of Bush's and Cheney's best jokes—and also the second-best jokes, which were the ones that usually got used. I once complained to Karl Rove after he had deleted a joke of mine from a presidential speech, "Karl, that was *funny.*"

"Yes, it was," he replied meditatively. "But presidents shouldn't be too funny."

In obedience to that rule, we cut from the Yale speech this joke: "It's great to return to New Haven. My car was followed all the way from the airport by a long line of police cars with slowly rotating lights. It was just like being an undergraduate again."

Gerson, McConnell, and Scully had written campaign speeches together sitting at a single computer, like Tin Pan Alley composers crowded around a piano. One of the campaign managers dubbed the three of them "the light bulbs"—not (as he told me) as a compliment to their brilliance, but because as they stared at their one screen, they looked like a reenactment of the old joke about the number of professors it takes to change a light bulb: three—one to hold the light bulb and two to turn the ladder.

Since the election, they had been joined by three other writers. The first two were Pete Wehner, a sweet-tempered, cerebral expert on education and social issues; and John Gibson, a career staffer from the Defense Department who seemed to know the insignia, history, and special cheers of every unit in the Armed Forces of the United States. I was the third.

Bush was an exacting editor. He usually reviewed his speeches early in the morning, directly after his intelligence briefing. He hated repetition and redundancy. (If he were editing this page, he would put a line through the words *repetition and*.) One of my first efforts for him included the phrase *I've seen with my own eyes*. The words *with my own eyes* were circled and a sarcastic "DUH" scrawled beside them with one of his heavy marking pens. He insisted on strict linear logic. If a sentence strayed from its proper sequence, it would be corralled with a furious inky lariat and directed back to its place with a big black arrow and a heavy explanation: EDUCATION goes HERE. TAX RELIEF over HERE. And DEFENSE SPENDING should all go THERE. Bush seldom cited statistics when he talked. But he demanded that they be included on the page. A sentence such as "We're increasing federal support for teacher training" would provoke the marking pen into paroxysms of exasperation. BY HOW MUCH?? FROM WHAT?? TO WHAT??

For most of the working hours since our first Oval Office meeting with Bush, the writing shop had labored on drafts of the joint session speech. We seized on it as an opportunity to lay out the governing philosophy of the administration, a new conservatism for a new century. We finished up our masterwork sometime around February 21 and sent it to Hughes for her review.

She hated it.

She read the writers' draft on the Thursday before the joint session speech, sighed with noisy disgust, and boarded a helicopter to Camp David the following morning to rewrite the whole thing. She used the writers' draft the way a Havana auto mechanic uses a defunct 1958 Chevrolet: as a source of spare parts. And I have to salute her. The speech she wrote that weekend up in the wintry hills was one of the most audacious and effective presidential speeches of the past two decades.

She finished by midday Sunday. Two and a half days later, the doors to the House of Representatives were flung open—the senators and representatives and cabinet secretaries and diplomats and justices of the Supreme Court rose to their feet—and the president of the United States walked into the hall, wearing the confident grin of a riverboat gambler ready to win the pot with a pair of sixes. The pot in this case was the biggest pile of money ever gathered in one place: $5.6 trillion, a decade's worth of projected federal surpluses. The Democrats in the hall hoped to spend much of that money; Bush wanted the bulk of it returned to the taxpayer. He would have less than sixty minutes to sway the public's mind.

He kept walking: past the outstretched hands, past the familiar and unfamiliar faces, into the well of the House chamber, and up the steps to the gleaming wood of the rostrum. He greeted Speaker Dennis Hastert and Vice President Cheney, opened the printed text of his speech (16-point type, Arial font), glanced at the clear plastic of the TelePrompTers on either side of him, and launched into a case as clear and simple as any of Euclid's propositions.

1. We have a big surplus.
2. We're going to use some of it to increase spending on education and defense.

3. Then we're going to use some more of it to repay debt.

4. And with the money left over, we'll cut taxes. Thank you, and good night.

Hughes even contributed the night's most quotable line: "Some say my tax plan is too big. Others say it's too small. I respectfully disagree. This plan is just right."

Hughes was absolutely right about the plan's intermediate size. The Reagan tax cut adopted in 1981 shrank the federal government's claim on the American economy by 3.3 percentage points over three years. The Kennedy tax cut Congress passed in 1964 reduced the federal government's claim by 2.0 percentage points, again over three years. Bush was proposing that the government scale back its demands by only 1.2 points over the next *ten* years.

Yet modest as the Bush cut was, its effects would be large. President Clinton had cunningly jiggered with the tax code to squeeze enormous sums of money out of comparatively tiny numbers of people. By 2001, the federal government was collecting more than 20 percent of the national income—the highest level in American history, more than it had taken even during World War II. The single most important source of this money was the federal income tax—and barely 2 percent of the nation's taxpayers, earning 21 percent of the nation's income, paid 27.5 percent of this tax.*

While Clinton was raising taxes as a share of the economy beyond their level at D-Day, he was cutting defense spending to

* Joint Economic Committee, U.S. Congress, "Distribution of Certain Federal Tax Liabilities by Income Class for Calendar Year 2000," April 11, 2000.

the lowest level since before Pearl Harbor. Soaring tax revenues plus plunging defense expenditures yielded giant surpluses. Had Clinton prevailed, the surpluses would have paid for some gigantic new domestic social program: national health insurance, perhaps, or a federal day care program.

Instead, the Democrats lost control of Congress in 1994, and for the next six years, American politics deadlocked. The Democrats could not force spending up as much as they wished; the Republicans could not push taxes down as far as they preferred; and the surplus between the tax line and the spending line grew and grew and grew. Between 1998 and 2001, the Treasury collected half a trillion dollars more than it spent. In January 2002, the Congressional Budget Office predicted that if nothing changed, the federal government would collect $5.6 trillion more over the next ten years than it would spend.

That colossal pile of money was the big unspoken issue in the 2000 elections. Should it be spent? Or should it be returned? The knife-edge result of the election left the issue just as undecided after the vote as it was before. Had Bush slipped or stumbled, the fiscal history of the 2000s would have been as stalemated as the 1990s, only in reverse: Instead of a Democratic president vetoing tax cuts to protect his hopes for future spending, a Republican president would have vetoed spending programs to preserve the possibility of future tax cuts.

But Bush did not slip, and he did not stumble. He triumphed. He signed his tax cut into law on June 7, 2001, eleven weeks after he took office—less than half the time it took

Ronald Reagan to pass his tax cut in 1981. Bush's opponents could only fulminate as he sent all that lovely money out of Washington forever, out of their reach, back home to its owners. The tax plan was the greatest domestic achievement of Bush's presidency. It would also be the last.

# 4

# "TYPICAL REPUBLICAN"

I N THE CABINET ROOM, on the two short walls between the Rose Garden and the corridor to the Oval Office, there is room for four paintings. Three of the four spaces are usually occupied by images of Founding Fathers; the fourth has been used by presidents since at least Jimmy Carter's day to make a political or personal statement. Jimmy Carter hung a portrait of Harry Truman in that fourth spot, to assert his affinity with the scrappy populist. Ronald Reagan replaced Truman with Coolidge, the great tax cutter of the 1920s. I had wondered whether George W. Bush would be sufficiently un-PC to hang James Polk, the laconic southern slaveholder who gained Texas for the Union. Instead, he chose Dwight D. Eisenhower. To emphasize the point, Bush installed a bronze bust of Eisenhower in the Oval Office as well, in approximately the spot where Bill Clinton had displayed a portrait of Andrew Jackson.

Why Ike? It might have been Bush's way of reminding his critics that he was not the first president to be ridiculed for his mangled syntax. But I think there was something more to Bush's choice: Eisenhower represented the kind of president that Bush wanted to be—a leader above party, a leader who drew his power from his personal authority. I suppose all presidents hanker for the larger-than-life prestige that Eisenhower possessed. But few presidents do possess it, and most do not crave it enough to make the compromises with their opponents that an Eisenhower-style presidency entails. Most prefer the benefits that come from whipping up tribal hatred of the opposing party, as Clinton did, and Harry Truman, and Theodore Roosevelt. Presidents who try to govern in nonpartisan ways forfeit a powerful weapon and usually come to bad ends: Think of Jimmy Carter and Herbert Hoover.

But George W. Bush was determined to try nonpartisanship anyway. He persuaded a Democrat to join his cabinet as transportation secretary—and not a conservative Democrat like those recruited by Ronald Reagan and Richard Nixon, but a Democrat's Democrat, Norman Mineta, formerly a liberal member of Congress and then Bill Clinton's secretary of commerce. Bush hosted more congressmen—Republican and Democrat—at the White House in a shorter span of time than any president on record. He solicited and accepted an invitation to the House and Senate Democratic retreats in February 2001. He even endorsed a bill to name the Department of Justice building after Robert Kennedy.

Bush would not criticize individual Democratic officeholders by name. He would not criticize the Democratic Party in general. In the late fall of 2001, when Bush's approval rating stood above 70 percent and Senate Majority Leader Tom Daschle was bottling up his economic agenda, the education bill, trade promotion authority, and even the increase in the debt ceiling necessary to finance the war in Afghanistan and the reconstruction of New York, Bush *still* squeezed his lips tight. He once reluctantly agreed to test FDR's old dodge and condemn the "Democratic leadership" in one of his Saturday morning radio addresses, but he almost immediately regretted this act of blatant politicking. Thereafter, he reverted to a blander phrase: "the leadership in the Senate"—with no mention of party labels at all.

When presidents talk about "bipartisanship" or "nonpartisanship," they usually mean that they wish the other party would roll over and play dead. Bush was by no means immune to this wish—who could be? But he meant something more by "bipartisanship" than "Do as I say." He meant respect, trust, and a good-faith effort to shrink political differences rather than maximize them for political advantage: in a word, "civility." "Civility," Bush said in his inaugural address, "is more than minding our manners. It is doing our duty."

"Duty" was a word Bush used often. Sigmund Freud imported the Latin pronoun *id* to describe the impulsive, carnal, unruly elements of the human personality. Among recent presidents, the first President Bush seemed not to have an id at all, while Bill Clinton's was given the run of the White House. George W. Bush's id seems to have been at least as powerful and destructive as the Clinton id. But sometime in Bush's middle years, his id was captured, shackled and manacled, and locked away. By the time he entered politics, he was the disciplined, guarded man I saw in the Oval Office in February. During the 2000 campaign, *New York Times* columnist Maureen Dowd ridiculed Bush for bringing a favorite pillow with him on his campaign plane; after the election, Dowd wannabes made fun of Bush's early bedtimes and his long August vacation. He was lazy, they said, or childish, or (alternatively) prematurely old. Bush mischievously enjoyed feeding that perception: Asked at his inaugural what record he hoped to set that evening—a reference to Clinton's record-breaking attendance at eleven different balls at *his* inaugural eight years before—Bush answered, "To get to bed earlier than any president in history."

But no president who rises at 5:45 every morning to have his first briefing at 6:30, who interrupts his day to run three miles in twenty-one minutes before lunch, and whose idea of a vacation is clearing brush in 110-degree West Texas heat can accurately be called "lazy." And a man who has overcome a drinking problem has good reason to shun parties and put himself to bed by 9:30. As for the pillow story, a candidate who intends to rise early and work long needs to use his hours of rest for sleeping, not thrashing around miserably. If he konks out ten minutes earlier on a pillow that fits his head than he would on one of those napkin-thin numbers they offer in campaign hotels—then he ought to bring the pillow.

The final weekend of the 2000 campaign nicely revealed the differences in the temperaments of the two men seeking to lead the country. Al Gore campaigned for thirty continuous hours, snatching what sleep he could on his campaign plane as he jetted from Philadelphia to Dearborn and then to Milwaukee, St. Louis, Flint, Miami, Miami Beach, and Tampa, before at last touching down in Carthage, Tennessee. It was a magnificent display of guts and stamina. On the other hand, an incumbent vice president blessed with a record of eight years of peace and prosperity should not *need* to campaign for thirty hours straight. Bush does not run his seven-minute miles by tripping at the beginning and sprinting at the end. He clicks them off at a steady pace of 8.5 miles an hour, one after another, with a gentle acceleration toward the very end. And he campaigned the same way: steady, efficient, controlled—recognizing that it was better to do two appearances right than to do five of them hoarse, incoherent, and exhausted.

Id control was the basis of Bush's approach to the presidency as well. Bush was a man of fierce anger. When he felt that he had been betrayed or ill-used, his face would go hard, his voice would go cold, and his words would be scathing. Yet he did not allow the anger to govern him. His feelings were as disciplined as his legs. That is what he meant by "doing his duty": not gloopy niceness, but mastery of his emotions. What he called "bipartisanship" flowed from that same self-mastery: He was prepared to work with—even lavishly praise—people he did not fully trust in order to achieve a common goal.

According to his more conservative supporters, Bush frequently emerged second best from some of these exercises in cooperation. Bush would not have agreed. He was not at all an ideological man, and he did not anguish over the sacrifice of this or that item of conservative principle in pursuit of his political goals.

On education, for instance, Bush was never as convinced of the merits of school choice as his ideological supporters were. The education problem that worried Bush most was the low performance of poor and minority children, and Bush doubted that heaping more responsibility on those children's often uneducated, often absent, often neglectful parents would improve the children's learning much. As governor, Bush had emphasized rigorous testing that carried real consequences for subpar schools, not school choice. As a candidate, he had offered an education plan that contained modest choice provisions. And as president, it was testing—not choice—that he fought hardest to preserve in his education bill.

In the same nonideological spirit, Bush was quite prepared to let his argument for his tax plan veer from folk libertarianism ("It's your money!") to the pop Keynesianism he presented to an audience in Billings, Montana, in late March 2001: "We want you to have more cash flow so you can expand your business when this economy is slowing down; we want you to have more money in your pocket so you can continue to employ more hardworking people in the great land of America." As the nominal author of remarks like these, I would receive anguished telephone calls afterward from free-market theorists.

"He's spouting gibberish!" they would complain. "You have to make him stop."

"I have a better idea," I'd reply. "*You* make him stop."

It often looked to conservatives as if Bush were surrendering treasured principles in order to obtain deals that were really not worth having. They could forgive him for reducing the size of his tax cut and adding a $300 rebate in which they did not much believe in order to gain the votes he needed to see the tax-relief plan through the Senate. But when he gave up the choice provisions of his education bill—or amended his faith-based bill to segregate religious activity from social services—many conservatives decided that he was putting politics ahead of principle.

But for Bush, getting things done *was* a principle, not only because the things to be done were important, although of course he believed they were, but because he wanted to prove that American politics still worked: that Democrats and Republicans did not have to destroy each other in an unending tit-for-tat game of scandal and counterscandal. Compromise was indispensable to the "new tone" he had promised to bring to Washington. For him, this "new tone" was a principle at least as important as any policy.

Unfortunately, it was precisely Bush's commitment to civility, to compromise, and to nonpartisanship that led him into the most politically damaging episode of his first year in office: the energy plan fiasco.

I T'S BEEN TEN years since I was in California," mused the president's energy adviser, Robert McNally, whom Bush had nicknamed "Electric Bob." "I had a job here just out of college. I worked in a parachute factory, stuffing chutes into jump bags. And now look," he concluded in a hushed voice. "I'm riding into Los Angeles in a presidential motorcade!"

"Congratulations," I answered. "Except . . . you were probably making more money in the parachute factory."

He calculated for a moment. "Pretty close."

It was the end of May, and Bush was paying his first visit to the largest city in the country's largest state. The mood inside the motorcade was edgy. Bush had lost California to Gore in November by 1.3 million votes. Six months later, the state seemed as unenchanted with him as ever. No well-wishers greeted the motorcade as it whizzed up Sepulveda Boulevard through Inglewood and Culver City; no schoolchildren waved flags outside his hotel. The only Angelenos who seemed interested in his visit were the protesters who thronged the sidewalks across from the Century Plaza Hotel, banging drums and chanting slogans.

I turned back to Electric Bob. "Do you think they're banging drums because they can't afford the electricity for a sound system?"

Half a decade before, the state's political leaders had devised a complex new electricity policy that promised Californians abundant power at low, regulated prices—all without having to build unsightly new power plants.

California's plan took effect in the spring of 1998 and almost immediately began to misfire. By mid-1999, national wholesale electricity prices were rising rapidly, and the state's utilities were losing money on every watt they imported from out of state. Gray Davis, who had won the governorship in 1998 proclaiming, "Boring is back!" opted to lie low and hope for the best. He had built his career by avoiding risks, and he was not going to start courting them now.

This time, however, doing nothing proved the riskiest course of all. The wholesale price of electricity rose and rose and rose: from $17 a megawatt-hour to $50, $100, $500, and finally $1,200. By the spring of 2001, the state's utilities verged on bankruptcy, blackouts were randomly closing factories and networks, business customers were gasping at the doubling and tripling of their power bills, and California's budget surplus had vanished into the pockets of out-of-state electricity exporters and brokers. Desperate and embattled, Davis at last shook off his passivity and boldly went looking for somebody to blame. He nominated Bush.

"Mr. President, you didn't create this problem, but you are the only one who can solve it. With all due respect, Mr. President, Californians want to know whether you are going to be on their side."

It was not only Californians who were worrying about energy prices in the spring and summer of 2001. Gasoline, which could be bought for less than $1.00 a gallon in many states in 1998, spiked up to as much as $2.00 in the Midwest and more than $1.80 in most of the rest of the country. Electricity and natural gas prices soared almost as high and as fast. Between 1998 and 2001, the average American family's expenditure on energy jumped by almost 25 percent. On Election Day 2000, energy had not figured at all on the pollsters' lists of public concerns; by July 2001, it ranked number one.

Shortly after taking office, Bush had ordered Vice President Cheney to draw up a plan to deal with the rise in energy prices and the insecurity of the nation's energy supply. In intense sessions around the long table in the Roosevelt Room, a dozen officials bashed out more than one hundred recommendations in a little less than four months. Cheney would sit at the table's head, frowning and nodding as he listened, seldom speaking even a single word. His words were all reserved for Bush's ears.

There has never been a vice president like Dick Cheney, and there probably never will be again. He abjured any independent political existence from the president. He had no political operation at all. He employed only a single communications aide,

Mary Matalin, and she answered at least as much to Karen Hughes as to him. He shared his sole speechwriter with the president. He built no power base within the party, and he shunned personal publicity. His strength depended entirely on Bush's trust in him—and he earned that trust by subordinating himself entirely to Bush.

Cheney was certainly a powerful figure within the administration. But those who identified him as a shadowy shogun who secretly controlled Bush, the weak mikado, could not have been more wrong. Even on energy, the domestic issue Cheney cared about most, Bush made the ultimate decisions—and Cheney's views, authoritative though they were, were often overridden.

The aide who tangled most often and most vociferously with Cheney was Karen Hughes. Cheney believed that the fundamental energy problem was not a short-term price spike, but a longer-term gap between the growth in American energy production and the growth in American energy use. In 2000, the United States for the first time imported more than half its oil; if the trends of the 1990s continued, the United States would import two-thirds of its oil by the year 2020. Cheney estimated that the United States would need to build between 1,300 and 1,900 new power plants over the next two decades to keep up with the projected demand for electricity. Conservation would obviously help. But as Cheney said in a speech in Toronto in April, while conservation might be a "personal virtue," conservation alone was not "a sufficient basis for a sound, comprehensive energy policy."

Hughes strenuously disagreed. In the 1990s, the environment had emerged as a defining issue for millions of voters, and especially women voters. These voters did not want power plants and power lines built near their homes. They did not like or trust energy companies. They wanted to believe in the promise of conservation and alternative energy. Nor were they worried about the energy outlook two decades out. They wanted price relief now—and they looked to their federal government to deliver it.

Hughes and Cheney battled over the energy policy page by page. And the outcome of their joint effort was—an incoherent mess.

The final report of the energy task force called for expanded oil drilling *and* for regulations to force companies to build costlier, more energy-efficient products. It called for reducing regulatory impediments to the use of coal, while subsidizing wind and solar power and other pet environmental schemes. It advocated careful consideration of an expansion of nuclear power—without ever quite endorsing that expansion.

American consumers wanted cheap, clean energy. The impasse between Hughes and Cheney produced a report that its opponents could plausibly describe as a formula for expensive, dirty energy. Democratic National Committee chairman Terry McAuliffe sighed that "it's clear that [Bush] cares more about oil industry profits than he does about working families' pocketbooks." The Sierra Club piled on: All the subsidies that Hughes had extracted from Cheney amounted merely to "hang[ing] a thin veil of energy efficiency over a cesspool of polluter giveaways."

Indecisiveness had produced a debacle. A CNN/*Time* poll

conducted after the plan's release found that only 38 percent of those surveyed approved of it. A few days after that, Bush's approval rating dropped below 50 percent for the first time in his presidency. A majority of those surveyed expressed doubts that Bush's leadership could be trusted. In the CBS/*New York Times* poll, 63 percent identified Bush as the one thing he most keenly wanted not to be: a "typical Republican."

Almost as soon as the task force delivered its report, Democrats in Congress began to huff and puff about "secret meetings" that Cheney and his people had with industry executives during their work. They demanded a list of all the attendees at these meetings in the hope of exposing the task force's nefarious entanglement with big business.

. This was goofy, even by the standards of Washington stuntsmanship. The task force's recommendations were all printed in black and white and illustrated in vivid color. The issue was surely the report itself, not the process by which it was written. If drilling in Alaska was a sellout to Big Oil, did it become any more a sellout if the members of the energy task force met with the head of Exxon for thirty minutes? Any less a sellout if they didn't? Environmental groups were angry that energy companies were granted better access to the task force than the enviros received. Would it really have made them feel better had they been invited in to rant and rave some more against an administration they had just finished spending millions of dollars to defeat?

Yet the pseudoscandal had its impact, and not only among the Democratic faithful. Bush's aversion to ideology had betrayed him. He had tried to please everybody—and unsurprisingly had pleased almost nobody.

He certainly had not pleased his conservative free-market base. One example: When Bush entered the White House, he found waiting for him a proposed regulation that ordered a big increase in the energy efficiency of washing machines. Free-marketeers hated the regulation: Energy-efficient machines were available on the market already, and consumers could buy them—*if* they were willing to pay hundreds of dollars more, and *if* they did not mind doing smaller and therefore more frequent loads, and *if* they did not mind bending over to fill and empty the machine from the front rather than the top. And if consumers were *not* willing to do those things, it was hard to see a justification for requiring them to do so. Energy is an important resource. So are time and money. It hardly made sense to force people to spend hundreds of dollars' worth of the latter to save a few pennies' worth of the former.

Nevertheless, Bush approved the regulation. Energy, he seemed to think, was too important to surrender to the economists.

I once made the mistake of suggesting to Bush that he use the phrase *cheap energy* to describe the aims of his energy policy. He gave me a sharp, squinting look, as if he were trying to decide whether I was the very stupidest person he had heard from all day or only one of the top five. Cheap energy, he answered, was how we had got into this mess. Every year from the early 1970s until the mid-1990s, American cars burned less and less oil per mile traveled. Then in about 1995 that progress stopped. Why? He answered his own question: Because of the gas-guzzling SUV. And what had made the SUV craze possible? This time I answered. "Um, cheap energy?" He nodded at me. Dismissed.

But if Bush was no energy free-marketeer, neither did he share the crusading zeal of the environmentalist Left. For Bush, the point of energy conservation was not for Americans to *use* less, but for Americans to *import* less. For him, energy was first and foremost a national security issue. In Michigan a month before the 2000 election, he had warned, "Oil consumption is increasing, our production is dropping, [and] our imports of foreign oil are skyrocketing. . . . As a result, America is at the mercy more than ever of foreign governments and cartels. . . ." He underscored this message in his speech unveiling his energy policy in St. Paul, Minnesota, on May 17: "Overdependence on any one energy source, especially a foreign source, leaves us vulnerable to price shocks, supply interruptions, and—in the worst case—blackmail." Even before September 11, Bush took a very skeptical view of the Arab oil powers, countries he described as "maybe our friends—maybe not." When critics of his energy policies pointed out that the Alaskan north shore would probably produce only about six hundred thousand barrels a day, Bush replied that this happened to be the amount that the United States was then purchasing from Iraq under the United Nations' oil-for-food program. Bush preferred to obtain that oil at home, or at least from countries that could emerge as stable new sources of supply: a Mexico tightly linked to a North American common market; a modernizing Russia under pro-Western leadership.

The energy issue stirred not only Bush's hawkish patriotism, but his ancestral puritanism. After finishing a speech practice in the Map Room one afternoon, he pointed with exasperation at a table lamp and demanded: "Do you think it's going to occur

to anybody to turn that lamp off when we leave the room?"
And he walked over and flicked it off himself. It vexed him to
look out the windows of the White House family quarters before sunrise and see the Executive Office Building bright with
lights that had been carelessly left burning overnight. In July,
Bush announced new federal efficiency standards for so-called
vampire devices—cell phone chargers, remote-controlled televi-
sions, and other machines that consume power even when
switched off. Bush proudly explained that by purchasing only
those appliances that met the new standard, the federal government would save enough electricity to power five thousand
homes. Or (I thought) even more homes than that if the home-
owners would just remember to turn off the lights when they
left the room.

The house he built on his Crawford ranch was a showcase
of enviro technology. Cold underground water was tapped and
piped to cool the limestone walls in summer without the use of
air-conditioning, and the house was positioned to be warmed
by the sun in winter. Bathwater was captured, treated, and
reused. Lawn grass was replaced with western wild grasses that
consumed less water; the little water the new plants needed was
provided through a sophisticated system of cisterns and sprin-
klers that relied on rainwater, not the underground aquifer. The
main fuel for the ranch's trucks and other vehicles was
propane, which emits 90 percent less carbon monoxide than
gasoline.

Bush's personal environmentalism did not, however, impel
him to cross himself before every article in the environmentalist
creed—not even article one, faith in the Kyoto Protocol on

global warming. Bush bluntly rejected Kyoto. Indeed, it would have been hard for the global bureaucrats who negotiated it to invent anything more offensive to his sensibilities. Kyoto imposed onerous burdens on the American economy, required Americans to pay taxes to other countries to buy the right to burn their own coal, and then exempted Mexicans, Indians, Chinese, and other industrializing countries from the rules that bound the United States. The Clinton administration had signed the thing in December 1997 but never dared submit it to the Senate for ratification: The Senate had by then put itself on record against a Kyoto-type treaty by a vote of 95–0. Signed but unratified, the protocol gathered dust for the next three years, as the Clintonites desperately hunted for some middle way between their treaty partners and the Senate. They never found it, and in March 2001, Bush at last settled the issue by withdrawing America's signature.

The withdrawal triggered international outrage. The French environment minister made headlines by calling Bush's act a "scandal," and European media reaction was even more violent. None of the European countries were actually abiding by the treaty themselves. But what did that matter? In the view of many European leaders, the decision to sign a treaty is a very different thing from the decision to honor it, and they were mortally offended by America's refusal to join them in their hypocrisy.

It was not only Europeans who felt that way. Reaction was pretty strong inside the United States as well. I happened to be at a conference with a big turnout of entertainment industry types a couple of weeks before the Kyoto repudiation and briefly found myself face-to-face with Barbra Streisand in a narrow auditorium corridor. Neither of us could go anywhere because the path in front of us was entirely obstructed by the vast bulk of the movie producer Harvey Weinstein. When Streisand heard what I did for a living, she released a small, disdainful "Ewwwwww." Streisand normally does not converse with anyone much below the executive producer level, so you can imagine how deeply moved she must have been to exchange words with me. But her rage against Bush had clearly been accumulating for weeks, and here was a Bush representative at hand and immobilized—so she let loose.

"So tell me: Why did Bush flip-flop on emissions standards?" (Bush had dropped a hint or two during the campaign that he might be willing to regard carbon dioxide as a pollutant. The week before the conference, the administration announced that it would not do so after all, at least not yet.) "I know why he did it," she continued. "It was because of all the campaign contributions he got from Enron."

"Wait a minute," I answered. "Enron was on *your* side of this fight." I explained: Most plans to control carbon dioxide envisioned that businesses would have to buy permits to emit the stuff—and Enron hoped to earn a lively sum running the market for these permits. I should probably have stopped there, but I tactlessly kept going. "This guy's not for sale, you know— not like the last one."

That detonated an explosion from Mount Weinstein.

"Barbra and I know this guy!" he bellowed. "Not one dollar went into his pockets! He never took anything!"

After a few minutes more of byplay, Streisand returned to global warming. "The snows on top of Mount Kilimanjaro are melting. There's no disagreement about that."

"Look," I said, "I don't know about that. I'm no kind of expert on climate change. But, Miss Streisand, I strongly suspect that neither are you. For you, this is religion, not science."

She looked at me with utter revulsion. "I know what I'm talking about. I give a lot of money to environmental causes," she huffed and followed Weinstein out the exit.

Yet while Bush disdained Kyoto, he could never quite bring himself to deny that climate change was very likely real and man-made. When he repudiated Kyoto, he promised to produce a climate change policy of his own. But when? Karl Rove and the administration's economists hoped he would postpone any action until the fall, or longer. Secretary of State Colin Powell, Secretary of the Treasury Paul O'Neill, National Security Adviser Condoleezza Rice, and Karen Hughes all pushed him to speak up before his first European trip in June. The green-green-lima-beans (as Bush called the enviros) had prevailed. Bush would give a speech. But what would he say?

Bush handed responsibility for the climate change brief to two midlevel aides who were absolutely convinced that the lima-beans had it right: John Bridgeland in the Domestic Policy Council and Gary Edson in the National Security Council. Bridgeland and Edson were two of the hardest-working men on the Bush staff: I got used to taking calls from Edson at ten o'clock at night and being invited over to see Bridgeland at three o'clock on Sunday afternoon. Bridgeland was a soft-spoken and idealistic moderate Republican from Ohio by way of Harvard, who was later promoted to run Bush's new Office of National Service. Edson, a brainy lawyer from Chicago, could not have been more different: talkative, impatient, sarcastic, a spicy jalapeño pepper in the midst of the smooth cream cheese of the Bush administration. In barely sixty days, they cobbled together an ambitious program of controls and trading permits intended to lower American carbon dioxide emissions by almost as much as Kyoto demanded, without international supervision or pay-offs to foreign entities.

They pushed their program all the way onto the president's desk before anyone else got much of a look at it. If Hollywood were writing the story, Edson and Bridgeland's ardor and enthusiasm would have won the respect of the president, carried the bureaucratic battle, and changed the course of history. In Washington, of course, they were crushed.

Their policy was tossed aside, the speech they wanted the president to deliver was ripped to shreds, and a new one was hastily cobbled together that promised to take the issue seriously—and study it some more. To celebrate their victory, Bridgeland and Edson's bureaucratic rivals leaked the whole story to columnist Robert Novak, who pilloried Bridgeland and Edson as a "contingent of greens inside the Administration . . . pressing the President to look more and more like Al Gore." That column, dated June 14, 2001, deserves a footnote in the history of the Bush administration: It is the first instance I can recall of anyone in the Bush White House leaking to the press to undermine someone else.

The press interpreted Bush's commitment to further study as a commitment to do nothing at all. But Bush had a climate change agenda: nuclear power, or, as Bush always said, "safe and clean nukular power." (This solecism may have been another tip of the hat to Eisenhower, who had always mispronounced the word in exactly the same way.) Nuclear power emits no greenhouse gases at all, and yet the United States had not brought a new nuclear plant on-line in nearly twenty years. As the capacity of America's existing nuclear plants maxed out, electrical utilities burned more and more coal, the dirtiest fuel of them all. By 2000, more than half the country's power was generated by coal.

Some enviros have hoped that the global warming issue could be used to force a simpler way of life on the overfed, overindulged people of the Western world. Bush, though, believed that technological problems demanded ultratechnological solutions. Again and again, in public and in private, he observed longingly that while the United States obtained only 20 percent of its power from nukes, France obtained 80 percent. If the United States could catch even halfway up to France, it could overfulfill its Kyoto commitments—without changing the American way of life at all.

Nuclear power in the United States was constrained by many forces, but probably the most daunting was the problem of waste disposal. For three decades, the problem had been studied and studied and studied—and every time a possible burying place was named, local people protested, national political leaders panicked, and the issue was sent out for one more round of study.

In the 1990s, the most intense studies yet had identified the best available site as Yucca Mountain, Nevada. The Nevada congressional delegation went wild—and since one of Nevada's senators, Harry Reid, was a powerful member of the Democratic leadership and a staunch defender of Clinton during the impeachment battle, Nevada's protests were heard. Clinton suavely positioned himself on both sides of the issue: In April 2000, he vetoed the Yucca Mountain site, not because he opposed it—which would have obliged him to identify another site he preferred—but because he felt that any decision would be premature. He wanted still more study—until, say, well past November 2000.

Bush declined to punt. His policies might flunk the test of market rationality. They might flunk the test of internal consistency. But they seldom flunked the test of courage. He gave the order: The waste would go to Yucca Mountain. The U.S. nuclear industry could grow again.

THAT GLOBAL WARMING leak to Robert Novak begat a summertime series of reprisal leaks. In the first week of July, *Time* magazine was given a whole arsenal of quotes, which together presented a glowing image of Karen Hughes and her efforts to save the administration from disaster.

*Time* opened with an anecdote about the Patients' Bill of Rights. Bush's congressional liaison, Nick Calio, had recommended that Bush threaten a veto if Congress approved the lawsuit-happy Democratic version of the bill. "Hughes," *Time* continued, "jumped into the fray. 'Once we say veto . . . that's all anyone's going to hear.' To Hughes . . . promising to veto a popular bill was sure to be a p.r. disaster. Bush had to be for the people, not the HMOs. 'This will hurt us,' she warned."

In fact, Calio's calculation proved exactly correct. Bush

threatened; Congress yielded; the Republican alternative passed. But Hughes was right, too. After weeks of winning at his ground game, Bush was now being clobbered in the passing game. She told *Time:* "Green issues are killing us." So they were. But then, by the end of June, *all* the issues were killing us.

# 5

# LIKE A FOX

Gᴇɴᴇʀᴀʟ . . . ɪ ᴄᴀɴ'ᴛ name the general. General . . ."
That was Bush's answer in November 1999, when an aggressive Boston television reporter named Andrew Hiller asked him to name the president of Pakistan. Bush whiffled equally dismally on the names of the prime minister of India and the president of Chechnya. He could summon up only one syllable of the name of the president of Taiwan: "Lee." Hiller scored his point—and for weeks afterward Bush mockers had a new favorite anecdote.

The Bush-mockers were not all Democrats. In the summer of 2001, I was invited to a large dinner party in New York City in honor of Governor George Pataki. It was a hot July evening, and the guests were standing on a brick terrace that ran the length of our hosts' apartment.

Before the meal, Pataki stepped onto a little platform to give a short speech. Our hosts had gathered a glittering crowd of opinion makers and fashion leaders. Pataki thanked them all for coming, talked for a while about his record as governor, and then noted that he had just welcomed George W. Bush to the Empire State for the first time since the 2000 election. "I realized," Pataki quipped, "that if *he* can be president, *I* certainly can be governor."

The crowd tittered appreciatively. As the others laughed, the few Republicans present exchanged weary glances. If Bush's old Yale acquaintance and the most prominent Republican governor in the country endorsed the dismissive view of Bush's abilities, how was anybody to be convinced otherwise?

A few weeks after the "can't name the general" incident, I had a chance to talk to one of Bush's old prep school classmates. What did he think? How smart was Bush? He considered the question carefully. He was not a political supporter of Bush's, but he was a fair-minded man.

"George is smart: not the smartest guy I've ever met, but smart. But as a boy, he always used his intelligence to hide his intelligence. And he's still doing it."

Every once in a while, Bush would lose his patience with aspersions upon his intellect. When Larry King asked Bush in December 1999 what he would say to those who doubted his capacities, Bush snapped that the same questions had been asked when he ran for governor of Texas in 1994. "They ignored the fact that I went to Yale and Harvard, and said my intelligence was [not] heavy enough to handle the job—and I won."

More often, though, Bush smiled and chuckled and told jokes about himself.

At Yale commencement 2001: "Take, for example, my old classmate, Dick Brodhead, the accomplished dean of this great university. I remember him as a young scholar, a bright lad, a hard worker. We both put in a lot of time at the Sterling Library, in the reading room, where they have those big leather couches. We had a mutual understanding—Dick wouldn't read aloud, and I wouldn't snore."

At the Al Smith dinner in New York in October 2000, standing beside Al Gore just after the presidential debates: "And I see Bill Buckley's here tonight, a fellow Yale man. We go way back, and have a lot in common. Bill wrote a book at Yale. I read one. He founded the Conservative Party. I started a few parties myself. Bill won every debate he ever had—and, well, I know how that feels."

He told a fellow Yale graduate about being spotted by the star of the Yale football team, the great Calvin Hill, in the back row of a class during the "shopping period" at the beginning of the semester. He said, "Hill shouted out to a half dozen of his nearby teammates: 'Hey! George Bush is in this class! This is the one for us!' "

Some of the jokes packed a punch. Frank Bruni, who covered the campaign for *The New York Times,* tells how Bush innocently asked him about his boss, Arthur Sulzberger, a great-great-grandson of the first Ochs Sulzberger to own the *Times.* "Do you think Sulzberger worked his way to the top?"

As Andy Hiller ascertained, Bush had a poor memory for facts and figures. He sometimes forgot whether his tax plan's last rate reduction went into effect in 2005 or 2006. He could not tell you how many families left the welfare rolls in Wisconsin in the 1990s. Fire a question at him about the specifics of his administration's policies, and he often appeared uncertain. Nobody would ever enroll him in a quiz show.

But memory is not the whole of intelligence and, for a president, probably not its most important attribute. More important than the ability to remember what has happened in the past is the ability to imagine what could happen in the future. As an English political scientist has well observed, the mind of a successful political leader "is more akin to the imagination of a creative artist than to any faculty that intellectuals possess."*

Bush himself must have wished he had remembered Lee Teng-hui's entire name. But the truth is that America's policy toward Taiwan has suffered from too much memory, not too little. It was the forgetful Bush who belatedly dragged it into the twenty-first century.

In 1978, President Carter abrogated the 1955 treaty that promised American aid to Taiwan should China attack. Carter substituted a policy he called "strategic ambiguity"—maintaining a close enough relationship with Taiwan to deter the Chinese, but not so close that the Taiwanese would feel free to provoke the mainland.

In the 1970s and 1980s, this policy possessed at least some modicum of plausibility. Taiwan's undemocratic leaders had not formally abandoned their claim to rule all of China. It was not utterly inconceivable that overconfidence could lead them to goad China—and since China was then an important ally in the cold war against the Soviet Union, such goading had to be avoided at all costs.

By the 1990s, though, "strategic ambiguity" had long ceased to make any sense at all. The Soviet Union had vanished, and China was rapidly evolving from a cold war ally into a re-

* David Marquand, "The Liberal Nation," *Prospect* (March 2002), pp. 23–24.

gional bully and international menace. Taiwan, meanwhile, had moved to full democracy. It staged the first free presidential election in the history of any Chinese-speaking country in 1995 and the second in 1999. In 1995, the mainland threatened to attack Taiwan if the Taiwanese proceeded with their election—and actually fired missiles across Taiwan's shipping lanes. In 1999, the mainland threatened war if the Taiwanese elected Lee Teng-hui, whom the Chinese disliked precisely because he wished to drop the ridiculous claim to rule all of China and instead declare Taiwan an independent democracy.

"Strategic ambiguity" emboldened an aggressive China and denied security to democratic Taiwan. Even so, almost every China expert—and virtually every Hiller-qualified politician and journalist—agreed that the policy must be continued. Not only that: They agreed that anybody who thought otherwise must be a certified bonehead.

Then, on the last day of March 2001, a Chinese fighter pilot rammed an American surveillance plane in international airspace over the South China Sea. The Chinese jet was destroyed and its pilot killed; the American surveillance plane crash-landed on Hainan Island. The Chinese detained the American crew for eleven days and extracted an apology from the United States before releasing them—and eventually a $50,000 payment to return the plane. It was an absolutely outrageous incident, and all the while it lasted, the Bush administration had to keep smiling and pretend that there was nothing amiss here but a little misunderstanding between friends.

During the campaign, George Shultz had promised conservatives that "this young man" would grow into the next Reagan. Now, as President Bush authorized his diplomats to negotiate the text of the apology that would free American aviators, the conservative press was mockingly comparing him instead to Jimmy Carter.

Twelve days after the release of the air crew, Bush announced a big new arms sale to Taiwan: four 1970s-vintage destroyers, eight diesel submarines, and a dozen sub-hunting aircraft. The Chinese squawked mightily, but they must have smiled inwardly. Bush had denied the Taiwanese the late-model missile-intercepting cruisers the islanders really wanted. The sale could not be described as a mere slap on the wrist, but neither was it the slap in the face the Chinese had earned.

They got that slap the very next day.

On April 24, Bush gave an unprecedented series of interviews to mark his hundredth day in office. The journalists predictably grilled Bush on the China incident and the Taiwan arms deal. Through the series of interviews, Bush stuck to the familiar talking points on China: China is not an enemy, we support the One China policy that denies Taiwan's right to statehood, the surveillance flights will resume at some future point. Perhaps Bush's attention slipped, or more likely, perhaps he could no longer bear the sound of his own voice mouthing the State Department's platitudes. But when interviewed by ABC's Charles Gibson, he dropped the talking points and spoke with startling candor.

Gibson asked: "[I]f Taiwan were attacked by China, do we have an obligation to defend the Taiwanese?"

"Yes, we do," Bush replied.

Astonished, Gibson tried to press for a clarification. He did not need to say a word, for Bush pressed on unprompted: "And the Chinese must understand that. Yes, I would."

Gibson, even more amazed: "With the full force of the American military?"

And Bush gave his final answer. "Whatever it took to help Taiwan defend herself."

"Strategic ambiguity" was dead.

Bush's words uncorked a whole jugful of complaints from allies, commentators, and foreign-policy wisemen. Didn't that nitwit in the White House realize how offended the Chinese would be—that he was discarding two decades of American foreign policy—that *he was playing with fire?*

State Department officials rushed to set the record straight, to deny that Bush intended any change in policy, and to reaffirm One China.

But the nitwit in the White House understood very well. The great British Conservative prime minister Lord Salisbury had observed a hundred years before that "the commonest error in politics is sticking to the carcass of dead policies"—and policies don't get any deader than strategic ambiguity after Hainan Island. It was the Chinese who had been playing with fire, and for far too long. Unprompted by his own administration—and to the horror of much of his own foreign-policy bureaucracy— Bush was informing the Chinese and the world that the fire marshals had returned to duty in East Asia.

B USH'S WORDS ON Taiwan showed imagination backed by courage. His new approach to Mexico displayed imagination infused by generosity.

For a Texan, the changes in Mexico since the mid-1980s were as exciting as—and probably even more consequential than—the changes in the Soviet Union. Mexico had lowered its protectionist barriers to join the General Agreement on Tariffs and Trade in 1986. It had entered the North American Free Trade Agreement with Canada and the United States in 1994. And in July 2000, the first truly free election in Mexican history had elected Vicente Fox to the presidency.

Bush and Fox had met while they were both still governors. Each of them was the first president in his country's history to have studied at a business school, Harvard in both cases, although unlike Bush, Fox did not complete a degree. Both were sons of wealthy men, both were businessmen turned ranchers, both espoused a politics that tried to fuse free enterprise and social conscience. The two seem genuinely to have liked each other's company. Yet they were linked by something much more solid than a shared background: mutual advantage.

Relations between the United States and Mexico had long ago ceased to be a purely foreign-policy matter. Some twenty million people of Mexican ancestry were by 2000 legally or illegally present in the United States, the fourth largest ethnic grouping after British, German, and Irish. The vast majority of those people had arrived recently. Many of them intended to return to Mexico someday; many more never would. Remittances from Mexicans working in the United States stabilized the Mexican economy; Mexican Americans were emerging as the single most powerful swing voting bloc in U.S. elections, but one that was increasingly tilting against Bush's Republican Party. If Mexican Americans were lured to the Democratic column by the promise of more lavish social spending and racial preferences for their children in college and on the job, the Republicans would be locked out of the White House forever. If, on the other hand, Bush somehow found a way to reverse the Mexican American voting trend, he would reelect himself and bequeath a strongly competitive party to his successor.

Fox and Bush were each therefore perfectly positioned to help the other with his problems. Fox was even more popular among Mexican Americans than among Mexican Mexicans. Every time Fox pronounced Bush "a friend of Mexico, a friend of the Mexican people, and a friend of mine," as he did at his ranch at San Cristóbal, Bush's numbers among Mexican American voters blipped upward. By April, Bush's approval rating among Hispanics had risen to 49 percent, according to the Harris poll, well below his approval among whites, but half as much again as his score during the election—and almost double his 26 percent among blacks.

Bush meanwhile had the power to grant Fox the thing Mexicans crave most: respect in the United States. Each time Bush rolled out the red carpet for Fox and treated him like the leader of a great power, every time Bush praised Fox's democratic reforms and promised the full cooperation of the United States, he strengthened Fox against the machine hacks and hard leftists who still controlled Mexico's federal Congress and most of its incorrigible bureaucracy. The two presidents covered each other's backs like soldiers working their way up a dangerous street.

U.S. presidents since Franklin Roosevelt have always selected Canada as the destination for their first foreign trip. Bush broke that custom and traveled instead to Fox's ranch. Fox and Bush saw each other again in Quebec City in April at the Summit of the Americas. Fox returned to Washington in May, toured the American Midwest in July, and paid a formal state visit with his new wife and much of his cabinet in the first week of September 2001.

Bush never wearied of wooing Hispanic voters with gestures of welcome and friendship: Spanish words in speeches, appointments of Spanish-surnamed officials, support for social services for legal immigrants, and the deployment of his Spanish-speaking nephew, George P. Bush. But Bush knew that Cinco de Mayo proclamations are not the stuff of enduring political coalitions. He would take the Republican Party where he knew the Democrats could not follow. He would reinvent the GOP as the party that advocated an ever closer relationship between Mexico and the United States—and that won Mexican American votes by delivering prosperity to people of Mexican ancestry on both sides of the border.

He envisioned a border open to labor, a border open to trade, and a border open to investment—especially investment in energy. Mexico had banned foreign investment in its energy industry in 1938, and ever since, Mexican oil production has been controlled by the creaky, corrupt, and polluting state monopoly, Pemex. As a result, even though Mexico's oil reserves are already known to be larger than those of the United States, Mexico provided less than 7 percent of America's 3.3 billion barrels of imports in the year 2000, one-seventh as much as OPEC's Arab members. If Mexico opened itself to the exploration and development of its oil resources by American entrepreneurs and technology, Mexican oil might possibly displace Arab oil from the U.S. market altogether. The United States would never be self-sufficient in oil again, but North America could be—a message that runs through the Cheney energy plan like a leitmotif through a Wagnerian opera.

For this energy "quid," Mexico would of course demand some equally valuable "quo"—and in Bush's mind that "quo" was immigration reform. Bush believed that immigration was valuable to the United States and praised it again and again in his public speeches and his private conversation. But if immigration was valuable to the United States, it was indispensable to Mexico. If all those eager young people who slipped across the border to earn dollars for their families were locked inside Mexico, the country would explode. Even after the economic reforms of the 1990s, Mexico would be burdened with more workers than it could employ for years to come.

So the Bush administration went to work to design some kind of system for regularizing the Mexican American labor relationship—not an amnesty like that of 1986, which simply invited a whole new generation of illegals to try their luck, but some grander system for enabling Mexicans to work in the United States temporarily and then to go home again. Regularization would help both economies. It would protect the United States from developing a submerged caste of workers without legal rights. And it would show Mexican American voters that President Bush wanted to help not only them, but also cousin Frederico who still toiled in Guanajuato and dreamed of working for two years in Chicago to earn the $15,000 it would cost to buy the gas station on Avenida Diaz.

As like-minded as Bush and Fox were, they envisioned very different futures for the continent. Bush saw Mexico evolving into a sunnier, spicier Canada—a country that retained its separate and distinct political system, even as it gradually merged seamlessly into the American economic system. Fox, on the other hand, imagined much more political integration: a North

America that looked like the European Union. Visiting Chicago in July, Fox proposed that Mexicans illegally present in the United States be allowed driver's licenses, access to American colleges and universities, and the right to vote by absentee ballot in Mexican elections. Bush believed that everybody who lived for any length of time in the United States had to become an American like everybody else. Fox dreamed of a future in which millions of people of Mexican ancestry lived in the United States and somehow identified with both Mexico and the United States at once.

These differences were not merely theoretical. They stymied negotiations all through 2001 and embittered Fox's state visit in September. Fox stepped out of his helicopter on the South Lawn on the morning of September 5, walked to the microphone, and without preliminaries assigned Bush a deadline for meeting his demands. "We must, and we can, reach an agreement on migration before the end of this very year."

Visitors do not usually talk in such a peremptory way to the president of the United States, especially not when they are standing on his lawn and getting ready to walk into his home. The objectionable tone of Fox's opening comments foreshadowed the entire disastrous visit. At the staff and cabinet meetings, Mexicans made blunt demands on their American counterparts for concessions on immigration, while refusing even to discuss the opening of their energy market.

I still remember that last week. The weather was hauntingly beautiful, a perfect Washington late summer. Mexican flags were bunched alongside the Stars and Stripes on the lampposts of West Executive and Pennsylvania Avenues. Dazzling boughs of flowers filled the White House. All was lovely—except for the grim-faced aides who stomped up and down the big staircases of the Executive Office Building, muttering about the intransigence of their Mexican counterparts. But in the photographs of the event that lined the halls of the West Wing for a week afterward, I could see Bush and Fox and the two First Ladies toasting one another jovially on the Truman balcony—and it occurred to me that the mutual exasperation of the two delegations was not the only reality of the week. Bush and Fox were of course not friends. They may have become fond of each other, even enjoyed each other's company, but two men with such large and often contradictory responsibilities can never truly be friends. But they were perhaps something more: collaborators in one of the greatest works of imagination ever essayed on this continent. That work might be obscured by the events to come, but its day would return. And if Bush sometimes blanked out on the details of Article 114.3(e)ii of the North American Free Trade Agreement, well, something has to be forgiven to the artistic temperament.

E VEN BUSH'S STERNEST critics were prepared to concede that he handled the relationship with Fox well. But Mexico, they complained, was too easy a test. The commanding Fox had made Bush look good. Set Bush a tougher challenge, and he was sure to fail. Bush's June meeting with Vladimir Putin in Slovenia seemed at the time to prove those critics right. The American and Russian leaders met in a baroque castle for two hours of face-to-face conversations, and their press conference afterward was instantly filed alongside the Hiller interview in the "Bush is a dunce" dossier.

"I looked the man in the eye," Bush said of Putin. "I found him to be very straightforward and trustworthy. We had a very good dialogue. I was able to get a sense of his soul."

His *soul*? Putin was a former KGB man who, according to some in U.S. intelligence, had helped the spy agency hide billions of dollars of assets before the collapse of the Soviet Union. Putin had pressured Yeltsin into appointing him vice president, most likely by threatening to publicize the graft and corruption of Yeltsin's family and friends. Yeltsin had then resigned six months before the scheduled election, enabling Putin to run for the presidency backed by all the sinister advantages of Russian incumbency. Putin had used an extremely peculiar series of bombings in Moscow to justify a war in Chechnya. He had laid flowers on the grave of Yuri Andropov, former KGB chief, former Communist Party general secretary, and the Soviet ambassador who urged the invasion of Hungary in 1956. Since taking office, Putin had stealthily moved to close or take control of every independent media source in Russia. Most ominous of all, Russian companies were selling nuclear technology to Iran— and Putin either could not or would not halt them. Had Bush known any of *this* when he pronounced Putin "straightforward" and "trustworthy"?

*The Washington Post*, a newspaper not reflexively hostile to the administration, complained that the president sounded "naïve."* The liberal *New Republic* complained, "Gush, gush, gush: Bush has mistaken big power summits for daytime television."† The popular television pundit Chris Matthews com-

---

* *Washington Post*, June 19, 2001, p. A-20.
† *New Republic*, July 2, 2001, p. 7.

mented sarcastically in his newspaper column, "Such powers of observation deserve our attention. George Reeves, the first Superman, could see whether a bad guy was hiding a gun under his coat. George W. Bush can see clear into a Russian ex-spymaster's 'soul.' "* Senator Joseph Lieberman complimented the president with heavy irony on his ability to gain such insights in two hours of conversation.

That hurt. And it did not help that Bush—stung by the criticism—gave an interview to Peggy Noonan of *The Wall Street Journal* and proceeded to expand at some length on what a fine job he had done in Slovenia. "I think Ronald Reagan would have been proud of how I conducted myself. I went to Europe as a humble leader of a great country, and stood my ground."

For the two months after the Slovenia summit, Bush's most ardent supporters and even his staff tacitly accepted the media's hostile verdict. Putin the ex-KGB man, the leader of a has-been country with an economy the size of the Netherlands, had been lavished with presidential praise in return for nothing at all that anybody could see. Bush's inexperience must have finally caught up with him.

Or had it? Bush told Noonan that he and Putin had identified one common supreme security interest: Islamic fundamentalism. And he described how he had given Putin a short introduction to the Bush preference for imagination over memory. Putin had told Bush that he loved to read history. Bush replied: " 'I do, too, I like history a lot. . . . You know, sometimes when you study history, you get stuck in the past.' I said, 'President Putin, you and I have a chance to make history. The rea-

* Syndicated column, June 22, 2001.

son one should love history is to determine how to make good history. And this meeting could be the beginning of making some fabulous history. We're young. Why do you want to stay stuck?'"

Sixty days later, America was at war. And at the head of the queue to help was . . . Vladimir Putin. Putin ordered up an increase in Russian oil production to help calm world markets. He kept his nuclear force on standby even as America went to the highest standard of alert—an act of trust in the United States that would once have been unthinkable for a Russian leader. Even when U.S. forces entered the territory of the former Soviet Union itself, in Uzbekistan and other newly independent states, Putin uttered not one word of protest. Bush had given Putin words of praise. Putin repaid him with coin more solid than words. And when in December Bush announced that the United States would withdraw from the Anti-Ballistic Missile Treaty it had signed with the Russians in 1972—and the Chinese and the French and everyone else with an interest in continued American vulnerability looked to the Russians to protest and resist— Putin mildly shrugged the decision off. "This step was not a surprise for us. However, we consider it a mistake."

And why should Putin not be calm? The day before the Slovenia summit, in a speech to the faculty and students of Warsaw University, Bush had offered Putin a much bigger prize than any arms control treaty: full membership in the Western world. "We look for[ward to] the day when Russia is fully reformed, fully democratic, and closely bound to the rest of Europe. . . . Russia is part of Europe."

In Bush's first six months in office, he had executed the most ambitious reorientation of America's grand strategy since

Nixon's time—away from China and toward Russia. He might be a little hazy about the details. But more than either of his immediate predecessors, he dared to discard obsolete ideas and habits and adapt himself to new times and new circumstances. And if Charles Darwin is to be believed, isn't adaptability the highest function and ultimate purpose of human intelligence?

"Bush isn't very smart—he just gets good advice." How often did we hear people say that in the first year, as if it were obvious which advice was good and which was not? Presidents are inundated by advice, and the very worst of it often sounds as beguiling and plausible as the very best. A president who consistently recognizes and heeds good advice will make good decisions. And about a president who consistently makes good decisions we can say: He's smart enough.

Bush was not a lightweight. He was, rather, a very unfamiliar type of heavyweight. Words often failed him, his memory sometimes betrayed him, but his vision was large and clear. And when he perceived new possibilities, he had the courage to act on them—a much less common virtue in politics than one might suppose.

On a visit to Crawford Elementary School later that summer, one of the students asked him whether he found it hard to make decisions.

His answer described the workings of his mind with more candor—and less false modesty—than he usually allowed himself.

"Is it hard to make decisions as president? Not really. If you know what you believe, decisions come pretty easy. If you're one of these types of people that are always trying to figure out which way the wind is blowing, decision making can be difficult. But I find that I know who I am. I know what I believe in, and I know where I want to lead the country. And most of the decisions come pretty easily for me, to be frank with you.

"I realize sometimes people don't like the decisions. That's okay. I've never been one to try to please everybody all the time. I just do what I think is right. The good thing about democracy, if people like the decisions you make, they let you stay. If they don't, they'll send me back to Crawford. Isn't all that bad a deal, by the way."

# 6

## SUMMER OF OUR
## DISCONTENT

KARL ROVE'S PLAN for the first year of the Bush administration looked like the diagram of a football play: charge
right—pivot—and then race down the field on the left-hand
side. The tax plan was the right charge, the faith-based initiative
the pivot, education the leftward streak. Complicated maneuvers like this depend on precise timing and good luck. And just
as Bush was executing his pivot, his luck ran out. Wham: He
was hit high and low first by the negative reception of the energy plan and then by the Jim Jeffords defection. For the next
three months, the administration was left to wander dazed
about the field, trying to shake the ringing out of its ears. The
playbook was played out.

Of the hundred senators of the 107th Congress, it would be
hard to name any one more perfectly ordinary than James Jeffords, Republican of Vermont. By the spring of 2001, Jeffords
had served in the upper house for a dozen years without doing
anything memorably awful or noticeably valuable.

Jeffords was usually described by the press as a "moderate Republican." If that phrase is supposed to imply that he found himself somewhere in the middle of the party, then it was very wrong. Jeffords was by far the most liberal Republican in the Senate, more liberal even than the late John Chafee of Rhode Island, and considerably more liberal than Olympia Snowe and Susan Collins of Maine. Despite his maverick voting record, Jeffords was not unpopular with his more conservative colleagues. They knew he was about the best they could hope for from Vermont, and they had learned to adjust to his quirks. One of those quirks was a more than ordinary fondness for the status and power of a committee chairman. In the spring of 2001, that human weakness turned the Bush administration on its ear.

Jeffords had originally joined the Republican Party out of tribal instinct. In Vermont in the 1960s, the Democrats were still the party of "rum, Romanism, and rebellion," and an old Yankee like Jeffords would no sooner join them than he would testify in church or talk about his "momma" in a campaign speech. Besides, the Republicans had more to offer. When a Senate seat opened up in 1988, the Vermont GOP handed its nomination to Jeffords on a platter. When the Republicans captured the Senate in 1994, Jeffords ascended to the chairmanship of one of the body's most powerful committees: Labor and Education.

The split result of the 2000 election threatened his agreeable position. Jeffords was now sixty-seven years old. He had just been reelected to a third and quite likely final term. He wanted to serve it out as a chairman. The loss of only a single seat would bump him out of his chair—and that seat could be lost tomorrow: South Carolina senator Strom Thurmond was ninety-eight years old, and if he passed on before his term ended in 2004, the state's Democratic governor would name his successor. And then good-bye chairmanship!

Senate Democrats understood Jeffords's problem—and his weakness. But they had a problem, too. They needed control of the Senate *now.* Thurmond could die tomorrow—but he could also last six more months. If he hung on until the tax bill passed, control of the Senate would do the Democrats little good: The surpluses would be returned and all their spending hopes would be dashed. They would give much to the man who could turn the Senate over to them before the tax bill passed—very, very much.

If Jeffords had been a better man or a worse one, he would have found his decision much easier. A better Jeffords would have stood up at once for his liberal principles and joined the Democrats while there was still time to stop the tax bill. A worse Jeffords would have appreciated that his vote became less valuable as the tax bill came closer and closer to final passage and would have sold out early for a whacking big price. But Jeffords was neither a liberal hero nor a cynical opportunist. He was a pleasant man, weak and vain, who wanted to keep his chairmanship but hesitated to break faith with old friends like Trent Lott and Olympia Snowe. So he hesitated—and thought—and hesitated some more. February passed into March. March gave way to April. April became May. The tax bill moved through the House. It passed through the Senate Finance Committee. Jeffords joined with John McCain and some of the more conservative Democrats to whittle down its size. But still he held back from taking the one step that could have killed it altogether.

Then, at the eleventh hour, Jeffords did what weak people often do—he moved his decision out of his own hands, by creating a crisis to shift responsibility away from himself.

About May 17, perhaps even a day or two earlier, rumors began to circulate inside the White House of Jeffords's impending defection. He was angry, he told the Democrats (who then told the press), that he had not been invited to the Rose Garden ceremony honoring the 2001 Teacher of the Year, a fellow Vermonter. Over the weekend of May 19–20, Jeffords reconsidered this story. Perhaps he felt it made him sound petty. In any case, by the time he met with Bush on May 22, Jeffords was poohpoohing the Teacher of the Year affront and pressing instead a new demand: He would remain loyal to the GOP if Bush scaled back his tax cut to make available $180 billion in special education funds over the next ten years.

This was an arresting proposition. Were the Bush administration even to consider reopening the tax bill, every senator would suddenly rush forward to demand *his* $180 billion special favor. And probably every single one of those special favors would possess a lot more merit than Jeffords's.

Since its creation in 1976, the federal special education program had evolved into a vast slush fund to pay for the warehousing of poor children and undeserved perks for rich ones—one of the most insidious forms of the "soft bigotry of low expectations" that George Bush had denounced in the 2000 campaign. Although the total number of physically and mentally disabled children has actually *dropped* over the past quarter-century (thanks to better prenatal care, better nutrition, better medicine, and the wider use of car seats and seat belts), the number of kids diagnosed as "special needs" has *tripled*. In the single decade 1991–1999, the number of special education children jumped from about four million to a little over six million.

Special education offered school districts their two favorite things: money and excuses. Diagnosing a child as "special needs" can gain a school up to $10,000 a year in extra state and local funds. And "special needs" kids can either be excused from state proficiency tests—or accommodated in ways that boost their scores.

"Special needs" diagnoses are especially common among two groups of children: the poorest and the richest. The eagerness of school districts to label their black children as abnormal and untestable is a familiar scandal. What is perhaps more surprising is the willingness of very affluent families to accept a "special needs" label in order to get their children free tutoring, free computers, and extra time on tests. One out of every three children in superwealthy Greenwich, Connecticut, is now diagnosed as learning-disabled. While only 13 percent of the students who took the SAT in 1999 came from families that earned more than $100,000 a year, 27 percent of the students who received extra time or other special favors came from the $100,000-plus bracket.*

And surprise, surprise: While most of the children who get the "special needs" diagnosis are poor and black, most of the special education money goes to children who are white and

* Clint Bolick, "A Bad IDEA Is Disabling Public Schools," *Education Week*, September 5, 2001.

rich. Oh: And the region of the country in which these affluent special needs students are most densely concentrated happens to be Jim Jeffords's own New England.

Bush told Jeffords that he did not oppose large, even very large, increases for a reformed special education program. His 2002 budget upped special education spending by $1 billion. In an October 2000 interview with *BusinessWeek,* Bush had endorsed future increases potentially as large as anything Jeffords was calling for—provided that the program was reformed of its notorious abuses. If Jeffords would endorse Bush's reform proposals, Bush would agree to find Jeffords the $180 billion he wanted.

Jeffords must have understood that by rebuffing Bush's offer and quitting the Republican Party he was shoving his pet cause to the very back of the cause queue. But there was something he wanted more than $180 billion for special ed. He wanted to be pushed into a step he could not bring himself to take on his own. He walked out of the Oval Office, told the waiting press that he would make a statement two days hence, and flew up to Montpelier to, as he said grandly, "declare my independence."

The big networks, the newsmagazines, and the top newspapers all eagerly accepted and uncritically repeated Jeffords's version of events. *Time* magazine's Margaret Carlson told CNN that Jeffords "is a man of principle . . . [who] gave word to what some of us have not been able to, which is that Bush campaigned as a moderate, but he's been governing as an arch-conservative." On NBC's *Today* program, Matt Lauer asked Karen Hughes, "Is this a chance for the [Republican] Party to look at itself and perhaps move more to the center, become more moderate in the wake of his defection?"

Almost nobody pointed out that Jeffords had made a fool of himself. Not only did he postpone his decision until it was too late to do the Democrats any good, but Bush even extracted a formal promise from him to delay his departure from the Republican Party until the tax bill was signed and sealed. Unsurprisingly, the Democrats now set a rather lower value on Jeffords's defection—especially since he could not in the end bring himself to identify with the party of Tammany Hall and Jefferson Davis. Instead he affiliated as an independent and caucused with the Democrats. They rewarded him, accordingly, with a distinctly second-tier chairmanship in the Senate: Environment and Public Works. His old gavel at Labor and Education was taken by Ted Kennedy.

Kennedy would spend the next six months trying to discover how high a price Bush would pay for something called "an education reform bill." Bush had floated his education proposals on the third day of his administration; now Kennedy could gnaw at them like the hungry shark eating the big fish in *The Old Man and the Sea*. Reform of special ed: Gulp! Tests with meaningful consequences for failing schools: Gulp! Gulp! Choices for children trapped in bad schools: Gulp! Gulp! Gulp! With every bite, Bush's conservative supporters wondered more and more whether the education bill was worth having.

By midsummer, they were wondering more than that. While Bush's position among Republicans outside Washington was unassailable, and while very few conservatives inside the capital were willing to speak on the record against him, at the six-month mark, questions about Bush's leadership were being asked persistently and loudly. All the old doubts about Bush were bubbling up again: Was he up to the job? Did he have any principles at all? Was he too soft, too naive, too inexperienced? I began avoiding parties where I expected the questions to be posed too persistently by my conservative friends, for I was not sure I would know how to answer. I felt strongly that the doubters were wrong, yet I lacked evidence to refute them. By the end of July, every single item on the Bush first-year agenda seemed to be blocked, stalemated, or doomed. On issue after issue, Bush himself seemed to have started a long retreat that threatened to end where his father's deal making had ended: back in Texas after a single term.

Jeffords's switch installed his fellow Vermonter Pat Leahy as chairman of the Judiciary Committee—and Leahy stopped approval of Bush's judges dead. In the year from June 2001 to June 2002, Bush would nominate eleven judges to the federal courts of appeal. Leahy would schedule hearings on just three of them, and two of these three were former Clinton nominees whose nominations had lapsed, and whom Bush had renominated in a gesture of goodwill. Over at the Pentagon, Rumsfeld's modernization initiative seemed to have been successfully thwarted by the admirals and generals. Bush's Social Security proposals had been passed off to a commission with a long, long deadline. The Senate voted again to ban all oil exploration on the Alaskan north shore.

Perhaps most ominous of all, Bush's signature faith-based initiative had stumbled into a quagmire of backbiting and recrimination. The initiative had begun as a brilliant ploy to unite conservative evangelicals, urban Catholics, minority pastors, and traditional noblesse oblige Republicans in a grand religiously inspired approach to social problems. It ended by casting doubt on George Bush's core political strategy.

To run his faith-based office, Bush had named a former colleague of mine from the Manhattan Institute, John DiIulio. DiIulio was a brilliant scholar, but an irascible man, who stumbled almost immediately into a series of fights with evangelical leaders. DiIulio disdained Washington's arcane etiquette: He saw no reason why if Pat Robertson criticized him, he should not slam Pat Robertson back in return. At a convention of evangelical ministers in March 2001, he dismissed Robertson and his allies as "white, exurban . . . parachurch leaders" and warned them not to "presume to speak for any persons other than themselves."

DiIulio wanted to direct faith-based dollars to black and Hispanic churches that "have benevolent traditions and histories that make them generally more dedicated to community-serving missions"—more dedicated, that is, than you-know-who—"and generally more confident about engaging public and secular partners in achieving their missions. . . ."

If evangelicals did not like it, well, nuts to them. They had nothing to offer people in need anyway: "Bible-thumping," DiIulio said, "doesn't cut it."

In July, the guerrilla struggle between DiIulio and the evangelicals burst into open warfare.

On the morning of July 10, *The Washington Post* reported on an internal Salvation Army memo that claimed the nation's largest Protestant charity had struck a deal with the White House: It would support the faith-based bill. In return, the White House would adopt a new regulation forbidding federal aid to state and local governments that required religious groups to adopt hiring practices that contradicted those groups' religious beliefs. English translation: No more federal dollars for San Francisco if the city continued its campaign to force the Salvation Army to offer gay domestic partner benefits to its employees.

The Salvation Army memo stoked House liberals' worst fears. On the day the *Post* story broke, John Conyers and Jerrold Nadler of the Judiciary Committee wrote to DiIulio, "[W]e have long been concerned" that faith-based plans "are merely tools to permit increased discrimination and which would inappropriately entangle religion in our political affairs."* Now they had their proof.

They had proof of something else, too: DiIulio's isolation and powerlessness. DiIulio immediately dismissed the *Post* story as "preposterous." DiIulio might have a Ph.D. from Princeton, but he saw himself as a tough guy from North Philadelphia, and now he swaggered into battle. There was no deal with the Salvation Army, he said, and never had been. The Salvation Army had made some proposals to junior aides at the Office of Management and Budget—but nobody had ever talked to *him* about the proposed regulation, and he was the man who called the shots. And as the man who called the shots, DiIulio said he had "no plans to pursue [the Salvation Army's regulation]. Period." No story here, fellows.

Except that the next day, the White House admitted there *was* a story. True, the Salvation Army had never discussed the matter with DiIulio. But they had discussed it with Karl Rove.

---

* Letter dated July 10, 2001, reprinted at www.house.gov/judiciary_democrats/dletters.htm.

Was there a deal? The Salvation Army denied it. But what could not be denied was that DiIulio was *not* the man calling the shots. Even more humiliating, he had not known that he was not calling the shots.

On August 17, DiIulio handed in his resignation, effective September 11.

DiIulio's departure was quietly celebrated by conservative evangelicals and noisily lamented by his would-be beneficiaries in the black churches. Eugene Rivers, one of DiIulio's favorite black ministers, told *The Washington Post* that DiIulio's resignation "sends a signal that the faith-based office will just be a financial watering hole for the right-wing white evangelicals." He told the *Boston Globe* that "with John DiIulio's departure, the Bush Administration has told the inner cities to go to hell."

The big idea that was supposed to bust the Republican Party out of its white evangelical box had blown itself up. Instead of drawing new people to the Republican Party, it had repelled them.

The introduction of the gay issue was especially damaging. Bush's instincts on gay rights issues were clear and emphatic: *Do not touch them.* During the campaign he had refused to comment on Vermont's civil unions. They were, he said, a local issue for local officeholders. He made a curt nod toward traditionalists by refusing to accept the support of the Log Cabin Republicans, an organization of gay Republicans—and then nodded equally curtly toward gay rights groups by meeting with a dozen prominent homosexuals in Austin after he had clinched the nomination. In office, he retained Clinton's Office of National AIDS Policy and named an openly gay man to run it, and he named a second open gay to the Advisory Commission on the Arts. He did not repeal any of the spousal benefits that Clinton had introduced for homosexual federal employees. He did not object when some of his cabinet secretaries participated in Gay Pride events in their departments—and he did not object when others did not.

Michael Gerson had a formula that nicely described the balance Bush was trying to strike: "morally traditional and socially inclusive." Gay issues demanded a choice between those two imperatives, and for that very reason Bush wished to have nothing to do with them.

All through the spring and summer, the faith-based initiative had been modified to mollify its secular critics. It had been titled "the Community Solutions Act," to stress its nonsectarianism. In his speeches Bush amended his language about "good people of all faiths" to "good people of all faiths and of no faith at all." That last phrase undercut some of the original logic of the faith-based initiative, which was premised on the claim that federal social-service grant making discriminated against the good works of people of faith in favor of the good works of people of no faith. Nonetheless, the House approved the Community Solutions Act on July 19 and sent it over to the Senate—to languish.

S TALEMATE, STUMBLES, and defeats: The first congressional session of Bush's presidency was ending badly. It was Karen Hughes who concocted the unusual remedy for Bush's midsummer slump: a vacation.

When the White House announced in July that Bush would

be spending the month of August on his ranch, the journalists cackled. A month-long holiday corroborated all their prejudices about Bush. *USA Today,* the administration's least disliked major paper, found a professor at the University of Missouri to sum up the conventional view: "Maybe he's lazy, maybe he's not determined. It feeds into the impression that he's not in charge."*

But the vacation was no vacation at all: It was a mini–political campaign. Hughes called it a "Home to the Heartland" tour and pronounced, "I don't want to see the president in a jacket and tie until Labor Day!" After the energy fiasco and the Jeffords defection, Bush would use August to reaffirm his connections to moderate, swing-voter America. Bush left Washington on August 4, 2001. On August 8, he traveled into Waco to build a house with Habitat for Humanity. On August 13, surrounded by Hispanic-looking farmers in open-necked shirts and cowboy hats, he signed the agriculture bill at his ranch. The next day he flew to Rocky Mountain National Park in Colorado to hoist a shovelful of dirt at a YMCA picnic. The day after that, he stopped by a heavily Hispanic elementary school in Albuquerque. On August 16, he issued a statement condemning bias against religious organizations in federal grant making.

Even when there was nothing on the schedule, Hughes released White House photographs of Bush striding the range like the Marlboro Man: clearing brush in the early morning hours or meeting with his advisers in checked shirt and blue jeans. He visited a Target store in Kansas and a Harley-Davidson factory

* Laurence McQuillan, "White House to Move to Texas for a While," *USA Today,* August 3, 2001, p. 10A.

in Wisconsin. And sure enough, his numbers began to climb up and up and up, back to where they had been in early May.

Hughes helped to drive those numbers up with Bush's most politically effective speech of the summer: his prime-time televised address on stem-cell research.

Six months earlier, probably not one American in fifty had ever heard of a stem cell. By the summer of 2001, stem cells had emerged as an issue with the power to shatter Bush's image as a social moderate.

In 1998, a biologist at the University of Wisconsin named James Thomson had discovered that the cells in four-day-old human embryos could be used in ways that might treat a range of terrifying diseases. Further research on these "stem cells" (so-called because, like a tree trunk, they could be made to branch out into thousands of different varieties of specialized cells) was barred, however, by a 1995 law that forbade the use of federal money for research that created or destroyed human embryos.

But it all depends on the meaning of the word *destroy,* doesn't it? Over the next two years, the Clinton administration sought—and found—loopholes in the 1995 law to permit research into embryonic stem cells to proceed.

As human embryo research advanced from theoretical possibility into imminent fact, the nation's pro-life groups mobilized against it. For pro-lifers, embryo research was as bright a moral line as human beings have ever been tempted to cross. Once we abandoned the moral rule against killing one innocent life to benefit another, they feared, we would plunge into a world without morality at all, where the powerful would use the weak as if they were so much inanimate meat.

On the campaign trail, Bush had denounced stem-cell experiments. In office, though, he delayed a final decision. The promised benefits from the research were so great that he hesitated to shut it down too hastily. He asked Health and Human Services Secretary Tommy Thompson to study the issue. In the meantime, the administration postponed all decisions on grant requests.

By July, the scientists had waited six months for Bush to make up his mind—and they were grumbling to sympathetic newspapers. U.S. STUDY HAILS STEM CELLS PROMISE, blared *The New York Times* at the end of June. A QUESTION OF LIFE AND DEATH, was *Newsweek*'s verdict in a July 9 cover story. (Just in case that headline left anyone in doubt as to which was the right side of the issue, the newsweekly explained on the inside that stem cells pitted "religion against science" and "pro-life purists against research.")

Polls taken after this press barrage showed that two-thirds of the public favored stem-cell research. So did many of the party's biggest donors. So did Nancy Reagan. So did a large majority of the White House senior staff. So did Vice President Cheney and Andy Card.

If Bush were the puppet of his staff or his vice president that so many journalists still believed him to be, now was the moment for him to snap to. But he didn't. He did something I had never seen him do: He brooded.

Very early one July morning, I was called into the Oval Office to receive some comments on a speech. After he finished, Bush paused and then said he had a question for me: Where did I come down on stem cells?

The Oval Office is a less chilling space in the early morning than in the afternoon. The sun streams in from the east-facing windows over the Rose Garden and through the tall windows to the south. Sometime in the spring, I'd noticed that my heart no longer jackhammered when I entered this space. I'd become used to speaking in here, even to making jokes—but not quite to speaking my mind. The jackhammering suddenly recommenced.

"Sir, I think when you are leading an outnumbered army, you have to be very careful about the ground you choose to defend. I don't know that you want to be seen as opposing research and knowledge—finding out what these stem cells can do. People are being offered some very tempting benefits, and it's going to be hard to persuade them to give them up."

"So you'd be practical, not moral?"

"No, sir, I'd just look for different ground. I wouldn't want the issue to be science versus religion. I'd want the issue to be human dignity versus commerce. Don't fight the scientists. Fight the biotech companies. What if you looked for a way to ban the purchase and sale of embryos? That would put a stop to most of the research you object to in a way that is very hard to answer back. People may not agree that embryos are human beings. But they'll agree that they're human life—and that human life should not be bought and sold."

I paused. He looked interested. So I kept talking.

"When I was a boy," I continued, "I attended a synagogue where the rabbi used to preach the same sermon every year. He used to say that if the current generation could live forever in exchange for no new generations coming into the world, we would of course say no. But would we really? Back then, what he was saying was a theoretical proposition. I think these days, though, you'd get a vote of eighty to twenty for the living."

The president laughed. "Yes, the living get their way, don't they?"

He made a motion, and I took my leave.

My advice had no influence whatsoever. I was suggesting a line of retreat from the political consequences of seeming too extremely pro-life. But Bush did not want to retreat. He held true to his principles—and trusted in Karen Hughes to explain them.

The specifics of the compromise that Bush adopted are usually credited to Karl Rove. I can't attest to that because the final hours of the process were so closely held, but it sure sounded like something he would propose: staunch on the content, cunning in the details. Research would be permitted on existing stem lines—that is, on cells taken from embryos that had already been killed—but it would be forbidden on new ones. And the federal government would massively fund research into adult stem cells, cells that came from the patient's own body and that required no killing at all.

The visuals of the stem-cell speech were less than inspiring. Bush looked ill at ease and nervous, and an incompetent cameraman pulled his lens too far from Bush's face, making the president look remote and small. But as a communication to the nation, the speech was inspired. Just as she had done on the first State of the Union, Hughes had distilled a complicated issue into extremely simple language—and presented it to the nation in terms that reassured the country's vast political center that their president was a moderate, reasonable, and thoughtful person.

The stem-cell speech had the simple structure that Hughes always preferred. Bush reviewed first the arguments for research, then the arguments against it, before finally presenting his own view. Instead of stressing what the government would forbid, the speech emphasized all that it would permit. And because Bush summarized all points of view so sympathetically, he was able to win the support of his viewers for his own not at all middle-of-the-road position.

The nation's Catholic bishops caviled rather ungenerously at the speech the next day. Then again, maybe they did him a favor. Bush had defended on national television the most unflinchingly pro-life position ever expressed by a president before a mass audience: "I . . . believe human life is a sacred gift from our Creator. I worry about a culture that devalues life, and believe as your president I have an important obligation to foster and encourage respect for life in America and throughout the world." And he had not only protected but actually expanded his image as a moderate. It was a masterstroke—and Hughes's finest hour.

A FTER STEM CELLS, a thick, sticky summertime quiet settled on the White House. The Washington summers are steamy and sultry. Inside the ancient offices of the Executive Office Building, the window air conditioners puffed out little jets of cool air like an asthmatic trying to blow out a birthday cake. The phones that never stopped ringing in the spring now kept their silence for hours at a stretch.

Being a White House speechwriter is a lot like being a fireman, without the heroics: Much of your time is spent waiting around in case you are needed. I would sit on the couch in my office to read and wake up fifteen minutes later with the book on my face, dreaming of suffocation and drowning. Staffers were vanishing for their holidays. My wife and children packed up and drove north to Canada. And then it was time for my holiday, too, and off I flew after them.

I landed in Toronto and boarded a train east to the pastureland of Prince Edward County, Ontario. I had a book with me, but I did not read it. I had some hard thinking to do. Over the previous six months, I had come to like and admire Bush, but I was not enjoying working in his White House. Since the tax battle, we had worked harder and harder on less and less—and since the loss of the Senate, the domestic agenda of the administration had filled up with gimmicks and dodges.

September would bring more of the same—only worse. The speechwriters had received early notice of a big new initiative for the fall. Under the title "Communities of Character," a grab bag of proposals would address a long and various list of ills: obscene music lyrics, children not eating dinner with their parents, racial intolerance, pervasive cynicism, school shootings, and so on. With the tax cut behind us and Social Security reform receding ever further into the distance, the administration would now take up school safety and character education. Somebody had written a policy paper suggesting that newspapers be encouraged to print more positive stories and that the federal government promote e-mail as a means for grandparents to keep in touch with grandchildren.

My heart sank at the thought of it all. The work ahead of me was not work I wanted to do, and I had come to like Bush too much to want to be a tourist inside his White House as his administration unraveled. As the train pulled into the little town of Belleville, I made up my mind: I would give myself a week or two after Labor Day to confirm that the next political season really was shaping up to be as dismal as I feared. Then it would be time to go.

# 7

## 9/11

Inside the white house, the events of September 11 began just the way they did for everyone else: on television. But for those of us who worked there, the events did not remain on the screen for very long.

I arrived at work late that morning. Washington's highway traffic, never good, was especially horrible that day, and I had to inch my way to the office from my children's school, too irritated even to listen to the radio. I did not pull into the little strip of parking spaces in front of the old Executive Office Building until a few minutes after nine.

My cell phone rang as I reached my desk. It was my wife's gentle voice that first introduced me to the hard facts of our new life: Two hijacked planes had crashed into the World Trade Center. The twin towers were burning. Thousands of people were in danger. The United States had been attacked.

Hours after the bombing of Pearl Harbor, Eleanor Roosevelt declared on the radio that "the moment we all dreaded had arrived." September 11 was a moment that had been dreaded by almost nobody except for a few terrorism experts. A quiet August was slipping unnoticeably into a golden September. Americans felt safe and remote from the troubles of the rest of the globe. The president's long vacation from Washington had ended; the country's long vacation from history had promised to go on and on.

Now history had exploded on us like a bomb, killing God knows how many thousands of people. I rushed to my desk and turned on my television. And there it was: the worst crime ever recorded on videotape.

I suddenly recollected that I was supposed to cross the Potomac River at noon to have lunch with a friend over at the Pentagon. I telephoned his office to cancel: Nobody, I thought unprophetically, would be leaving his or her desk today. My friend's assistant picked up the phone. I began to say that something terrible in New York had happened, we would all be needed at our posts . . . but she cut me off. "They're evacuating this building," she said grimly. "I cannot talk. We must leave."

I turned the television's sound back on. They were reporting that a third plane had struck the Pentagon—a truck bombing was reported at the State Department—fires had been set on the National Mall. My wife called again, her voice taut and strained. "The White House will be next! You have to get out of there—don't wait, please hurry!"

I felt a surge of . . . what? Battle fever? Mulishness? I only remember how hot my ears felt. "No!" I said fiercely. "*No!* I am not leaving!" I clicked off the phone, ready to . . . well, I don't know what I was ready to do—whatever it is that speechwriters do in times of war. Type, I suppose—but type with renewed patriotism and zeal. And at precisely that blood-boiling moment, a Secret Service agent was pounding on my door, shouting, "Everybody must evacuate this building now—this is an order—everybody must evacuate now!" A face popped through the doorway. *"You!* Out—now! *Now!"*

My heroic moment had lasted less than two minutes. I stepped out into the corridor. The tiled hallways of the Executive Office Building are wide enough and high enough for a chariot race. No matter how many people they hold, they always look and sound half-empty . . . but not that day. Little streams of clicking feet merged into rivers of footsteps, and then into a torrent. "Don't run!" the guards shouted, and the torrent slowed. We poured through the tall, carved oak doors of the building onto the avenue between the Executive Office Building and the West Wing of the White House and were reinforced by another rivulet of secretaries and staffers.

The guards suddenly changed their minds. *"Run!"* they now shouted. "Ladies—if you can't run in heels, kick off your shoes."

The northwest gate to the White House was thrown open, and out we all raced. More guards waited for us on Lafayette Square. "Keep going!" The offices in the town houses along the west side of the square emptied themselves into the crowd. "Don't stop!"

We ran past the statues of Count Rochambeau, the hero of Yorktown, and General Steuben, who drilled Washington's army. We ran alongside Andrew Jackson astride his horse, Sam Patch. We ran under the windows of the house of Commodore Stephen Decatur ("Our country! . . . may she always be in the right—but our country, right or wrong!"). We finally halted on the south side of H Street. "Take your badges off!" shouted another guard, and we pulled over our heads the blue or orange plastic cards that might mark us for a sniper. And there we stood: banished from our offices, stripped of our identifiers, helpless and baffled.

During the fighting in Afghanistan, it became popular for White House staffers to wear red, white, and blue plastic cards around their necks with the motto "These colors don't run." But that day they did run, and I ran with them, and I will never fully extract the sting of that memory.

The crowd of staffers milled aimlessly about the streets. Senior directors of the National Security Council, presidential assistants, and officers in uniform stood on the sidewalks, punching again and again at the dial pads of their cell phones, unable to get a signal, unable to keep a signal if they did get it, uncertain of where to go or what to do. The White House's emergency plans dated back to the cold war and were intended to protect the president, the vice president, and a handful of top aides against a nuclear attack. The rest of the staff, it was quietly assumed, would have been vaporized into radioactive dust.

But here we all were, alive but shaken, knowing less about what was going on in the world than a CNN viewer in Tasmania. I spotted John McConnell, the vice president's speechwriter. "We're just a couple of blocks from the American Enterprise Institute," I proposed. "They'll have land lines and television sets. And maybe we'll be able to think of something useful to do." We struck off across Farragut Square—and arrived to the news that the south tower of the World Trade Center had collapsed, killing unknown thousands of people inside.

Chris DeMuth, AEI's president, greeted McConnell and me

like sailors hauled in from the water. He offered us offices and telephones, Internet connections and e-mail—"Whatever you need," he said urgently.

McConnell and I had been trying for an hour to reach Michael Gerson by pager, by phone, by e-mail. We would have sent pigeons if we had had them. We finally found him at his home in Alexandria. He had been late to work that morning, too—and had been stuck in a traffic jam underneath the flight path of American Airlines Flight 77 when it crashed into the Pentagon.

Gerson told us that DaimlerChrysler had volunteered its Washington office as an improvised headquarters for the White House staff. We should walk over and get to work at once on a statement the president could issue on his return to Washington. It would be impossible for Gerson to enter the city. He would work from home.

A statement for the president. But what would it say? What *could* it say?

McConnell and I set off again. It was drawing close to noon. A security perimeter was being drawn around the center of Washington, D.C. To reach the DaimlerChrysler building we had to cross a police line, guarded by uniformed Secret Service agents who scrutinized our passes with unusual minuteness.

I had assumed that the federal government had designated these offices in advance for emergency use. In fact, the only reason we were here was that somebody on the White House staff was married to somebody in DaimlerChrysler's management, who offered up the premises in a spontaneous gesture. It was about 11:45. I was pointed to an office and told it was mine for the day. Its regular tenant gave me his long-distance dialing codes, showed me how to work his e-mail, packed his briefcase, and shook my hand on his way through the door.

There's an old political—okay, Republican—joke about the biggest lie in the world being "I'm from the government, and I'm here to help you." The joke didn't seem very funny on September 11. We were from the government, and as far as the people at DaimlerChrysler were concerned, we *were* here to help them—by helping their president defend their country. And they in turn wanted to help us.

Somehow they had contrived to set out trays of sandwiches, bowls of salad, cookies, cake, coffee, and soft drinks before they left. Anxious, weary, and parched, the ravenous White House staffers wolfed down the food and then settled at Daimler-Chrysler's computers and telephones.

The White House was now distributed in three principal places, with stragglers spread throughout the capital. The mid-level staff was here at 1401 H Street. The vice president and his chief of staff, Lewis Libby; National Security Adviser Condoleezza Rice; Deputy Chief of Staff Josh Bolten—they were all beneath the White House in a hardened bunker. And the president, Chief of Staff Andy Card, and the top political and communications aides were flying westward on Air Force One.

The president had been reading to the second-grade class at the Emma E. Booker Elementary School in Sarasota, Florida, when Card whispered into his ear the confirmation that the plane crashes in New York City were terrorist attacks. He finished reading and then approached the microphones. Reprising a line of his father's from ten years before, he declared that terrorism against the United States "would not stand."

It is hard to govern during an age of instantaneous broadcast. There were no microphones to preserve every quaver in Abraham Lincoln's voice after the firing on Fort Sumter; we cannot study Franklin Delano Roosevelt's face for traces of uncertainty in the seconds after Pearl Harbor. There would be much criticism of Bush's seeming disorientation and unease in the early hours after the attack. Well, who that day *wasn't* disoriented and uneasy? Yet we do live in an age of instantaneous media and have no choice but to play by its rules—and those rules would treat Bush harshly from his first remarks that morning until he returned to Washington that night.

The president ordered Air Force One to fly back to Washington as swiftly as possible. But as the president's plane approached the capital, the Secret Service received intelligence suggesting that the plane was a terrorist target, too. It would take many days for that intelligence to be proved false. So the big jet was rerouted to Barksdale Air Force Base in Louisiana. The president disembarked there to address a shocked and terrified nation at 12:40 eastern time: "The resolve of our great nation is being tested," he said. "But make no mistake: We will show the world that we will pass this test. God bless."

The words were correct and reassuring. The images were not. Air force bases do not come equipped with television studios, so the president was obliged to record his message in a bare room over a herky-jerky digital connection. He looked and sounded like the hunted, not the hunter. Even such a good friend of the administration as the editorial page of *The Wall Street Journal* cuttingly commented that Bush's flight from air force base to air force base before finally returning to the capital showed that he "could not be frightened away for long, if at all."

With Air Force One apparently a target, and the White House shuttered and largely useless, Bush proceeded to Strategic Command at Offutt Air Force Base in Nebraska. From Offutt the president can command the defense of the nation's airspace, if need be, and teleconference with his National Security Council.

As Bush flew westward, taking phone calls, gathering information, and deciding upon his and the nation's course, his writers were pacing and talking and drafting and redrafting a formal message that the president could deliver to the nation from the Oval Office that evening.

By now, Matthew Scully had made his way to the Daimler-Chrysler building, and he, McConnell, and I gathered around a computer screen, with Gerson on the other end of a phone line. When we finished, we fired the text to Gerson's home; he edited it some more and then forwarded it to Hughes.

Our work was interrupted by a terrible bulletin. McConnell had said to me on our walk through the empty city: "There are going to be thousands and thousands of funerals in this country over the next week. Everybody is going to know someone among the dead." Now it was our turn. My wife telephoned into our office. She could barely speak. She had learned that Barbara Olson, wife of Solicitor General Theodore Olson, had been one of the passengers aboard the flight that crashed into the Pentagon. In the confusion and terror of the hijacking, Barbara Olson had somehow found the cool and courage to call her husband on her cell phone. Her call gave the government early notice of the seizure of a third plane. Her last words expressed her infinite faith in Ted: "The pilot is here with me. Tell him what to do."

I keep a transliteration of the Kaddish, the Jewish prayer for the dead, on my PalmPilot. I stepped out of our little office, retreated to the photocopy room, closed the door, and looked around for something with which to cover my head. I could find nothing, so I pulled my arms out of my jacket, pulled it up and over my head like a shawl, recited the ancient words, and mourned my brave and beautiful friend.

The sun was setting. Information circulated that the president would be returning to Washington at about eight o'clock and that the White House would be reopened to staff. McConnell, Scully, and I decided to return to the office in case we were needed for something. We cleared our desks and gathered up our notes and copies of our e-mails for the presidential record keepers. I left a short note of thanks for the man whose desk I had occupied all day, but I have a bad feeling that the record keepers scooped it up, too. We stepped out of the office, into the elevator, and out of the building—into a world transformed.

Washington was empty and silent, save for the screams of sirens far off in the distance and the periodic roar of F-16s overhead. Entire city blocks were cordoned off by yellow police tape. Uniformed guards checked our passes every fifty feet. Black-clad paramilitary agents clutching murderous automatic weapons surveyed us skeptically. Otherwise, there were no people to be seen. A sad and lonely stillness had settled upon the central precinct of American power.

We were all weary from the emotions that had surged through us that day: fear and rage and grief. But we were not depleted. The fear and the rage receded, the grief had to be postponed. What was left was a budding tenderness toward every symbol of this wounded country. The lights that illuminated the monuments of the capital had been defiantly switched on. The evening air was sweet and soft. And we looked with new and more loving eyes at the familiar streets. There! There was the Treasury Department—where they would mobilize the limitless resources of the nation for war. There! There was the East Wing, the office of the First Lady, who had visited Congress that morning—and who could have easily numbered among the dead had the fourth hijacked jet struck the Capitol. And there! There! There was the flag over the White House. Tomorrow it would be lowered to half-staff. Today it flew high, brilliantly lit, in defiance of all terror—still gallantly streaming, just as it had for an imprisoned poet on the deck of an enemy warship two centuries ago.

The day's violence seemed to be over for the moment. The night was quiet. But tomorrow? What would happen tomorrow? And the next day?

McConnell, Scully, and I drew near the black iron fence around the White House. We showed our passes once more, and a guard radioed our names to some authority inside. A long wait—and then one by one we were permitted to step through the gate.

Even on the dullest day, stepping from the outside to the inside of the White House gate feels like crossing into a forbidden city. But never before had the line of separation felt so thick and high. The silent, patrolled city beyond the lush lawn and the still-thick greenery of the trees, beyond the sensors, the fence, and the gates, fell away behind us into remoteness and invisibility as we trudged along West Executive Avenue to the entrance to the West Wing. We stepped under the white canopy that extends from the side doorway to the avenue—and into a building that was humming back to life after the longest session of inactivity perhaps in its existence.

We entered the small basement suite of offices that Gerson and his assistant shared with another senior staffer and his assistant. We turned on the television, sat on a couch, and watched the president walk briskly across the South Lawn to the Oval Office. There was an hour to wait before he would speak to the country.

The screens began to flash images of the White House as the networks readied themselves for the president's message. My mind traveled backward through all the images of this president those same networks had shown the American people since he had emerged on the national scene two years before. Had they seen a man in whom they could place their trust? It was nine o'clock. We were about to learn.

# 8

## TEN DAYS
## IN SEPTEMBER

THE AMERICAN PEOPLE always rally to their president in times of danger. They rallied to John F. Kennedy during the Cuban missile crisis, to Richard Nixon when he imposed wage and price controls, even to Jimmy Carter during the Iranian hostage crisis. But they do not necessarily *stay* rallied. Carter lost them. So did Nixon.

Bush kept them.

Before the terrorist attacks, the American public had warmed to Bush's honesty and good nature. He had benefited too from the final reverberations of the Clinton boom. But the roots of Bush's personal popularity had not reached deep, and when gasoline prices rose and industrial employment slumped, those roots shriveled. In the ten days after September 11, however, Bush made one of those mysterious connections with the public that some leaders make and others—sometimes equally admirable men—simply cannot.

John F. Kennedy was the outstanding modern example of the leader who made that connection. To this day, polls find that Americans rate him the greatest president in their history, ahead even of that onetime favorite, Franklin Delano Roosevelt. Some professional historians tut-tut when they read those polls. The historians remind us that Kennedy was a rather aimless and callow young man, elevated to the presidency by his family's money and power and the good luck that paired him with a uniquely unattractive opponent; they say that his domestic policies were cautious and vague, his foreign policy unnecessarily confrontational. They say, in short, the same things that the same kind of person says now about George W. Bush.

And in fact, despite the Ike-onography on his walls, Bush does curiously resemble Kennedy. They were both sons of privilege, they both professed religions that unnerved the secularists of their day, they both won the presidency in a squeaker, and they were both defined by foreign crises. And one more thing: Both owed their connections with the public above all to the power of their words. John F. Kennedy's gorgeous speeches still resound forty years later; Bush's oratory in the ten days after the terrorist attacks transformed his leadership—and may perhaps last as long.

But he did not get off to a promising start. When Bush finished speaking to the nation on the night of September 11, Scully, McConnell, and I rose from the couch in Gerson's outer office and said good night to one another—nothing more than good night, because there was nothing more to say. When I think of this story now, I ask myself why we did not walk along the basement corridor, up the half flight of stairs to the main floor, and then wait to greet the president on his route from the Oval Office back to the mansion. It had been a hard day for everyone, but surely hardest of all for him—the support of his staff might have meant something to him. Why did we not do it? Because we did not even think of it. We were too crushed with misery, too despondent and downcast, to meet his eye.

The words Scully, McConnell, Gerson, and I had written together in the DaimlerChrysler building had been chucked and replaced by Karen Hughes. Machiavelli says somewhere that it is the universal tragedy of man that circumstances change—but he does not. The same could be said for woman, too. Hughes had helped Bush win two gubernatorial elections and then the presidency by teaching him the political language of the 1990s. But the country had changed more in the past ten hours than it had in ten years, and the political language of the 1990s was now as dead as Hittite.

Bush spoke to the nation from the Oval Office—the first time he had ever done so. He opened with a jarringly conversational greeting: "Good evening." The expression on his face was all wrong, too: He tried a half smile when he said his "good evening," and throughout the broadcast there was something weak and tentative about the set of his jaw. Bush sometimes chewed at the inside of his lips when he was nervous, and it caused his mouth to shift about when it ought to have been fixed and hard.

Then: "Today, our fellow citizens, our way of life, our very freedom, came under attack in a series of deliberate and deadly terrorist acts. The victims were in airplanes, or in their offices; secretaries, businessmen and -women, military and federal workers; moms and dads, friends and neighbors."

That was not good. There was something condescending about this particularizing of the dead, as if we did not trust our listeners to feel sufficient grief for the murdered unless we summoned up the images of their orphaned children. At their funerals, we would mourn them as individuals. Tonight, all that needed to be said about the dead was what Franklin Roosevelt said in his Pearl Harbor message of December 8, 1941: "Very many American lives have been lost."

Although Bush referred in passing to a "war on terrorism," he offered no explanation of the attack and promised no retaliation against the attacker. He referred glancingly to unspecified action by the "intelligence and law enforcement communities," but he said nothing about the use of armed force. At the center of the speech, where Bush ought to have explained who the enemy was—and then pledged to destroy him utterly—the public was offered instead a doughy pudding of stale metaphors.

"Terrorist attacks can shake the foundations of our biggest buildings, but they cannot touch the foundation of America. These acts shattered steel, but they cannot dent the steel of American resolve. America was targeted for attack because we're the brightest beacon for freedom and opportunity in the world. And no one will keep that light from shining."

After the bit about the light, Bush paused to deliver a thank-you to members of Congress, the sort of thank-you a president might insert in a signing ceremony for a farm bill or tax cut. "I appreciate so very much the members of Congress who have joined me in strongly condemning these attacks." *Strongly condemning?* We strongly condemn stock-market fraud—not mass murder.

Then at last he signed off with a peroration that drowned all meaning in a warm bath of bathos. "This is a day when all Americans from every walk of life unite in our resolve for justice and peace. America has stood down enemies before, and we will do so this time. None of us will ever forget this day. Yet we go forward to defend freedom and all that is good and just in our world."

Americans had been slaughtered in a horrible fiery massacre. The country was stunned, terrified, furious, and ready for war against anyone and everyone in any way connected to the attack. But the speech Bush had delivered was not a war speech. It was a hastily revised compassionate conservatism speech. As I walked out of the West Wing into the mockingly beautiful September evening, and looked south down West Executive in the direction of the smoking Pentagon, I could imagine Americans switching off their television sets and looking at one another with the same dismay I felt. I could imagine them thinking: Bush was a nice fellow, a perfectly adequate president for a time of peace and quiet; but this was war, real war, and he had given not one indication all day long of readiness for his terrible new responsibilities.

I drove home through the deserted streets of my city. *My city.* I had never thought of Washington that way before. I had lived here for five years like a sojourner. I paid my taxes, I knew the name of my city councilor. But I never thought of Washington as mine. Had you asked me when I left the house that morning where my home was, I would have thought for a moment and answered: Toronto. But Toronto was not burning. Toronto was not bracing for death by gas or by germs or by nuclear explosion. Toronto was where we could take refuge if we wanted out of this war.

But I wanted *into* this war. That plane that crashed in the Pennsylvania countryside—it was probably heading for the White House. The world did not yet know about the brave men who had crashed United Flight 93 into the earth. But we already knew that if the terrorists' plans had succeeded, the White House might well have been a smoldering ruin tonight, and the wife and children to whom I was driving home would then probably have numbered among the day's widows and orphans. Ninety-one of the day's widows were carrying children. My wife was six months pregnant. She might have been the ninety-second.*

It was my home that was burning. Those were my F-16s I heard roaring overhead, my police guarding my roads, my soldiers protecting my president. I was too old to join the army. The least I could do was join my fate to that of the country in which I lived. I had become eligible for American citizenship in the spring of 2001. I had sent away for the naturalization papers—and I'd carried them around in my briefcase for months, unable to bring myself to complete them. In an interval of quiet in the DaimlerChrysler offices, I signed and sealed them.

I pulled into my driveway. The house was dark, as if the people inside were expecting an air raid. I opened the door. My daughter and son and my wife and my dogs bounded down the long, narrow stairway. We all embraced desperately, right there in the middle of the slope, jumbled one on top of another, and

* The Infant Care Program of the Independent Women's Forum of Washington, D.C., has tallied and aided these ninety-one women.

we did not stop squeezing until we had walked in a huddle back up the flight of stairs, back into the bedroom, where my wife had dragged mattresses and sleeping bags for the children, so that we could all sleep in one place, and listen to the planes, and feel at least the illusion of safety.

I woke up very early the next morning and tiptoed around the children to watch the news and read the newspapers. Grief had inundated the country.

My neighborhood in northwest Washington is not exactly an abode of superhawks. Before September 11, when the impulse to wave a flag came upon my neighbors, they would fly theme banners: pumpkins, turkeys, soccer balls, Easter bunnies. But that morning, Wesley Heights looked like Childe Hassam's painting of Fifth Avenue in 1917. There were flags up and down every road and street, flags on all the cars and vans. There were flags on the flagpoles, too—and they all flew half-staff.

The blocks around the White House were closed to traffic. I had to show my pass two full blocks from the White House, and again at the corner of Seventeenth and E. I had to show my pass to enter the little strip of street on which I parked, and then one last time to enter the White House complex. Guards in body armor patrolled the grounds. Cars choked West Executive Avenue. Early in the morning, the basement entryway was already crowded with cabinet secretaries and undersecretaries, generals and admirals, and men in dark suits with anonymous faces.

I walked to the mess takeout window for a coffee. Then I crossed West Executive Avenue, walked up the stairs to the Executive Office Building—and was overwhelmed by quiet. No clutches of people in the corners. Nobody walking through the halls. No conversation drifting over the high transoms of the heavy doors. The EOB never felt crowded: It was built on too vast a scale for that—hallways twenty feet wide, ceilings twenty feet high, doorways through which three big men could pass abreast. But it had always felt busy, bustling with aides, thronged with visitors. Now visitors had been banned, and would be banned for months. Aides were sitting in their offices . . . waiting for orders. The West Wing is the brain of the presidency; the Executive Office Building, its arms and legs. While the brain was planning, the limbs could only strum and tap. Fortunately, a blood bank opened on the fourth floor; the underemployed EOB staff queued all day to donate. There was something medieval about it: drawing blood in order to quiet the staff's agitated mood.

During the sleepy summer of 2001, I would sometimes bring my ten-year-old daughter with me to the office when I had a weekend task. The guards at the gate would jocularly issue her an "intern" pass. She would order a hamburger at the mess takeout window, then wander out onto the South Lawn to eat it. The president was away, and the guards were indulgent. No more of that now.

The White House was swaddled in an ever heavier blanket of security. Bomb-sniffing dogs were added to the checkpoint at Seventeenth and E. For fear of truck bombs, the whole Seventeenth Street wing of the Executive Office Building was evacuated. The EOB is built out of solid granite, and its walls were invulnerable to pretty much anything short of a tactical nuclear weapon. But the windows set into the wall were built on the same gigantic scale as that of the rest of the building. An explosion on the street would blow the windows in, and the shards of glass would shred anybody inside the room. The ground floor on Seventeenth Street had been Karl Rove's empire: His special assistants had occupied a line of vast, square offices, decorated with grand fireplaces and ornate plasterwork. Now they were reassigned three to a room, their desks shoved together like the work groups in an elementary school.

The quiet of September 12 lasted only a single day. By the thirteenth, there was work to do all over the building: Supplemental budget requests had to be written and sent to Congress, emergency aid found for the grounded airlines, a decade's backlog of counterterrorism initiatives to be revived, and on and on and on.

Uniforms filled the halls, and even many of the men in civilian clothes wore haircuts that told of very recent departure from the ranks. Clutches of flags appeared on the street lamps throughout the compound, and four gigantic multistory flags spread themselves from the second to the third floors of the east, west, north, and south facades of the Executive Office Building. Some weeks after September 11, I stopped by the office of Budget Director Mitch Daniels. It is an impressive room: If you could stand in the director's doorway and sink a basketball in a hoop nailed to the opposite wall, you would be a welcome addition to any college team in the country. Now the office looked different, strange—and I realized after a moment that all natural light into the office was filtered through a field of red-and-white stripes, each of them four feet high. A giant flag had blocked off every square inch of his gigantic windows.

The writers too had their work to do. I was relieved at least that everyone understood that the speech on the evening of the eleventh had been a failure. Well, almost everyone. "Everybody complains about the Tuesday address," Hughes erupted one morning. "I just don't agree." Somebody (not in the writers' shop, I should say) nicknamed it the "Awful Office Address," and the name stuck.

Now the damage done by that speech needed to be un-stuck—and there was not much time to unstick it.

Presidents are either in command of events or at their mercy. Bush's failure to take command on September 11 left him desperately vulnerable on September 12. To what precisely he would be vulnerable, few on the White House staff were in a position to say: Nobody outside the innermost circle then had any inkling of the revelations that would later emerge about the disregarded warnings at the FBI and CIA. But we did know, or rather could easily predict, that a disaster as horrible as 9/11 would produce commensurately horrible accusations against the people in charge at the time of the disaster. If Bush did not seize control of the situation, those accusations would find listeners in the angry public.

In 1941, those Americans who did not want to fight the Nazis accused Franklin Roosevelt of complicity in Pearl Harbor—and no matter how often and how brutally their conspiracy theories are demolished, sixty years later they still find believers. In 2001, it was to be expected that those Americans who did not wish to fight terrorism would generate conspiracy theories of their own—and those theories would hurt a damaged president much more than an admired one.

Georgia congresswoman Cynthia McKinney gave voice to one such theory in April 2002, when she charged: "I am not aware of any evidence showing that President Bush or members of his administration have personally profited from the attacks of 9/11. A complete investigation might reveal that to be the case. . . . On the other hand, what is undeniable is that corporations close to the administration have directly benefited from the increased defense spending arising from the aftermath of September 11." As McKinney's own hometown newspaper, the *Atlanta Journal-Constitution,* documented in August 2002, McKinney's accusation was an example of what the psychologists call "projection." The person in American government who most immediately "profited" from 9/11 was McKinney herself: Her office recorded $13,850 in contributions on September 11, 2001, her third best fund-raising day between January 1999 and the end of March 2002. Among her donors that day were six people investigated by the federal government for their terrorist links, one of whom served time in jail. They must have realized that they would need friends in the days ahead. (McKinney's second best fund-raising day of the three-year period was October 25, 2001, the day she published her open letter denouncing New York mayor Rudy Giuliani for refusing a check from a Saudi prince who wanted to make an anti-Israel statement at the presentation ceremony.)*

McKinney's was an extreme case, and her vituperative words eventually lost her her congressional seat. But there were other dangers that could easily be imagined if the administration fumbled in the future as badly as it had on the eleventh. We had to do better—and we had to sound better.

---

* Bill Torpy, "Some McKinney Donors Probed for Terror Ties," *Atlanta Journal-Constitution,* August 3, 2002, www.accessatlanta.com/ajc/metro/0802/03mcmoney. html; see also *The Wall Street Journal*'s "Best of the Web" for August 3, 2002, www.opinionjournal.com/best/, for other relevant links.

Two opportunities for sounding better were swiftly placed on the calendar: a memorial service for the victims on September 14 and a speech to a joint session of Congress on September 20. The joint session speech was Rove's idea. He knew that Bush spoke best in front of a live audience and was at his worst when he had to address the silent eye of the television camera.

Perhaps Rove appreciated something else as well. When Bush spoke to the nation from the Oval Office, alone and uninterrupted, he was adopting a form that presidents had used during the cold war. It was alone from the Oval Office that John F. Kennedy justified his actions in the Cuban missile crisis in 1962 and that Lyndon Johnson announced his escalations in Vietnam; thus did Richard Nixon defend his attack on North Vietnamese bases in Cambodia in 1970, and thus did Ronald Reagan present his Strategic Defense Initiative. Those dramatic solo addresses emphasized the power and authority of the president. And that was also their problem: The president was often explaining actions he had already taken, rather than asking for a mandate to take action. He was speaking *to* the nation—but not always *for* the nation.

But this war was not the cold war.

Some weeks after the attacks, an aide asked Karl Rove whether he believed that the American people thought the war on terrorism was like World War II. He considered for a moment before replying. "No, they don't—but they want *us* to think it's like World War Two." So he suggested that Bush revert to older forms and speak not from his solitary desk, but from the rostrum from which Woodrow Wilson and Franklin Roosevelt asked for their declarations of war and Harry Truman announced the Truman Doctrine. It was a brilliant idea—but what would Bush say up there?

We had a little more than one week to work it out. In the meantime, we had dead to mourn.

It will someday be difficult to describe to people who did not live through the 9/11 attacks the blood-red fury that swept the country in the days afterward. The famously delicate *New Yorker* published a cartoon in which one tweedy New Yorker tells another, "I agree we have to avoid overkill, but not at the risk of underkill." Professor Alan Dershowitz, the prominent civil libertarian of Harvard Law School, published an op-ed in the *Los Angeles Times* arguing that judges should be empowered by law to issue "torture warrants." A friend of mine told me about a friend of his, a liberal-minded professor of literature who happened to be visiting a foreign university the week of the attack. One of the academics there repeated some glib comment about America bringing the attack on itself—and my friend's friend lunged at him and knocked him down. His wife asked him later whether he was sorry. He answered, "I'm sorry I didn't hit him harder."

Bush's great gift to the country after September 11 was his calm and self-restraint. His speech on the night of the eleventh had been wrecked by his failure to fuse his message of calm with the appropriate wrath and resolution. But when in the subsequent days he allowed himself to voice those emotions of war, his instinctive moderation served him well. He seemed to feel not the rage that the rest of the country felt, but the quiet determination it knew it ought to feel. He made it clear to his writers that he would pronounce no words of vengefulness or anger. When he spoke off-the-cuff, he again and again paraphrased the commandment of Romans 12:21: "Be not overcome by evil, but overcome evil with good."

The spirit of goodness filled the first of his great war speeches, the speech in the National Cathedral. McConnell and Scully started at work on it first thing on the morning of September 12 in McConnell's office in the vice president's suite. It is very hard to write a flawless presidential speech. Too many and too powerful people wish to insert a pet sentence and paragraph, and a writer who tries to push them all away has soon propelled himself out of a job. Even the very finest speeches almost invariably contain a clumsy or banal or kitschy line or two. But the cathedral speech was flawless. And when someday it is chiseled in marble on a national memorial, Matthew Scully and John McConnell should receive at least a footnote.

"God's signs are not always the ones we look for. We learn in tragedy that His purposes are not always our own. Yet the prayers of private suffering, whether in our homes or in this great cathedral, are known and heard, and understood. . . . Grief and tragedy and hatred are only for a time. Goodness, remembrance, and love have no end. And the Lord of life holds all who die, and all who mourn.

"It is said that adversity introduces us to ourselves. This is true of a nation as well."

McConnell had dredged from his vast memory of American political lore a speech that Franklin Roosevelt had given in October 1941, ten days after the sinking of the destroyer USS *Kearney* by Hitler's U-boats: "History has recorded who fired the first shot. In the long run, however, all that will matter is who fired the last shot." McConnell adapted Roosevelt's words to insert into the elegy in the cathedral the war message that ought to have been delivered three days before. "This conflict," Bush said, "was begun on the timing and terms of others. It will end in a way, and at an hour, of our choosing."

Tickets for the cathedral were distributed to officers on the afternoon of September 13. I gave mine away: I suspected that my rank in the bureaucratic hierarchy would entitle me to a folding chair directly behind one of the cathedral's stone pillars. I watched instead on the television in my little office so I could see the president's face as he spoke. The dignity and authority that had been missing on the eleventh had settled upon him now. When he finished, the trap drums of the marine drum struck up a menacing *rat-a-tat-tat, rat-a-tat-tat,* and a military choir burst into "The Battle Hymn of the Republic"—and not one of the soulful renditions that had become popular in the 1990s, but the full-throated anthem of Protestant righteousness militant.

> *I have read a fiery gospel writ in burnish'd rows of steel,*
> *"As ye deal with my contemners, So with you my grace*
>   *shall deal";*
> *Let the Hero, born of woman, crush the serpent with his*
>   *heel,*
> *Since God is marching on.*

And as the vast congregation took up the fierce words of the old song, I recalled with grim satisfaction George Patton's words before the invasion of Normandy: "Why, by God, I almost pity these poor sons of bitches we are going up against. By God, I do!"

That service was the first time the nation saw a new Bush. A few hours later came the second—and this time, the encounter was entirely unscripted.

Immediately after the service, Bush flew up to New York City. He had wanted to go earlier but had to wait until the over-burdened city could cope with a presidential visit. Three days after the attack, New York was still broken and bleeding. The dust of the annihilated towers still covered every surface in lower Manhattan. The Brooks Brothers store on Liberty Street was still a hastily converted hospital and morgue. Manhattan below Fourteenth Street was ghostly and empty, bridges and tunnels were closed to inessential traffic, photocopied photo-graphs of the missing were plastered to every surface, and the sidewalks in front of the city's fire stations were invisible under masses of flowers.

Giuliani and Governor George Pataki met Bush at McGuire Air Force Base, south of Princeton, New Jersey. They heli-coptered to the Wall Street heliport on the East River, then drove in a tightly guarded motorcade around the bottom of the island to ground zero. All along the short route, rescue workers, police, firefighters, and medics cheered wildly, waved flags, chanted, "USA! USA!" Giuliani pointed out the window of the limousine at the shouting crowd. "You see those people cheer-ing you?" he asked Bush. "Not one of them voted for you."

Bush stepped out of the limo and toured the ruin. He was dressed casually in a dun-colored windbreaker. The ground was still shifting and unstable, dangerous and fiery. No preparation had been made for Bush to speak: The plan had been for him to deliver remarks later in the day, at a meeting with families of the missing at the Javits Convention Center, uptown in the West

Thirties. At ground zero, there was no microphone, no sound system. Bush had no notes. But the crowd of workers pressed in close upon him, seething with emotion, and Bush decided he had to speak. Somebody passed him a bullhorn. A retired firefighter, Bill Beckwith, climbed atop a wrecked fire truck and jumped up and down on it to check its strength. Bush climbed up beside him. He put an arm around Beckwith's shoulders to help him keep his balance—and then left it there. He began to speak, to tell the workers that the whole nation was praying for them and for the city of New York. But his mouth was too close to the mouthpiece and the sound garbled. A worker shouted, "We can't hear you!" So Bush pulled the bullhorn away from his face and replied with a characteristic Bush joke: "Well, I can hear you." Then his face grew serious.

"I can hear you.

"The rest of the world hears you.

"And the people who knocked these buildings down will hear all of us soon."

Was the crowd shouting before? It was roaring now. *USA! USA! USA!*

In the cathedral, Bush had spoken in the high tones of the American religious tradition. "War has been waged against us by stealth and deceit and murder," he said in the cathedral. He described the murderers as "the evil ones." In a country where almost two-thirds of the population believes in the existence of the devil,* Bush was identifying Osama bin Laden and his gang as literally satanic.

Now in New York, he was speaking in the American ver-

---

* "Believer Nation," *Public Perspectives* (May–June 2000), pp. 24–25, www.ropercenter.uconn.edu/pubper/pdf/pp113c.pdf.

nacular, the plain language of the frontier. It was the language he had used when he promised that he would "smoke out" the killers and "git 'em"—when he said he wanted them "dead or alive." The first language reassured Americans that the war would be fought for just purposes. The second promised that it would be fought with decisive methods. But what were those purposes? And what would be those methods? Those were the questions for which the country was still awaiting answers.

In his speech before Congress on September 20, Bush faced a much more daunting challenge than Roosevelt had on December 8, 1941. There was no mystery then about who had attacked Pearl Harbor—or how the United States would respond. In 2001, nothing seemed clear: not the identity of America's enemy, not the nature of the conflict, not the definition of victory.

Soon after I joined the White House, I was handed back a speech draft that Bush had slashed apart. When I next saw him, I said I had not understood his edits: The material he had hacked out of the speech seemed to me the headline story of the event. Bush shook his head at me. "The headline is: BUSH LEADS."

He was leading now. Within hours of the attack, he had made two crucial decisions that would determine the aims and conduct of the whole war in terror. The decisions had not been well explained that first night. But they had been taken. Inside the gooey mess of one bad speech had been the hard strength of two great innovations in American foreign policy.

The first crucial decision was to recognize that this war *was* a war. Bush had taken that decision almost instantly. When he stepped aboard Air Force One in Florida to jet north and west, he told the staff there, "We are at war," and he repeated that message in a statement he read to the press in the Cabinet Room on the morning of September 12: "The deliberate and deadly attacks which were carried out yesterday against our country were more than acts of terror. They were acts of war."

The second big decision was to hold responsible for these acts of war not merely the terrorists who committed them, but also the governments that aided, abetted, financed, and shielded terrorism. I had inserted this thought into every draft we sent off from the DaimlerChrysler offices in the afternoon. Only one sentence out of all of that labor had survived into Bush's speech that evening, but it was the one that mattered: "We will make no distinction between the terrorists who committed these acts and those who harbor them." With those words, Bush upgraded the "war on terror" from metaphor to fact.

Together, Bush's two fundamental decisions discarded thirty-five years of American policy in the Middle East and repudiated the foreign policies of at least six of the previous seven U.S. presidents.

In the thirty-three years before September 2001, close to one thousand Americans had been killed by Arab and Islamic terrorists. That's four times as many as died in 1898 aboard the USS *Maine*—the ship whose destruction triggered the Spanish-American War—and more than five times as many as died at the Alamo. The roster of the dead begins with Robert Kennedy, assassinated by a Palestinian gunman in June 1968, and Cleo Noel, the U.S. ambassador to Sudan, machine-gunned to death on the orders of Yasser Arafat in 1973. The dead include the 241 marines killed in the bombing of the barracks in Beirut and the 18 airmen killed in a bomb attack near the U.S. base in Torrejon, Spain, in 1983; the diplomats and soldiers killed in three Iranian-sponsored bomb attacks on the U.S. embassies in Lebanon in 1983 and 1984; and the 17 soldiers killed by Islamic terrorists at the Khobar Towers in Saudi Arabia. Civilians have suffered, too: Leon Klinghoffer, a wheelchair-bound vacationer aboard the *Achille Lauro* cruise liner, who was shot and shoved into the sea by Palestinian terrorists in 1985; the passengers on Pan Am Flight 103, blown up by Libyan agents over Lockerbie, Scotland, in 1988; and the 6 office workers killed in the first bombing of the World Trade Center in 1993. The attackers grew bolder and deadlier in the 1990s. They killed hundreds in the bombing of the U.S. embassies in East Africa in 1998 and dared a direct attack on a U.S. warship, the USS *Cole,* when it put ashore in Yemen in 2000.

Only once in all those thirty-three years did an American president interpret a terrorist atrocity as an act of war, demanding a proportionately warlike response: in April 1986, when Ronald Reagan ordered the bombing of Tripoli after Libyan agents detonated a bomb in a Berlin discotheque, killing two American servicemen and injuring dozens more. All the rest of the time, the United States chose to treat terrorism as a crime to be investigated by police, or a clandestine threat to be dealt with by covert means, or an irritant to be negotiated by diplomats.

And for the same three decades in which the United States had shrugged off terrorism, it also had drawn a sharp distinction between terrorists and their sponsors. Terrorists might sometimes be pursued; sponsors rarely faced anything worse than sanctions—if that. Syria harbors some of the world's deadliest terrorists, including George Habash, the Palestinian who introduced the hijacking of airplanes and the murder of passengers to Middle Eastern politics. Yet seven of the past nine secretaries of state and two presidents, Nixon and Clinton, have traveled to Damascus to visit Syrian dictator Hafez al-Assad and his son and successor, Bashar. Iran has the blood of hundreds of Americans on its hands and is busily trying to acquire the nuclear weapons that would enable it to kill hundreds of thousands more. The Clinton administration nonetheless wooed Iran in the 1990s, offering to lift economic sanctions and praising President Mohammed Khatami as a "moderate" and "reformer." Saudi Arabia is terrorism's paymaster and recruiting sergeant, yet Saudi Arabia is an honored ally of the United States. And of course the Palestinian Authority is the epicenter of world terrorism, the entity by and for whose sake hundreds of heartless terrorist acts are committed every year—and since at least 1991, America's Middle East policy has aimed at promoting the Authority into a state into which billions of dollars of U.S. and European aid could be poured.

How much of all of this past policy did Bush intend to discard? When he spoke of "those who harbor" terrorism on September 11, he may well have contemplated nobody except the Taliban of Afghanistan. I cannot imagine that he expected those words to lead him into conflict with the Saudis and plunge him into the Israeli-Palestinian dispute. But they did—and he followed where his words led.

Bush had made a moral commitment to wage the fight against terror to ultimate victory. And when Bush makes commitments, he honors them. This fact of Bush's psychology imbued his speech on September 20 with vast significance. An important presidential speech is not produced by a writer sharpening his pencil and then letting his fancy roam over the next two dozen pages. The speech begins with direct instructions from the president—and no matter how fine the writer, it is those instructions that ultimately determine whether the speech succeeds or fails. As it happens, Jimmy Carter's notorious "malaise" speech was extremely well written: lucid, thoughtful, and in spots poetic. But well-written whining remains whining.

There was no whining on September 20. Bush's speech to the joint session of Congress was remarkable equally for what it did not say and for what it did say. Here is the most important thing it did not say: It did not accept—it did not even deign to acknowledge—the argument that the United States somehow brought the terror attacks on itself. In the fall of 2001, many people who by any definition count as mainstream felt some urge to excuse or palliate the 9/11 crime. At Georgetown University on November 7, 2001, former president Clinton prefaced otherwise sensible remarks on terror with the observation that "those of us who come from various European lineages are not blameless" and proceeded to describe America's record of slavery, dispossession of the Indians, and individual hate crimes as part of terrorism's "long history." *

---

* Lest there be any doubt that I have quoted Clinton fairly, here is the relevant paragraph in full:

First of all, terror, the killing of noncombatants for economic, political, or religious reasons, has a very long history, as long as organized combat itself, and yet it has never succeeded as a military strategy standing on its own. But it has been around a long time. Those of us who come from various European lineages are not blameless. Indeed, in the First Crusade, when the Christian soldiers took Jerusalem, they first burned a synagogue with three hundred Jews in it, and proceeded to kill every woman and child who was Muslim on the Temple Mount. The contemporaneous descriptions of the event describe soldiers walking on the Temple Mount, a holy place to Christians, with blood running up to their knees. I can tell you that that story is still being told today in the Middle East and we are still paying for it. Here in the United States, we were founded as a nation that practiced slavery, and slaves

Clinton was not the only serious, thoughtful American who could not quite bring himself or herself to regard September 11 as an act of absolutely unjustified wrong. Had the Florida recount turned out only slightly differently, some of these people could well have been in positions of power or influence on September 11, 2001. Instead, the man in charge was a man whose moral vision was not occluded by guilt or self-doubt. Bush's speech of September 20 fused his two crucial decisions of September 11 and 12 into an ultimatum to the world: "Every nation, in every region, now has a decision to make. Either you are with us, or you are with the terrorists. From this day forward, any nation that continues to harbor or support terrorism will be regarded by the United States as a hostile regime."

It was Bush's own policy and moral strength that made it possible for the joint session speech to be great. It was Michael Gerson's word processor that turned the possibility into fact.

Normally, Karen Hughes would have assumed sole responsibility for a speech as important as September 20. This time, however, chastened by the poor reviews of the Awful Office Address, she conceded the drafting of the speech to Gerson, reserving to herself only the final edit. From that concession came a speech that was not only bold but beautiful.

---

were, quite frequently, killed even though they were innocent. This country once looked the other way when significant numbers of Native Americans were dispossessed and killed to get their land or their mineral rights or because they were thought of as less than fully human, and we are still paying the price today. Even in the twentieth century in America people were terrorized or killed because of their race. And even today, though we have continued to walk, sometimes to stumble, in the right direction, we still have the occasional hate crime rooted in race, religion, or sexual orientation. So terror has a long history.

The transcript can be read in its entirety at www.georgetown.edu/admin/publicaffairs/protocol_events/events/clinton_glfl10701.htm.

Big presidential speeches are constructed the way the Romans built their temples: The major components are carved in workshops all around the site and then hoisted into place according to the architect's plan. John McConnell penned the speech's single most powerful line: the observation that political Islam would follow Nazism and communism (the latter hastily renamed "totalitarianism" for fear of offending China, whose UN Security Council vote the United States needed) into "history's graveyard of discarded lies." But everybody pitched in, working tirelessly and generously and with growing pride.

Each component of a major speech can represent a whole vast field of national policy, the work of hundreds or thousands of people. The struggle between the policy experts to whom the component is a life's work and the writer who must squeeze it into place can sometimes be intense—and sometimes absurd.

It fell to me, for example, to ask the intelligence expert on the National Security Council what the agencies would like said about their role in the battles to come. The man I spoke to was very pleased to be asked—so pleased that he offered to work up a memo for me on the subject. The memo arrived six hours later. It was divided into three parts. Part one stressed that intelligence (the CIA's domain) would be very important in the war on terrorism. Part two added that counterintelligence (the FBI's domain) would be very important in the war on terrorism. Part three repeated points one and two. The NSC man stood proudly in my office as I read the note through. "So," I said, "if I understand you correctly, you want the president to say that both intelligence and counterintelligence will be very important in the war on terrorism." He nodded enthusiastically. "And that's it? That's all you want him to say?"

Well, he said reluctantly, of course there's more. . . .

"What?" I asked.

"I can't tell you. It's classified."

"You can't tell me what you want the president to tell a national television audience?"

He did not agree that this was funny.

As all the components were worked up, Gerson gathered them together and integrated them into an eloquent whole. He revised and rewrote, harmonizing all the elements, wrapping them in his lovely prose. After the speech, Bush called Gerson at home to thank him for his work. Gerson said, "Mr. President, when I saw you on television, I thought—God wanted you there."

"He wants us all here, Gerson," Bush answered. "But thank you."

A poll taken immediately after the attacks suggested that only about half the country felt "highly confident" of Bush's ability to cope with the crisis. After the joint session address, a great tsunami of faith lofted Bush up to levels of trust no leader in American history had ever previously achieved. The bitterest Bush hater I knew at the time of the Florida recount e-mailed me to ask how he could help organize a Manhattan chapter of "Democrats for Bush" in time for 2004. In Philadelphia, the first ten minutes of the speech were piped into the monitors of the local arena during the break between the second and third periods of a Flyers-Rangers game. At the end of ten minutes, the speech cut out so play could resume—and the fans booed and then chanted in unison, "Leave it on, leave it on." Management hastily resumed the broadcast, and the crowd watched to the end, thirty-six minutes later, cheering the most exciting lines with chants of "USA! USA!" The game was declared a 2–2 tie, and the players skated onto center ice to shake hands.

For me, there was one sad detail in that handshake. Half the players on the ice that night were Canadians, including both team captains. Over their heads hung both America's Stars and Stripes and Canada's Maple Leaf. And this was fitting. In no nation on earth, not even Britain, did ordinary people take 9/11 more to heart than the people of my native Canada. When the Federal Aviation Administration ordered the closing of U.S. airspace on September 11, 224 planes and 33,000 people were diverted to airports in Canada. All across Canada, people drove to the airports to offer stranded passengers a place to stay. The single small town of Gander, Newfoundland, population 10,000, found beds for 6,595 travelers. One hundred thousand Canadians flocked spontaneously to Parliament Hill in Ottawa on the evening of September 14, in the largest vigil ever seen in Canada's capital.

Yet although Bush's speech found room to thank Egyptians for their prayers and to mention the death toll among El Salvadoreans, there was no reference at all to these acts of fellow feeling in Canada. I got my copy of the final draft of the speech about three hours before it was to be delivered. My stomach plunged as I read it: All references to Canada had been cut. The speech had been running long, and somebody had reasoned that if we mentioned Canada, we'd have to praise all the other NATO countries by name, too, and many of them had been much quicker than Canada to offer aid and assistance. I could anticipate all the rest. The omission stung and shamed Canadians with the power of a savage and unexpected slap, and the Canadians who felt the blow most keenly were America's best friends. I spent hours on the phone over the next week, taking calls from Canadians pleading for some explanation for the omission. Had Bush been offended by Prime Minister Jean Chrétien's boorishness in not attending the Ottawa vigil? Was the Pentagon annoyed that Canada had not matched Britain's and Australia's offer of military assistance? Had Americans at last reacted against the lax refugee laws that had made Canada a haven for Islamic terrorists? The answer was yes, yes, and yes—and no. Canada was not omitted to send some elliptical message. Canada was omitted because it is easy to forget friends whose governments give you no cause to remember them.

Bush, despite achieving the highest approval rating of any political leader in American history, was in some ways not much of a politician at all. The politician's mind is an archive of checklists. He does not say "farmer" without also saying "rancher"; "church" without saying "synagogue" and now "mosque"; "business leaders" without adding "labor leaders." Bush did not always check his list as carefully as he should have, and September 20 was one occasion when his carelessness inflicted an unintended injury.

There is a Holden Caulfield streak to Bush's personality: a deep distaste for the necessary insincerities of political life. From this streak come many of his best decisions—and from it have come some of his worst troubles. Yet troubled though he was, Holden articulated the feelings and captured the sympathy of a nation and a generation—and so, in those ten days in September, did George W. Bush. In the aftermath of the speech, his approval rating would climb to the highest level ever recorded. It would remain at that supernatural level for weeks, before gently subsiding to the incredible and thence to the merely astonishing. He had transformed himself. He had won America's trust. Now he had to prove himself worthy of it.

# 9

## RELIGION OF PEACE

I RONICALLY, AT PRECISELY the moment that Bush's popularity was ascending to fantastic heights with the general public, it was slumping among the conservative elite in Washington. For all his reputation on the Left as a right-wing ogre, and for all his fabulous post-9/11 popularity among the conservative rank and file, Bush had not won the unquestioning support of the conservative intelligentsia in Washington and New York City in the way that Barry Goldwater, Ronald Reagan, and for a time Jack Kemp had done. Conservative elites were perpetually sniffing the air around Bush for the scent of sellout—and in the seven weeks from the joint session speech to the fall of Mazar-i-Sharif, the scent was strong in their nostrils.

They did not like Colin Powell's attempt to recruit Syria and Iran to the antiterror coalition. They did not like the talk of delaying the war until after Ramadan. When the war commenced despite Ramadan, they complained that it was being prosecuted too tentatively. Most of all, however, they did not like Bush's lavish praise of the religion in whose name more than three thousand Americans had been murdered.

Six days after September 11, Bush visited Washington's Islamic Center near the vice president's mansion to meet with Muslim community leaders. After the meeting, Bush emerged to denounce hate crimes and to compliment Islam: "Islam," he said, "is peace." Three nights later, in his joint session speech, Bush defended the Muslim faith even more emphatically: Osama bin Laden and his followers "practice a fringe form of Islamic extremism that has been rejected by Muslim scholars and the vast majority of Muslim clerics—a fringe movement that perverts the peaceful teachings of Islam." The terrorists, Bush said, had "hijacked" the Muslim religion.

Bush restated these conciliatory opinions after his September 26 meeting with Muslim religious leaders at the White House, in radio broadcasts, and in official government statements. His words were echoed and amplified by America's great and good—newspaper editorial writers, university professors, television talking heads—all of them seemingly determined to convince the American public (in Bernard Lewis's mordant words) that Islam was a religion like Quakerism, only less violent.

This advertising campaign on behalf of the faith of Muhammad drove conservative leaders almost wild with vexation. Charles Krauthammer spoke for many when he demanded in a November column, "Who attacked whom? Who should be doing the soul-searching and the breast-beating? Why are we acting as if we bear guilt for our own victimization?" While Bush privately characterized the al-Qaeda terrorists as a "bunch of nuts," conservatives perceived them as the logical products of a culture of extremism within modern Islam—a culture that had taken root inside the United States. They feared that Bush's friendly overtures signaled that the president intended to appease Islamic extremism rather than confront it.

The signals were indeed disturbing. Only two days before September 11, Hamza Yusuf, a charismatic American-born convert to Islam, gave a speech in Irvine, California, in which he defended Sheik Omar Abdel Rahman (the blind Egyptian preacher convicted of masterminding the 1993 bombing of the World Trade Center) and cop killer Jamil al-Amin, the former H. Rap Brown, as victims of miscarriages of justice. "This country is facing a very terrible fate," Yusuf said. "The reason for that is that this country stands condemned. It stands condemned like Europe stood condemned . . . after conquering the Muslim lands." Hamza Yusuf was invited to meet with the president in advance of the September 20 speech and to sit in the gallery that night with the First Lady—and it was he who suggested the "hijacked" line.

On the afternoon of September 11, Salam al-Marayati, executive director of the Muslim Public Affairs Council, said on a Los Angeles radio program that the state of Israel belonged on any list of suspects for the World Trade Center attack. Fifteen days later, al-Marayati was one of the Muslim leaders invited to meet with President Bush.

Even Muzammil Siddiqi, the California imam who joined the prayer service in National Cathedral, had an equivocal record on the subject of religious violence. When asked by the *Los Angeles Times* in 1989 whether Salman Rushdie deserved to die for publishing *The Satanic Verses,* Siddiqi "was noncommittal, saying that would have to be determined in the due course of Islamic law."*

In the weeks after September 11, full-throated, unequivocal condemnation of Osama bin Laden by the leaders of American Islam was startlingly rare; condemnation of the culture of extremism inside American mosques was rarer still. Muslim leaders condemned "these acts" or "terrorism"—and then added "whoever committed them," a wink to those in their community who believed that the Mossad was the real culprit. They would express sympathy for the victims—and then add that America needed to "understand why it was hated" in the Muslim world.

Sheik Muhammed al-Gamei'a, imam of the largest and wealthiest mosque in America, on East Ninety-sixth Street in Manhattan, decamped to his native Egypt after September 11 and gave an interview there on October 4, 2001, in which he claimed that Muslims were being murdered in the streets of New York and poisoned by Jewish doctors in the city's hospitals. He alleged that his home had been attacked by an angry mob. "I went out to them and asked why they were doing this. . . . During my conversations with this group, it became clear to me that they knew very well that the Jews were behind these ugly acts." He repeated the fantasy that four thousand Jews had received word to stay home from work on September 11—and then advised the world's Muslims "not to offer any aid whatsoever to the [American military intervention in Afghanistan], because this is a betrayal of Allah and his Prophet. . . ."†

---

* John Dark, "L.A. Area Muslims Disagree with Khomeini's Call to Kill Rushdie," *Los Angeles Times*, February 22, 1989, page 13.

† The full text of the interview can be read at www.memri.org/bin/articles.cgi?Page= archives&Area=sd&ID=SP28801.

The sheik's antiwar pronouncements found an audience in America: The most visible and effective American Muslim organization, the Council on American Islamic Relations, announced its opposition to the war in Afghanistan on October 7, 2001. A Zogby International poll of American Muslims at the end of November found that 43 percent opposed the war in Afghanistan. Four-fifths of American Muslims identified support for Israel as the main cause of the September 11 attacks. And two-thirds of those surveyed thought the best way to fight terrorism was by changing American foreign policy in the Middle East rather than by the use of military force.*

As September 11 receded, American Muslim opposition to the war grew and intensified. By May 2002, Zogby found that almost half of American Muslims opposed the U.S. involvement in Afghanistan. One-third now regarded the war on terrorism as in reality a war on Islam. Only about one-third of American Muslims still believed that Osama bin Laden was responsible for the attack on America; 22 percent blamed "somebody else"; and 40 percent of them declined to answer the question at all.[†] After his September 17 mosque visit, Bush had asserted that America's Muslims "love this country as much as I do." To conservative eyes, that increasingly looked like wishful thinking at best, willful blindness at worst.

So why was Bush mouthing these words? According to *The Washington Post,* it was all the fault of . . . a speechwriter named David Frum.

A couple of days after September 11, I had received a fax

---

* www.projectmaps.com/PMReport.htm.

† The survey can be read in .pdf form by following the links at www.hamilton.edu/news/more_news/display.cfm?ID=4607.

from Michael Horowitz, an alumnus of the first Bush administration now working at a think tank in Washington. Horowitz
urged me to meet with a friend of his, a law professor at Cleveland State University named David Forte. Forte's ideas on how
the president should speak about Islam would be worth,
Horowitz promised, a squadron of fighter aircraft to the United
States. I had known Horowitz for a long time as a man with an
unusually fertile mind, so I quickly called him back and said I
would be glad to meet with his friend. In advance of the meeting, Horowitz sent over a package of Forte's writings.

Those first days after the attack on America were a franti-
cally busy time, and in the end I was not able to see Forte until
September 21, the morning after Bush's joint session speech. On
my way out the door to the Starbucks on Pennsylvania Avenue—with all but the highest-priority visitors banned from the
White House, the coffee shop across the street from the Executive Office Building became the administration's unofficial conference room—I grabbed Horowitz's still unopened envelope
and hastily flipped through the articles inside.

They made the familiar points: Osama bin Laden represented
an extreme form of Islam rejected by most Muslims; Islam's
teachings are good and peaceful; the president should avoid criticizing Islam as a religion. Still, I had promised Horowitz that I
would listen to his friend. Forte and I drank a cup of coffee together. When we were done, I thanked him for his time, returned
to my office, and dropped his articles into a file folder.

Four days later, my phone rang: It was Dana Milbank, a reporter for *The Washington Post*. I told him that the press ban
was still in effect and that I could not speak, but he insisted he
had just one short question for me: Had I ever met a David Forte?

That question hardly seemed to implicate any state secrets. I acknowledged that I had indeed met Forte and then said good-bye.

Two mornings after that, I picked up my morning *Washington Post* and read with amazement a headline on page A-6:

PROFESSOR SHAPES BUSH RHETORIC:
WHITE HOUSE TAPS OHIO SCHOLAR'S WRITINGS
ON RADICAL ISLAM

The story was even more sensational than the header:

In the first days after the Sept. 11 attacks, the writings of . . . David F. Forte landed on desks in the White House and throughout the national security apparatus. Those words would form the moral and rhetorical basis of the U.S. war effort.

Milbank mentioned four specific administration officials as recipients of Forte's work: one at State, one at NSC, one at Defense, and, er, me. He then quoted an unnamed White House speechwriter who, Milbank said, "acknowledge[d] the scholar's influence, saying Bush's speech was 'Forte-ed.' "

By the time I arrived at work, my voice mail and e-mail were blinking with exasperated messages from Gerson, Ari Fleischer, and Communications Director Dan Bartlett. They all wanted to know the same thing: Who in the world is David Forte? And why was I telling *The Washington Post* that this man nobody had ever heard of had inspired the president's speech?

It was a very awkward morning.

I left an angry message on Milbank's voice mail at the *Post.* Milbank replied by e-mail that he had been given the "Forte-ed" quote by Horowitz, who had solemnly assured him that he had heard it from the speechwriting staff himself. To their credit, Milbank's editors found this "two degrees of separation" method of quotation less acceptable than he did, and the *Post* ran a correction the following day.

The correction arrived, as corrections usually do, too late. The *Post* had launched Forte on a spurious but glittering media career. He was invited to lecture at campuses around the country, where he was presented as an "adviser on Islamic affairs for the Bush administration."* He was interviewed on radio and television. And when critics stepped forward, they gave him even more credit than his admirers. In an article in *The New York Times Magazine,* Andrew Sullivan mocked Forte as Bush's "Catholic ghostwriter." All in all, it was the most impressive PR achievement since Ransom Stoddard snagged the credit for shooting Liberty Valance. Even more impressive, really: Stoddard had at least been in the vicinity of the gunfight.

In truth, Bush hardly needed to send to Cleveland for advice to speak nicely about Islam. That advice was pouring in upon him from every quarter. His pro-Muslim words were, as the literary critics say, overdetermined.

His words were determined first by his own conscience. After September 11, Muslim groups reported a horrifying wave of hate crimes against their co-religionists: shootings, stabbings, the desecration of mosques, and the intimidation of women who wore head coverings. These reports enraged Bush. He expressed his feelings with sincere scorn after his visit to the Washington mosque. "Those who feel like they can intimidate our

* That was Forte's billing in a March speech at Washington University in St. Louis, http://news-info.wustl.edu/News/2002/forte.html.

fellow citizens to take out their anger don't represent the best of America, they represent the worst of humankind."

Bush's second motive for speaking out was strategic. The unpleasant truth was that Osama bin Laden's attack on the United States had detonated a big bang of joy and triumph throughout the Muslim world. Palestinians danced with glee, Pakistani merchants sold Osama T-shirts, proud Kuwaiti parents named their newborns after him. The Bush foreign-policy team keenly wanted to pry Osama's support away, and the Middle East experts at the State Department and on the National Security Council insisted that the best way to do that was to deny his Islamic bona-fides and insist on America's great respect for the Muslim faith.

There was a third, more political, motive. Bush had campaigned hard to win Muslim and Arab American votes in the 2000 presidential year. It's possible, in fact, that Muslim votes may have tipped the balance of the whole election. The Tampa Bay Islamic Center claimed that its exit polls showed that fifty thousand Muslims came to the polls in Florida in November 2000 and voted 88 percent for Bush, 8 percent for Nader, and only 4 percent for Gore. Those numbers may not have been wholly reliable, but they were widely accepted inside the Bush camp. The leaders of the American Muslim community had a lot of Bush operatives' phone numbers in their PalmPilots—and a hefty positive balance in the favor bank.

None of these motives—not the conscientious, not the strategic, and not the political—much impressed those members of the conservative intelligentsia alarmed by Bush's soft line.

As for the first, conservatives were quick to note that the reports of a hate crime wave had been grossly exaggerated. In the six months after September 11, the FBI was called to investigate 350 suspected hate crimes against Arabs and Muslims. State and local authorities investigated 70. Some 65 of these 420 complaints proved to have any merit, and the large majority of them turned out to be very minor offenses—anonymous threats, graffiti, and so on. In the entire United States, there were three proven hate homicides after September 11, and one of them was committed by a man with a long history of mental illness. (His victim was an Arizona gasoline station owner named Balbir Singh Sodhi, an American Sikh.) The other two slayings were committed by a career criminal named Mark Anthony Stroman in the course of robberies. Stroman was apprehended, convicted, and in June 2002 sentenced to death by a Texas jury.

America in the twenty-first century offered no impunity for racist killers. But a closer look at the details of alleged hate crimes often revealed a context more complicated than the antiracist morality tales the media liked to highlight. A story: After the September 20 speech, Bush asked his staff to look for examples of American tolerance and understanding that he could showcase. They found a beauty. Some thug had smashed the window of a Muslim shop owner in a town near Washington. The shop owner was a new immigrant to the country and underinsured. A nearby merchant who was Jewish heard of his neighbor's distress and took up a collection along the shopping strip to replace the vandalized glass. Bush had been delighted by the story. That, he said, is "what this country is all about." Bush wanted every merchant in the group—Muslim, Jewish, Christian—invited to the White House to be honored together. I happened to be in the Oval Office on the day he pressed the staffer in charge to tell him when the ceremony would occur.

There was an awkward pause.

"Well, sir, we've come across a problem."

A problem?

"Yes, well—it seems the guy with the broken window—well, it seems he's been giving money to some of these terrorist groups in the Middle East."

We dropped the event.

Conservatives saw even less merit in the strategic motive for the soft line. Far from winning friends for the United States, it was actually giving encouragement to the nation's enemies, by making the United States look overeager and therefore weak. According to a massive Gallup survey of Muslims in nine Middle Eastern countries conducted in early 2002, after months of relentless pro-Muslim messaging by the United States:

- More Muslims condemned the American war in Afghanistan than condemned the September 11 attack on America (77 percent vs. 67 percent).
- Almost two-thirds refused to believe that Muslims carried out the September 11 attacks.
- Those hostile to the United States outnumbered those friendly by a margin of two to one.
- Among the most hostile of the nine societies were the two the United States had fought to defend in 1991: Kuwait and Saudi Arabia.

America's compassion and concern for the sensibilities of Arabs and Muslims went entirely unreciprocated. Secretary of State Colin Powell implicitly recognized this sad fact in a September 17 interview with the Arabic-language television station al-Jazeera, when he offered this reason that Arabs and Muslims should condemn the September 11 attacks: Not only, he said, "thousands of Americans were lost, but also hundreds of Arabs were lost." This statement wildly overstated the Arab death toll—but it very accurately assessed how little sympathy could be expected from the Arab world for an attack in which only Americans perished.

Worst of all, conservatives complained, in an effort to avoid offending Muslims at home and abroad, the Bush administration had blinded the country to the identity of its enemy. All this talk of fighting "terrorism" made as much sense as a war against "sneak-attackism" would have made after Pearl Harbor. Terror was a tactic, not an enemy, and it was the administration's insistence on pretending otherwise that obliged airport screeners to search pigtailed seven-year-old girls and former vice presidents of the United States, all to uphold the fiction that the terrorists could be anybody, from anywhere.

As for the Bush administration's political motives, they too alarmed the conservative hard core. It was easier for people unaffiliated with the administration to acknowledge the obvious: If Bush had indeed swept 88 percent of the Muslim vote, he did not do so because of his faith-based initiative, his education plans, or his support for small business. Other socially conservative immigrant groups had reasons to like all those things, too, but Bush seldom won even as much as 35 percent of their votes. What made this one constituency an exception to the usual rules of American politics? Only this: Al Gore's decision to put a Jew on the Democratic ticket.

As one political operative who had assisted Republican candidates with Muslim votes in 2000 put it to me: "This is a very diverse community. They come from all over the world. Some are very rich, others very poor; some very educated, others not educated at all. Really, there is only one thing that unites them: They all hate your people." He did not mean Canadians. No less a spokesman for the Muslim community than Bush's guest Hamza Yusuf admitted the centrality of anti-Semitism to the politics of American Muslims: He told *The Wall Street Journal* in October 2001 that he regretted that the "political animosity" he and many American Muslims felt toward Jews had become a "racial and ethnic animosity." He added piously, "We have to change that,"* although the evidence that he himself did anything to change it is scanty at best.

When you draw support from a constituency overwhelmingly motivated by what its own chieftains describe as "hatred" for another constituency,† you tend to draw some very questionable supporters. Bush did not escape this fate. During the 2000 campaign, Bush accepted the backing of Sami al-Arian, a professor at Southern Florida University. Al-Arian's campaign help was rewarded with a photo session with the candidate. Al-Arian was best known, however, not for his academic work, but for his leadership of a south Florida Islamic organization that sponsored conferences attended by a number of extremists, among them Sheik Rahman. Sami al-Arian had also raised money for a group later identified by the FBI as a front for the terrorist group Hamas and had himself urged jihad against Israel. Al-Arian's brother-in-law, Mazen al-Najjar, an illegal immigrant to the United States, was deported

---

* http://online.wsj.com/article_email/0,,SB101372652597775160,00.html.
† Hamza Yusuf's word in an October interview with the British newspaper the *Guardian,* http://www.guardian.co.uk/g2/story/0,3604,564960,00.html.

in August 2002 for what the Department of Justice called "established ties to terrorist organizations."*

Nevertheless, Sami al-Arian was invited to the White House for a political briefing in the summer of 2001. And when objections from the Secret Service prevented al-Arian's son Abdullah from attending a meeting with John DiIulio in June, President Bush responded swiftly: He condemned Abdullah al-Arian's removal as "wrong" and "inappropriate" and ordered the deputy director of the Secret Service to apologize to Abdullah al-Arian in person. Young al-Arian later detailed the incident in *Newsweek*'s on-line edition. He said he had been excluded only because of his "name and physical features."† Although the al-Arian family's political connections were by then well known to the White House, the normally hypersensitive political operation let the allegations go unrebutted.

Connections like these, merely troubling before September 11, began to look distinctly ominous afterward. In the 1990s, conservatives had often (and not always fairly) connected the dots between Clinton's soft line on China and his fund-raising among people who did business with China; conservatives feared that it was trusting too much to the ineptitude of the Democrats to assume that they would refrain from connecting dots in the same way between the Bush administration's refusal to profile at the airports and its hopes for votes from the potential profilees.

That, as I say, was the reaction of conservatives—and I was

---

* Department of Justice Statement Regarding the Arrest of Mazen Al Najjar, November 24, 2001, www.usdoj.gov/opa/pr/2001/November/01__ins__606.htm.

† Abdullah al-Arian, "We Are the Targets of Misdirected Anger," http://www.msnbc.com/news/629237.asp?0sp=w12b2.

among them. But in retrospect, Bush was right, and we were wrong.

Bill Clinton's former campaign consultant Dick Morris has compared the Republican Party to a tank: big and strong, but not very nimble. Under Clinton, Morris delighted in luring the tank into battles it could not win—but that its drivers would not be clever enough to avoid. After the Oklahoma City bombing, for instance, Clinton proposed adding special chemicals to any potential explosives sold in the United States to help investigators trace their place of origin if they were used in a crime. It was one of those ideas that probably would not do much good (what if the explosives were stolen?) but would not do much harm, either. Journalists scoffed at the ideas as typical of Morris's useless symbolism. But the idea was not useless at all: Morris was counting on at least some Republicans being stupid enough to oppose the plan, thus enabling him and Clinton to hang the responsibility for Oklahoma City around their necks.

All through the 1990s, Bush had watched the GOP lumber into one such trap after another. And the conclusion he had reached from his observation was that Republicans must discipline themselves to stop biting at sucker bait.

Racial profiling at the airports was sucker bait. It would add little to the country's security, because Middle Eastern terrorists have often found non–Middle Easterners willing to do their terrorism for them—think of the Germans responsible for the Entebbe hijacking back in 1976 and the alleged dirty bomber Jose Padilla as recently as 2002. And the price for the small increment of security offered by racial profiling would be horrendous—a shattering of the nation's unity, the defection of many Democrats from the pro-security coalition, and a revival of the endless

American debate over race and ethnicity right in the middle of a war. Better to keep to the high ground of nondiscrimination, enforced by a secretary of transportation who had been confined as a boy to an internment camp—and instead to concentrate the administration's energies on projects more likely to achieve results.

Where it was necessary to do so, Bush was more than willing to defy ethnic lobbies. His administration wrote and put into effect new internal-security legislation, the USA Patriot Act of 2001, that expanded the government's power to deport noncitizens associated with terrorist organizations. The Bush Justice Department detained more than a thousand people who might have relevant information about the terror attacks. His FBI summoned Middle Eastern students for voluntary questioning. His Immigration and Naturalization Service directed enforcement resources toward Middle Easterners who had overstayed their visas. Bush added Hamas and Hezbollah to the State Department's list of terrorist organizations, to the dismay of the leading American Muslim organizations. On December 4, Bush ordered that the assets of the nation's largest Muslim charity, the Holy Land Foundation in Richardson, Texas, be frozen because of the group's long record of support for Hamas.

Yet Bush took all these strong actions in ways that reassured the country—which is, after all, home to liberals as well as to conservatives—that its security was in the hands of moderate, unhysterical, unbigoted people.

In the past, efforts to protect the country against internal threats had been tainted by prejudice and panic. The FBI had disgraced itself with its espionage against Martin Luther King, and that disgrace still hobbled the agency almost forty years later. The FBI had overcompensated for past sins by building racial ultrasensitivity into its operations: That was one reason that all those warnings about Arabs at flight academies were disregarded. The country needed a less obtuse law enforcement culture—but it needed also to be assured that the bad old days would not return. The conspicuous religious and ethnic sensitivity of the man at the top of the government helped achieve a public consensus in favor of a little less sensitivity in the ranks.

Bush's guiding philosophy in so many areas of politics was this: There were other ways of entering a room than charging headfirst through the wall. It was not always a betrayal of conservative principle to knock politely at the door.

Bush had another guiding principle, and it helped to explain many of the foreign-policy actions that irked his conservative supporters: He would not commit himself to any one course of action until he must. If Colin Powell wanted to try a diplomatic solution to a problem—and Donald Rumsfeld promised to have a military solution ready to go within three weeks—Bush would not say, "Right—we're doing it Don's way." He would say: "Colin—you have three weeks."

Sometimes, instead of trying one course of action first and then another later, Bush would allow both to develop, to give himself more time to decide which was superior. And that is the story behind the internal White House battle that probably caused more conservatives more heartburn than any other: the great "Why do they hate us?" debate of 2001.

By early October, it was no longer possible to pretend that bin Ladenism was a fringe phenomenon in the Muslim world. If not yet a majority ideology, it certainly counted many millions, perhaps even many tens of millions, of supporters among Muslims from the Philippines to Pittsburgh—Pittsburgh being, as it happened, the home base of *Assirat Al-Mustaqeem,* or the *Straight Path,* a glossy magazine that between 1991 and 2000 published more than one hundred issues advocating jihad against the United States and the mass murder of Jews and Christians.

So the next logical question was: Where does this phenomenon come from? And then: What do we do about it?

Arab and European leaders, and many of the American academics who specialized in the Middle East, were quick with an answer. The Muslim world, they argued, hates the United States because of America's unjust and anti-Islamic policies, and especially because of America's support for Israel. The appropriate response to the attack on the World Trade Center was, therefore—a Palestinian state. The State Department agreed. Within days of September 11, the State Department began leaking a story that Colin Powell was about to make a big speech on the Middle East, presumably one staking out a new, more pro-Palestinian line. Almost everyone in the Bush White House reacted to Powell's project with horror. One of my speechwriting colleagues put it nicely: "Let's see: They kill six thousand Americans [the best estimate of the casualties at that time], and we give the Palestinians a state. If they kill six thousand more Americans, do we give the Palestinians twice as big a state?" Powell's speech was postponed and postponed again, and when he finally delivered it in November, Condoleezza Rice managed to boil all its policy content away. What remained after she finished with it was a speech announcing "a positive vision" of a Middle East peace: two states, Israel and Palestine, living side by side in peace. And a very lovely thought it is, too.

But if America and Israel were not to blame for 9/11, what was? Two competing theories soon divided the Bush White

House. As usual, each theory was backed by its own little team. Again as usual, the teams were captained by Karen Hughes and Karl Rove.

Hughes answered the question "Why do they hate us?" with characteristic cheerfulness. They hate us, she believed, because they don't understand us. They think we are godless, materialistic immoralists. The solution, then, is to convince them that Americans are good, decent, God-fearing people. To that end, Hughes built a vast communications effort, run from the State Department by former advertising executive Charlotte Beers, the newly confirmed undersecretary of state for public diplomacy, but ultimately controlled by herself.

Rove was drawn to a very different answer, the answer given by the eminent academic Bernard Lewis: They hate us because they resent us. Islam—to summarize some very sophisticated ideas in my own crude words—is not merely one of the world's great religions; it was also one of the world's great empires. And unlike the former imperial states of Europe, the heirs to the Islamic empire have never reconciled themselves to the loss of their power and dominion. They regard the two great English-speaking world powers, Britain in the first half of the century and the United States since 1956, as usurpers who possess what they ought to possess. It is unlikely, therefore, that Muslim hatred of the United States will abate until Islam itself changes. While waiting for that change to occur, the United States should recognize that although it cannot expect to be loved, it can enforce respect—and that the surest way to forfeit this respect is to seem overeager to please. Western attempts to ingratiate ourselves were interpreted in the Muslim world as signs of weakness and fear, not of friendship and goodwill.

Rove invited Bernard Lewis to the White House in November to explain his views. That in itself was an amazing fact. Lewis is the world's greatest living authority on the Muslim world, a master not only of Arabic, but of Persian, Ottoman, Modern Turkish, and French and German for good measure, whose historical and philological knowledge extends across twenty centuries. For that very reason, Lewis has become a demon figure to many Arab nationalists. He is the villain of Edward Said's famous book *Orientalism,* which argues that there is something not only sinister but imperialist and even larcenous in the study of Arabs by non-Arabs. For the mastermind of the Muslim outreach campaign of 2000 to wish to listen to what Lewis had to say—well, that was something.

Hughes arrived at the Lewis briefing fifteen minutes late, departed half an hour early, and listened in between with ill-concealed impatience. Who could blame her? The grand old man's message was that everything the White House had done up to that point to sell its case was wrong.

Myself, I was not sure that Lewis's harsh assessment was entirely fair. Much of the campaign of understanding that Hughes had advocated since September 11 had done real good. Surely one reason so few hate crimes were reported after 9/11 was precisely President Bush's swift and decisive condemnation of them. Even if bin Ladenism had attracted a wider following in the Middle East than the administration cared to admit, it was also true that the large majority of Muslims in the United States and the world lived by humane values—and the United States had little to lose and much to gain by speaking to those people.

Hughes had breathed new life into American public diplomacy. Hughes and Beers had won the president's support for

Radio Sawa, a new Arab-language radio station that replaced the Arabic service of the Voice of America with a new format that broadcast attractive, modern music from both Western and Middle Eastern pop artists (no clash of civilizations here!), interspersed with short news bulletins. To American ears, the Radio Sawa format sounded very familiar, and understandably so: Radio Sawa was the brain wave of Norman Pattiz, who headed the largest distributor of radio programming in the United States. Bush had appointed Pattiz to the Board of Broadcast Governors, which supervises the Voice of America, Radio Liberty, Radio Marti, and the American government's other radio services. But in the Arab Middle East, Radio Sawa's bulletins were a novelty: concise and truthful information without propaganda, paranoia, or anti-American and anti-Semitic incitement.

On the other hand, it was true that some of the "it's all a big misunderstanding" initiatives were embarrassing, if not dangerous. On October 25, with the Taliban still in control of almost every inch of Afghan territory, Bush traveled to Thurgood Marshall Elementary School in Washington, D.C., to announce a new program to encourage American children to find pen pals in the Islamic world. It was like a *Saturday Night Live* parody of compassionate conservatism at war: "We want," the president said, "to be friends with Muslims and with Muslim children." By writing back and forth, "you can let boys and girls know what you think are [*sic*] important. You can let boys and girls know what your dreams are, and ask them about theirs, too." Unfortunately, since there was that small problem of deadly anthrax pouring through America's mail slots, the communication would have to be by e-mail only.

After the "e-mail a Muslim pen pal" initiative, a note of ridicule began for the first time to be heard in press coverage of the "I ❤ Islam" campaign. By then, too, media outlets including *The Washington Post,* the *New York Post,* Fox News, and even the left-wing on-line magazine *Salon* had mustered the nerve to report more frankly on the backgrounds and public statements of the leaders of American Muslim groups like the Council on American Islamic Relations and the American Muslim Council. For two months, administration spokesmen had given interviews to al-Jazeera, in hope of winning friends via the region's most virulently anti-American broadcaster. For two months, the heads of the very same American Muslim organizations who had professed their patriotism and loyalty in the immediate shock of 9/11 had denounced the administration's internal security measures and the war in Afghanistan as "Islamophobic" and racist. For two months, Americans had been learning how much support al-Qaeda had drawn from Saudi Arabia—and not merely from individual Saudis, but from the royal family and the government. After two months of testing Karen, Bush decided it was now time to try Karl.

On November 9, the Taliban army began to disintegrate, and the Northern Alliance entered Mazar-i-Sharif. Bush addressed the United Nations General Assembly the following morning. That speech attracted less attention than his September 20 speech, but it deserved as much. Though not as spellbindingly written, it made explicit the arresting new doctrines Bush had announced at the war's beginning—and it expanded them.

The war on terror, he told the United Nations, would not end in Afghanistan. There would be no more tolerance for the corrupt side arrangements that many Islamic governments had made with terror. And terror did not become more tolerable when it targeted Israelis rather than Americans.

"We're asking for a comprehensive commitment to this fight. We must unite in opposing all terrorists, not just some of them. In this world there are good causes and bad causes, and we may disagree on where the line is drawn. Yet there is no such thing as a good terrorist. No national aspiration, no remembered wrong, can ever justify the deliberate murder of the innocent. Any government that rejects this principle, trying to pick and choose its terrorist friends, will know the consequences."

It was a breathtaking statement. Everyone understood who the governments were that rejected Bush's principle: They included the greater part of the governments of the Arab world, including many of America's traditional Arab allies. For thirty years, the United Nations had been the playpen of these Arab states. In May 2001, member states voted the United States off the UN Human Rights Commission—and voted to add slave-owning Sudan in America's place, alongside Syria, China, and Cuba. In 2002, Libya was elected to the commission's chairmanship. The UN ran the Palestinian refugee camps in which terrorism was incubated. It had bent its rules to allow Yasser Arafat to wear a gun holster on his hip in 1974. On November 9, 1974, the anniversary of the Nazi Kristallnacht, the United Nations had voted to condemn Zionism as a form of racism. Now, on the same day as that infamous vote, Bush stood on the same rostrum on which Arafat had stood and delivered an ultimatum to the Arab world: The terrorism must stop—or else.

Three days after Bush's UN speech, Kabul fell to the U.S.-backed Northern Alliance, then Herāt, then Kandahār. Sometime after that, I noticed a marked-up copy of one of Bernard Lewis's articles in the clutch of papers the president held in his hand. Bush's remarks at the Ramadan Iftar dinner in the White House dining room on November 19 were friendly but restrained. "America respects people of all faiths, and America seeks peace with people of all faiths."

In the end, Bush was simultaneously generous and respectful toward the Islamic faith and unillusioned about and unwilling to appease domestic Muslim organizations. Some critics on the Right thought that the second set of impulses conflicted with the first. Many on the Left thought that the first was nothing more than a cynical cover for the second. Bush never understood why he could not honor both impulses at the same time. And that is just what he did.

# 10

## DEATH IN THE AIR

I N FORTY-FIVE DAYS from the beginning of October to the middle of November, the American nation traveled from terror to euphoria. October was the month of the American Blitz; November was the month of the modern Midway.

On October 4, 2001, a sixty-two-year-old British-born photographer named Robert Stevens showed up at a Boca Raton, Florida, hospital complaining of difficulty in breathing. At first the doctors thought he was suffering from meningitis. They X-rayed him and discovered instead the first anthrax infection to be diagnosed on American soil since 1976. They applied antibiotics, but not in time: Stevens died the next day. On Monday, October 8, a fellow employee in the building where Stevens worked—the headquarters of the *National Enquirer*, the *Star*, and other tabloid titles owned by American Media Inc.—was found to have anthrax spores in his nasal passages. On October 10, a third employee in the building, this time a woman, was found to be infected. There could now be no doubt: Somebody had deliberately released a weapon of bioterror against American Media Inc.

But who? And how? The means by which anthrax was delivered to the American Media offices were never found.

Then, on October 12, New York mayor Rudy Giuliani announced that the NBC News staffer who opened anchorman Tom Brokaw's mail had tested positive for anthrax. Her case proved that the spores were being sent through the post. Over the next four weeks, anthrax would be found at the offices of the Microsoft Corporation, CBS News and ABC News, the *New York Post,* New York governor George Pataki, and Senate Majority Leader Tom Daschle and in the off-site mailrooms of the CIA, the Supreme Court, and the White House. The Hart Senate Office Building would be closed; later, the Capitol itself would (briefly) be evacuated. A total of eighteen people would be found to be infected with anthrax disease; five would die before the anthrax wave faded away in early December: Stevens himself, two postal employees, a New York hospital worker, and a ninety-four-year-old woman in the small town of Oxford, Connecticut.

The September 11 attacks had broken the country's heart; anthrax shook its nerve. Nobody then knew much about al-Qaeda and Osama bin Laden. Americans were ready to believe he was a real-life Dr. No: infinitely resourceful and cunning. American power was already striking Afghanistan—but Osama bin Laden had nonetheless managed to deliver boastful videotapes to al-Jazeera; why could he not have readied a second strike—and then a third?

Czech intelligence claimed to have observed a meeting between Mohammed Atta, the lead 9/11 hijacker, and an Iraqi intelligence officer in Prague in April 2001, suggesting some degree of cooperation between al-Qaeda and the Iraqi dictator. The Iraqis themselves did not quite deny it. "Even if such an incident had taken place, it doesn't mean anything," said Deputy Prime Minister Tariq Aziz in October 2001. "Any diplomat in any mission might meet people in a restaurant here or there and talk to them. . . ." Saddam Hussein had produced arsenals of anthrax. Might he have shared it with Osama bin Laden, as some believe he supported the Islamic extremists who bombed the World Trade Center in 1993?

If bin Laden—or the Iraqis or other terrorists inside the United States—could send death through the mail, what else might they do? Infect suicide couriers with smallpox? Blow up a nuclear power plant? Commit random machine-gun massacres in shopping malls? Poison the reservoirs? Detonate a dirty bomb a block or two from the White House?

Fear gripped Washington in October even more tightly than in September. Jitters and false alarms hit the city twice and thrice in a day. One October afternoon, I met my wife for lunch about five blocks from the White House, and on my short walk I passed two clusters of buildings emptied out by bomb scares. Their workers thronged the sidewalks, half amused, half frightened. Residents of the capital had discovered on September 11 how utterly unready our municipal government was for disaster, and in some part of our minds, we feared that the terrorists had discovered the same fact and had therefore marked out downtown Washington as their next target for attack.

On October 3, Sally Quinn published an article in *The Washington Post* coolly describing her hunt for secondhand gas masks left over from Saddam Hussein's 1991 Scud attacks on

Israel: "The prices, if you're on a waiting list, range from $50 to $500, and nobody can tell you why the more expensive mask is better than the less expensive ones except for how long they last. (I got the ones that operate for 12 hours.)"

Maureen Dowd, always a useful indicator of the Washington media mood, could not muster even Quinn's degree of sangfroid. In her column for October 10, she wrote: "The noise of military planes roaring over the capital at 4 A.M. unnerves me. My gas mask ominously stares back at me from the bedpost where it hangs, scaring me even more." Quinn and Dowd set the tone for the city: From Georgetown up to Potomac and out to Great Falls, nervous people stockpiled tinned foods, flashlights and bottled water. They bought Cipio to protect themselves from anthrax and iodine to treat radiation sickness. Parents' night at my children's school was twice canceled because of bomb threats. One of the infected post offices was the Friendship Heights Station, on upper Wisconsin Avenue, the station that serves the sector of northwest Washington in which journalists and government officials congregate most densely. For a month, I opened my mail with rubber gloves.

My wife packed a suitcase and a boxful of emergency supplies and put them in the basement, so that we could escape the city quickly if we must. We designated a place of rendezvous a hundred miles away in case we were separated. We asked ourselves whether we did right to keep our children in a city that might be attacked and at a school that might be a target. My wife bravely said, "Compared to what people in Israel live through, not so much is being asked of us. We stay together." I doubled my life insurance and wrote a new will. I made a tense little joke about these preparations in the mess one day ("What do you think I should have said when the insurance company asked whether I worked in a high-risk job?") and discovered that everybody at the table had done, or was about to do, the same.

A week into the anthrax attacks, Andy Card summoned the officers to the fourth floor for one of his cheery briefings. He wanted to know how our staffs were bearing the strain. He wanted to assure us that every possible precaution was being taken to protect the safety of the White House staff. I had noticed that "every possible precaution" a day or two before. An unmarked white van had suddenly appeared one day in the parking lot on West Executive Avenue, its engine idling twenty-four hours a day. A long white flexible tube snaked out from the van's rear. An odd little plastic pipe emerged from its top. It was a biological warfare detector.

One liked to believe that the White House was protected from germ warfare by supersophisticated high technology. It was a little unnerving to discover that this huffing-puffing windowless Good Humor truck was our first line of defense. How effective was this mechanical air sniffer? Card turned the briefing over to a security officer, who proved a glib master of the art of question evasion.

"Can you detect the presence of anthrax inside the White House complex?"

"The White House is protected by the most advanced technology available."

"What would happen if you did detect it?"

"We have prepared extensive contingency plans."

"Is the president safe?"

"The president is safe."

"Are *we* safe?"

"We have taken every possible precaution."

I had noticed the unguarded fences around the District of Columbia's reservoir and asked, "Is it safe to drink D.C. tapwater?"

The Secret Service man answered mockingly: "You drink D.C. tapwater?"

We were urged by the White House doctor not to let terrorism alter our personal lives: It was important to continue to spend time with our families, to exercise, and to pray, if we were in the habit of praying. And we were urged by an adviser from the FBI to be sure to scramble our personal routines: not to leave for work at the same time every day, not to travel by the same routes, and to change our e-mail and other personal passwords regularly. We all did our best to live exactly as we had lived before, only completely different.

One thing we knew for certain was this: People at large believe that White House staffers know much more than they really do. If we showed anxiety, our friends and neighbors would infer that we must know some *reason* for anxiety. If we expressed an opinion, our friends and neighbors would suppose that we were relying on secret knowledge. So our most important duty was to seem calm and confident, while actually saying as little as possible, to do our part to thwart the spread of rumors and to allay panic.

But it was hard to stay calm when we were surrounded by so much grief.

Thirteen days after September 11, Bush invited to the White House the families of the passengers and crew of United Flight 93, the flight that the passengers forced to earth in Pennsylvania before it could reach Washington. Bush asked the staff to line the hallway between the mansion and the East Wing, from which the families would exit, to say thank you on their way out of the building: Very possibly, it was to the husbands, fathers, sons, and brothers of these families that we in the White House owed our lives.

At about two o'clock the first of the relatives emerged, in a small cluster of four or five. They looked dazed by sorrow, dumbfounded by the tragedy that had brought them to the president's house. They saw more than one hundred staffers lining both sides of the corridor, holding little American flags, and they shook our hands absently, as if their minds still had not absorbed what had happened to them.

A minute or two passed—and then another half dozen stepped out, their faces sunk in the same shell-shocked expression. Another long pause, and then another little group. A pause again, and then another group passed by. Some of the staffers began to cry. A few peeled away to sit for a minute on the benches in the Kennedy garden to the south of the corridor, to stare at the grass and paving stones. I felt as if I'd swallowed a burr that was tearing open my throat from the inside. The families seemed to expect the staffers to say something—but what was there to say? I found myself repeating over and over: "We won't forget, we won't forget." Then there was another long pause, and then another small group, and it was sadder than ever, and the families with their straight faces still kept coming and coming and coming.

It took an hour for them all to walk by. I shook the hand of Lisa Beamer, who fixed every one of us with her beautiful eyes and whispered, "Thank you, thank you," with the poise of a bereaved queen. The tall, handsome family of Tom Burnett marched by in a purposeful phalanx. And at the very end of the long procession, one older woman hiked painfully up the short flight of stairs from the corridor to the lobby of the East Wing, turned, waved a big wide wave at us, and shouted, "God bless you all!" Somebody shouted back, "God bless America!" And still clutching the little American flags we'd been waving, we returned to our offices to try to do something that might be described as work.

Shortly after that visit, Gerson relayed a complaint from the president to the writers. For the first time since September 11, Bush had recorded some video greetings for events and gatherings around the country. The script for one of these greetings described a great athlete as a "real American hero." The presidential marking pen slashed out the phrase. We must choose our words more carefully, he told Gerson: The country had greater heroes now, and the title was to be reserved for them.

Bush was hopeless at faking emotion. He was equally hopeless at controlling his emotions when he truly did feel them. The whole country had observed the intensity of Bush's feelings of grief and loss at the televised memorial service on October 11 for those killed at the Pentagon. The death toll in Virginia was of course less enormous than that in New York, but because the structure of the Pentagon stood intact, the visible devastation had been in some ways even more gruesome than at ground zero in New York. Rescue workers had discovered the charred skeleton of a woman still sitting at the keyboard of her half-melted computer and the remains of a group of people who had been burned to death in front of a television set—they had been watching the destruction in New York, unaware that the same death was at that very moment plunging out of the sky toward them.

Unlike the National Cathedral speech, Bush's remarks at the Pentagon were unrehearsed. And whereas the front pews of the cathedral had been filled with the nation's mighty and powerful, at the Pentagon, the nearest seats were reserved for the families of the dead. Bush's speech at the Pentagon was not as oratorically superb as his speech in the National Cathedral. It did not need to be. Those who saw that speech will not remember Bush's words; they will remember the expression on his face as he waited to deliver them. As he stood on the grandstand, clutching another of those forlorn little American flags in his hand, he looked so overwhelmed by sadness that I wondered whether he would be able to speak at all. He looked like an eleven-year-old boy who had promised himself that he would not cry. He pulled his lips into his mouth in the hope that nobody could see them tremble. He blinked his eyes as rapidly as a Spanish dancer clicks her castanets. He fixed his gaze upon a point somewhere over and above the sobbing families in front of him lest he see something that might wreck his self-control. His voice trembled at the beginning of his speech, but he recovered his poise as he spoke. "Within sight of this building is Arlington Cemetery, the final resting place of many thousands who died for our country over the generations. Enemies of America have now added to these graves, and they wish to add more. Unlike our enemies, we value every life, and we mourn every loss. Yet we're not afraid."

Nor was the mourning finished. On November 12, an American Airlines jet bound for Santo Domingo crashed at

Rockaway Beach, New York, killing 265 people. Was it a bomb? Sabotage? The National Transportation Safety Board quickly ruled the crash an accident caused by cracks in the jet's tailfin, not terrorism. The verdict was believed, but the pain of the city and the country, already so terrible, grew more terrible still.

Bush had assigned the mission of securing the home front to his friend Pennsylvania governor Tom Ridge. Ridge had been short-listed for the vice presidency in 2000. He was a Catholic, a wounded veteran of Vietnam, a former athlete, and still a man of commanding appearance. He had ultimately been barred from the ticket by his pro-choice views on abortion and his strangely weak voting record on national security issues during his congressional career in the 1980s.

Now, as governor of one of the 9/11 states—for so Pennsylvania was because of Flight 93—his record could no longer be assailed, and Bush hired him as assistant to the president and homeland security adviser. This weighty new title carried little actual power: Homeland security responsibilities were scattered all over the government and concentrated in some of the country's oldest and most ornery bureaucracies: the Immigration Service, the Coast Guard, the FBI, and so on. Ridge was supposed to coordinate the work of all these agencies—but with a staff of barely a dozen, he had almost no capacity to discover what that work *was*.

Ridge was squeezed into a small, windowless office in the center of the first floor of the West Wing. The office was tiny, perhaps eight feet by seven feet, with a low ceiling that Ridge—a big man—cleared with only inches to spare. The man responsible for averting the next 9/11 occupied a space that in any substantial private sector company would be used to store the paper and toner. But almost nobody's office was closer to the Oval than his, and in the White House, people will endure almost any discomfort to shift even a foot or two closer to the boss's chair.

Mary Matalin, the vice president's communications director, had unintentionally set Ridge up for trouble with her unfortunate comment—off the record, but alas immediately recognizable—that the White House wanted to "brand" Ridge: not in the Texas sense of the word, searing a "W" in his flank with a red-hot iron, but in the Madison Avenue sense. "When people see him, we want them to think: My babies are safe." In that hope, she would be disappointed. Ridge and Attorney General Ashcroft issued a series of vague but urgent alerts in the fall of 2001: one on October 11, a second on October 29, a third on December 3. By the time of the third alert, the press and the public were getting irritable. What was the point of these vague, contentless warnings? Why tell people to be on the alert without telling them what to be on the alert for? After the third all-points alert, Ridge acknowledged, "The threats we are picking up are very generic. They warn of more attacks but are not specific about where or what type." This vague information put him in an almost impossible position. If he passed it on, he would be blamed for frightening people unnecessarily. If he kept quiet about it, he would be accused of withholding vital information from the public.

Occasionally, I would do some writing for Ridge and his team. I'd arrive with my notepad, and they would detail the appalling list of ways that America was vulnerable to terror and mass murder. I never wrote down any of these macabre conversations, but I can still remember some of the grisliest moments.

"I don't know why they sent the anthrax through the mail," one of them said to me. "It would have been much more effective if they had just doused themselves with penicillin, put the anthrax in a salt shaker, and emptied it out the back of a New York subway train."

"What if you coordinated a terror attack with a cyber-attack?" suggested another. "Phones would go down, traffic lights would stop working, 911 systems would crash. They could paralyze a whole city."

"You could have the same effect by sending in a series of credible false alarms. Responders would soon be hopelessly overextended to a real strike."

"Yeah—and you've got a choice of targets. They would not have to do anything as fancy as a bioattack. Just hijack a dozen trucks and fill 'em with explosives."

"Or a ship—and then sail it into the middle of Seattle."

"I still think the shopping mall suicide bombers would work best."

The conversations would weigh on me for hours afterward. "Isn't there some way we could end this on a more positive note?" I'd ask. "It sure would be nice if we could say, 'We've looked at these problems and we're finding solutions,' not, 'We've looked at these problems and they're even worse than we feared.' "

They just fixed me with a grave look and answered: "The problems *are* even worse than we feared."

Ridge and his staff reminded me of environmentalists: another group of people haunted by impending catastrophes to which they can never persuade the rest of the world to pay sufficient attention. One small example: When a visitor enters the

White House complex, he or she must give both name and ID to a guard, who then issues a temporary pass. The visitor's purse or briefcase must pass through an X-ray machine; then the visitor must wave the pass in front of an electronic scanner and walk through a metal detector. Pretty stringent. Except for this: All afternoon, dozens of visitors enter the White House complex carrying paper cups of coffee sealed with opaque lids. And when those visitors remove their keys and cell phones from their pockets before stepping into the X-ray machine, they typically rest their coffee on the same little shelf. Then, after they have been thoroughly checked out, they turn around, retrieve their cup, and proceed on their way. Probably a couple hundred cups enter the building this way every day—almost any of which could hold more plastic explosive than the Libyans used to blow up Pan Am Flight 103 over Lockerbie. A year after September 11, the cups went as uninspected as ever.

It was things like those coffee cups that kept the homeland security people up at night. Homeland defense was an attempt to protect the country with a strategy that a basketball coach would call "playing zone"—a zone that happened to include dozens of nuclear power plants, hundreds of oil refineries, thousands of miles of border and coastline, tens of thousands of commercial aircraft, trucks, and trains, and hundreds of thousands of unpredictable targets of opportunity. In basketball, the alternative to zone defense is playing the man—marking the man with the ball and blocking his shot. For the nation, the only realistic way to make homeland security effective is to stop trying to fortify every potential target—and to begin hunting down the men who would wish to attack those targets.

Playing the man, however, is not "homeland security." It is

intelligence work—and in the 1990s, American intelligence had deteriorated to the point of imbecility. The FBI was stripped of its ability to monitor extremist organizations. When it needed to know what was being said inside the radical mosques, it was obliged to telephone freelance investigators like journalist Steve Emerson and ask to take a look at his files. In 1995, strict new restrictions were imposed on the CIA's ability to employ as an agent or informant anyone with a record of human rights violations. Managers at both the FBI and the CIA were rewarded for hiring and promoting minorities and women—but nobody seemed much to care whether they hired and promoted people who spoke the languages of America's enemies.

Experts debated whether the CIA or the FBI was the more incompetent agency, and it seemed that everyone who had contact with either agency quickly acquired his own inventory of horror stories. I had a doozy myself. One day in early spring, the doorbell rang at my home. The caller showed his FBI badge and asked my wife if she would answer a few questions. He nodded at the house next door. Your neighbor over there, he said, is going to be working for the president, and we want to know what you can tell us about him.

"Mr. G——?" my wife asked.

"Is that his name?" the agent said.

"Yes," she said. How strange, she thought, that our neighbor had not said anything about his new job to us. Still, she answered the FBI man's questions to the best of her ability: No, we knew of nothing unusual, they had regular habits, steady employment, and so on. It was only after she spoke to the neighbors, who told her that Mr. G—— had no plans to work for the president, that she realized what had happened: The FBI man had gone to the wrong door. He was supposed to have gone to the G—— house to ask about *me.*

After the Bay of Pigs fiasco, President Kennedy is supposed to have said to CIA director Allen Dulles, "If we lived under a parliamentary system, I'd have to resign. We don't, so you have to." September 11 was a debacle that made the Bay of Pigs look like MacArthur's triumphant landing at Inchŏn, yet Bush insisted that both FBI director Robert Mueller and CIA director George Tenet stay at their posts. In the case of Mueller, Bush's forbearance was hard to gainsay: The FBI man had been sworn in only nine days before September 11. Keeping Tenet was a tougher call. Tenet had run the CIA for six years. If there was any obvious candidate to bear the blame for the 9/11 catastrophe, Tenet was the guy.

Yet Bush protected him. Why?

The very toughest decisions a president makes are often the decisions to do nothing. When the country's blood is running hot, and the press is twitching, and the aides are panicking, it's tempting to quell the crisis with a bold, audacious maneuver. In the very short run, these maneuvers often seem to work. The president is seen to be *leading,* and people are so impressed that they don't ask too many questions about *where* he is leading them.

But the problems of a great country are exactly the kinds of problems most resistant to bold strokes. America was caught by surprise on September 11 because of a great many mistakes by very many people over a long period of years. Firing the guy who happened to be sitting in the big office on the day of the disaster might feel good for a minute—but then the president would have to find somebody else to sit in that big office, and he'd face exactly the same problems that the old guy did. And before the new guy took his seat, he would have to be confirmed by the U.S. Senate—and the Senate being the Senate, those hearings would turn into a bloody battle of accusation and counter-accusation over who had failed and why. Bush might want to replace the man at the wheel of U.S. intelligence, but the Senate would dismantle the entire car—at exactly the moment the country needed to race it.

Bush made it plain that he was not pleased with the performance of the FBI and the CIA, especially not with that of the FBI. In his public appearances, he stressed that a "new culture" was emerging at the FBI; in his first private meeting with Ashcroft and Mueller after September 11, he solemnly told them that they must never, ever, allow the nation to be taken by surprise like this again. But he also made a point of visiting the headquarters of both agencies to praise the work of the ordinary agents. The CIA and FBI might be lemons, but Bush operated on the theory that lemons give more juice if you stroke them a little before squeezing them.

We now know that elements of the U.S. government had received some advance warning that some kind of terrorist operation was coming. The president was briefed in August about unusual activity in Osama bin Laden's network, and the FBI, the CIA, and the NSA had each picked up indications of trouble, although none of them seem to have shared that information with anybody else.

I caught my own brief glimpse of the mechanics of that failure in the late fall. Toward the end of November, I met the writer Salman Rushdie. Rushdie had published a new novel in the fall of 2001 and had been about to launch a book tour when his publisher told him he would not be traveling after all: The Federal Aviation Administration had issued an order forbidding all U.S. airlines to carry him or others on a short list of known targets of Islamic terrorism. Three months later, the ban still stood.

The story enraged me. Responding to bin Laden's terrorism by grounding Salman Rushdie was as reasonable as responding to the Ku Klux Klan by placing Martin Luther King under house arrest. It was unfair. It was cowardly. And it was ultimately demoralizing, for by banning Rushdie, the FAA was conceding that not only could we not protect randomly chosen aircraft, we could not even protect aircraft that we knew our enemies might wish to attack.

Everyone in government to whom I told this story agreed that it was an absolute outrage. Yet it still took a whole month of phone calls to regain Rushdie's right to fly.

The Rushdie incident shows both where conspiracy theories come from—and what is wrong with them. It shows that, yes, the U.S. government had some advance knowledge that something bad might be about to happen. It also shows that the government had no idea of what that "something" might be—and that it interpreted the little information it had through the distorting lens of its preconceived ideas. A dozen years before, one set of Islamic extremists tried to murder Salman Rushdie. Confronted with warnings of new activity by a different set of Islamic extremists, government agencies blow the dust off their files and prepare for . . . another attempt to murder Salman Rushdie.

Yet there were government agencies that did learn from the past. At Defense, Donald Rumsfeld had demanded that the Pentagon produce something more imaginative than a replay of the Gulf War—and what he got was the most dazzling set of new ideas since Billy Mitchell's aviators sank a steel battleship with biplanes made of canvas and wood.

Donald Rumsfeld joked that he knew the armed forces had taken to heart his call for new ideas when he received a requisition form for saddles and horse feed. The photograph of U.S. Special Forces in Afghan tribal garb on horseback captured the imagination of the country. It also opened its eyes to the possibility of a new kind of war, a war fought by smart weapons and smarter soldiers, by small units operating independently while linked by instantaneous communications, calling in airpower as their striking arm.

In this new kind of war, political, military, and humanitarian concerns fused together almost indistinguishably. In September and October, aid groups like France's Médecins sans Frontières and Britain's Oxfam and Christian Aid warned that an attack on the Taliban would trigger famine in Afghanistan. In an October 18 speech, Noam Chomsky predicted: "Looks like what's happening is some sort of silent genocide. . . . Plans are being made and programs implemented on the assumption that they may lead to the death of several million people [from starvation] in the next couple of weeks. . . ." In fact, Bush's war *saved* millions of Afghans. At the outset of the war, American planes used their control of the sky to air-drop tons of emergency rations and supplies. As the Taliban retreated, American forces opened Afghanistan's roads and trails to truckloads of American food aid—aid that the Taliban had stolen or tried to frighten away in five hungry years of self-embargo. Even as the war was being waged, American and European diplomats were working in Berlin to assemble the first representative government in Afghanistan's history.

We read much in those same months about the certain doom of the American enterprise in Afghanistan. "Whatever happened to the 'brutal Afghan winter'?" asked the Canadian journalist Mark Steyn in December 2001. "It was 'fast approaching' back in late September, and apparently it's still 'fast approaching' today. 'Winter is fast, fast approaching,' reported ABC's *Nightline* on September 26. . . . 'Winter is approaching fast,' said Thomas McDermott, UNICEF regional director, on December 9. And not just any old approaching winter, but the 'brutal Afghan winter,' according to National Public Radio, the *Boston Globe,* Associated Press, etc. . . . 'The temperatures can drop to 50 below, so cold that eyelids crust and saliva turns to sludge in the mouth,' said Tom Ifield of Knight-Ridder newspapers.

"As I write, it's 45 (above) in Kabul. . . . Ghurian and Herat check in at 48. Bost, Laskar, and Kandahar report 61 and sunny. . . ."

Yet you can see why the ill-wishers moaned and groaned. Afghanistan *had* been the graveyard of empires, almost the last place on earth anyone would wish to fight, and for that very reason the ultimate refuge of the world's bandits, drug lords, and terrorists—who often happened to be the very same people. Yet with less than a month to prepare, American troops and aircraft had charged into this country, overthrown its government, destroyed its terrorist bases, and hunted down their enemies, while losing only fifteen of their own to enemy action. The operation was not a total success, of course. Probably a majority of the twenty most-wanted terrorists had escaped alive, possibly including Osama bin Laden himself. But the terrorists' ability to do harm had been greatly diminished after their humiliation in Afghanistan and the rolling up of their overseas networks—and of course the war was not over yet.

As American forces advanced, Europe's left-wing press invented atrocity stories to keep them company. The left-wing British tabloid the *Mirror* accused the United States of torture for the offense of handcuffing al-Qaeda terrorists in transit to Guantánamo Bay and issuing them plugs to protect their ears from engine noise en route. A professor at the University of New Hampshire toted up every Taliban claim of civilian casualties, counting some of them twice or thrice, accepted them all as true, and produced an estimate of civilian deaths in Afghanistan larger than the death toll of September 11—and for his trouble, he was promoted into a major celebrity in Europe and the Middle East. A French author went further and claimed that the 9/11 attacks were a hoax intended to justify military spending.

You can see why America's many detractors, ill-wishers, and enemies would be alarmed by the Afghan victory. If a few hundred men and a few dozen planes could overthrow the Taliban, what might ten thousand men and a few hundred planes do in Iraq? Or a hundred thousand men and a thousand planes do to the whole Gulf? It suddenly seemed that American power could do *anything*. The next great question facing the Bush administration was: What precisely *did* it wish to do?

Should it call off the war after Afghanistan and entrust the continuing struggle against Islamic terrorism to an international police and intelligence effort? That option would minimize the disruption of the Middle Eastern status quo, pleasing many of America's European allies and all the Arab and Muslim Middle

Eastern states. On the other hand, it would leave the war on terror as unfinished as the Gulf War had been left in 1991. Saddam Hussein would continue to build nukes and germ bombs. The Iranian mullahs would continue to sponsor Hezbollah and shelter the remnants of al-Qaeda. And Saudi Arabia and Egypt would continue to incubate deranged fanatics bent on jihad.

Alternatively, should the United States take President Bush's words literally and continue the war on terror until terrorism was entirely uprooted from Middle Eastern and Muslim politics? If the United States overthrew Saddam Hussein next, it could create a reliable American ally in the potential superpower of the Arab world. With American troops so close, the Iranian people would be emboldened to rise against the mullahs. And as Iran and Iraq built moderate, representative, pro-Western regimes, the pressure on the Saudis and the other Arab states to liberalize and modernize would intensify. It was quite a gamble—but also quite a prize.

Donald Rumsfeld and his Defense Department became the advocates of the bold second option; Colin Powell and his State Department espoused the cautious first one.

The Rumsfeld-Powell split was often described in shorthand as a split between "hawks" and "doves," as if it were a rerun of the bureaucratic battles of the cold war. It might be more illuminating, though, to reach back even further in time, to an even earlier debate: the debate within the U.S. Army over the right way to fight the Civil War.

Then as now, opinion divided between those who wanted to fight the smallest possible war and those who wanted to win the biggest possible victory. The leader of the small-war faction was

George McClellan. The leader of the big-victory group was Ulysses S. Grant.

People nowadays remember General McClellan as a coward. That is not at all fair. Personally, McClellan was a very brave man. He opposed a big war not because he feared for his own life, but because he accurately foresaw that a big war would end with the abolition of slavery, the smashing of the Old South, and the reconstruction of the American Union. McClellan dreaded such an outcome. He yearned for the restoration of "the Union as it was"—his slogan when he ran for president against Lincoln in 1864.

People sometimes think of General Grant as a butcher. That is not fair, either. Grant was a gentle and sensitive man. But he perceived that the only way to preserve the country was by fighting a total war that would upend the old social order and destroy the old elites. "The Union as it was" was gone forever. The only choices were a new Union or a new disunion.

The choice that divided Grant from McClellan in 1862 was the same choice that divided Powell from Rumsfeld after the fall of Kabul. The "Middle East as it was"? Or victory over terror? McClellan's war? Or Grant's?

Powell's and Rumsfeld's views were known. Cheney sided with Rumsfeld. That left only one member of the foreign-policy first team in play: Condoleezza Rice.

By all rights, Rice ought to have sided with Powell. She was a protégée of Brent Scowcroft's, and Scowcroft was America's most ardent advocate of "the Middle East as it was." As national security adviser to the elder Bush, Scowcroft had endeavored to preserve the old Soviet Union and the former Yugoslavia.

Those two projects had failed, but his third had succeeded: He had urged President Bush to halt the Gulf War early so as to preserve the stability of the Iraqi state. Snowcroft had hoped, of course, that Saddam Hussein would be bumped off and replaced by a less disagreeable dictator. But as an aide to Henry Kissinger in the 1970s, Scowcroft had absorbed the old maestro's rule that instability is usually more dangerous than tyranny. Applying this rule to Saddam Hussein was extending Kissinger's rule too far even for Kissinger himself. But Scowcroft lacked his mentor's ingenuity and flexibility. He was not a man to whom ideas came easily, and when one finally did pass his way, he would not readily let it go again. And Scowcroft's favorite aide was his senior director for Soviet affairs: Condoleezza Rice.

In the eight years' interval between the two Bush presidencies, Rice had grown close to the younger Bush and his wife, Laura, and when Bush stepped into his father's old office, Rice stepped naturally into Scowcroft's. Rice is not a person whose profile could ever be low. It's news when a president appoints the first black woman national security adviser—and when that woman is not only unusually attractive, but also unusually charming, she stays news. You would sometimes see male foreign dignitaries emerging from the West Wing into their limousines after a meeting with her, still smiling goofy, ingratiating smiles.

But while Rice's personal influence was unmistakable, her views were not. She had published little before returning to government, and those publications revealed less. She practiced an almost steely discretion—which it was part of her charm to let slip from time to time. About a month after September 11, I was one of a small group of staffers called to her office to help her prepare for an international meeting. She nodded to one of the aides working on her schedule. "So which thugs have you got for me to meet?"

Because of Rice's extraordinary tight-lippedness, even her own National Security Council senior directors confessed themselves unable to predict whether she would align herself with Rumsfeld's big-victory or Powell's small-war point of view. But with every passing day after September 11, she seemed to edge closer and closer to Rumsfeld. She resisted Powell's plan for a Middle East speech in September, protected Bush's with-us-or-with-the-terrorists language against outraged would-be editors in the State Department, opposed the postponement of the war beyond Ramadan, and urged that fighting begin in Afghanistan as soon as the military was ready—rather than after the State Department completed its negotiations.

She was notably less eager than Powell to ingratiate herself with Arab opinion. In an interview on al-Jazeera on October 12, for instance, she was asked whether "people in the Arab world look forward for the middle of November as something—a U.S. plan for the Middle East would be announced then, something similar to the Madrid Conference after immediately the Gulf War of '91?" She answered diffidently, "Well, we are constantly evaluating how we can best push the process of Middle East peace forward. I wouldn't put any time line on what the United States might do next."

How had this foreign policy professional drifted so far away from the State Department consensus?

Perhaps her academic career influenced her. She had specialized in Russia and would have witnessed firsthand how often people who began their careers as exponents of "stability" in Soviet-American relations ended as apologists for evil.

Perhaps September 11 changed her. Colin Powell had spent the day on a plane flying back into Washington from Peru. Rice had spent it in the bunker underneath the White House. After such an experience, it could not have been easy to take seriously the claim that America's top priority in the Middle East remained the defense of the Saudi monarchy.

Or perhaps it was just that she was convinced by the better argument.

Whatever the cause, sometime in November, Condoleezza Rice threw in her lot with the Rumsfeld faction against the Powell faction. She remained exceedingly cautious. She was more likely to say "I don't oppose this" than "I favor it." If a bold idea failed, the finger of blame—which zooms around any White House like the deadly Blue Glove in the Beatles' *Yellow Submarine*—would point out Rumsfeld or Paul Wolfowitz or Cheney, not her. But in her careful way, she was decisive.

Defying Powell took tremendous courage. Powell was the deadliest bureaucratic knife fighter in the whole Bush administration. It was all very well for Rumsfeld to butt heads with the secretary of state: Rumsfeld had the weight and might of the Pentagon bureaucracy behind him, decades of connections throughout Washington, and if worst came to worst, a brilliant record and hundreds of millions of dollars in the bank to console him. A national security adviser commands little institutional weight, and because of her relative youth and her years in California, Rice had a relatively flimsy personal network in the capital to call on. True, she had a personal rapport with the president. But so did Powell—and he also had the press in his pocket and control of much of the flow of information on which the National Security Council relies. And Powell had the atomic bomb: He was the only person in the whole government whose resignation would seriously damage the Bush presidency.

Yet Rice broke with him all the same. At the highest level of the government, there were now three votes for the Grant big-victory strategy: Cheney, Rumsfeld, and Rice. Powell was left alone to champion the McClellan "Middle East as it was" alternative.

It was now up to Bush to cast the only vote that counted.

# 11

# POLITICS RETURNS

YOU NOTICED THE quiet. For three weeks after September 11, planes were banned from Washington's Reagan National Airport. Commercial jets approached no closer to the capital than Baltimore or Dulles Airport. The skies above the city were empty except for the occasional shriek of an F-16 on patrol.

You noticed the quiet on the ground, too—but here the sound that was missing was not the roar of jet engines, but the clatter of politics. Politics did not go away, of course. It never does. But its volume and shrillness had abated. From September until January, the nation's business was debated in hushed, decorous tones.

Some of us were naive enough to expect that the change might even be permanent, or at any rate lasting. Shortly after September 11, C-SPAN's Brian Lamb interviewed the Republican and Democratic leaders in the House and Senate. They had been whisked to safety that day and had ended up spending hours together in a bunker somewhere. They had never before, they said, spent so much time in each other's company.

For a short time, it seemed possible that such experiences might mitigate, if only a little, the ferocity of Washington's political wars. George Bush hoped that could be so. He made extraordinary overtures to the congressional leadership: He scheduled regular breakfasts with the four top congressional leaders in the Family Dining Room at the White House. He courted the Democrats with extra assiduity. He thanked them loud and often for their cooperation. "It is oftentimes said," he observed while taking questions at the cabinet table on October 21, "that when it comes to foreign policy, partisanship stops, and that's exactly what has happened . . . because whether you're Republican or Democrat, we all want to win this war." And he offered concession after concession to maintain that cooperation. The Democratic leaders wanted airport security screeners to join the federal workforce. Bush assented. They wanted federal unemployment and health care benefits for workers displaced by the terror attacks. They got them. They asked that New York's emergency aid pay not just to rebuild lower Manhattan, but to improve it. So it was done. They urged Bush to focus his postattack economic stimulus on low-wage workers. He did that, too.

What did Bush get in return? On January 4, 2002, Tom Daschle gave a much publicized economic address in which he accused Bush of responsibility for the "most dramatic fiscal deterioration in our nation's history." Daschle's speech was an extremely strange one: Hundreds of thousands of people were losing their jobs every month, the U.S. airline industry was plunging toward bankruptcy, the stock market was twitching, the dollar was slumping—and Daschle was worried, not about the American economy, but about the disappearance of that great pile of money he had mentally earmarked for his postwar spending spree.

I assume that the Democrats' internal polls showed what the Republicans' polls did: When you asked Americans whom or what they blamed for the economic downturn, they fingered terrorism first, Bill Clinton second, and Bush third. Daschle attempted to convince them otherwise by praising Bill Clinton's 1993 tax increase as the foundation of the prosperity of the 1990s. That move goaded Bush into doing something very remarkable.

To understand how remarkable, you need to understand this: We had a lot of rules in the Bush speechwriting department, but the supreme rule of rules was so obvious, so necessary, so absolute that nobody ever needed to utter it aloud. We just knew it. Never, never, ever was the word "taxes" to appear in any proximity at all to any reference to the President's anatomy: not his feet, not his hands, not his head, and most certainly not his lips. Bush was scheduled to speak at a town hall in California the day after Daschle's speech. I was asked to draft his remarks. I knew the Daschle speech was coming and I correctly guessed what he was likely to say. I was keen to insert just a little mild zinger about Daschle's eagerness to raise taxes—and Bush's determination to stop him. I didn't do it. I knew it would be useless. Somebody would send the text back to me with a big circle around my words and a query sarcastically demanding, "Read my lips?"

On the Saturday afternoon that Bush delivered his reply to Daschle, I was in my car, the radio tuned to C-SPAN. The crowd was cheering, Bush was getting excited, and he was drifting further and further away from my suggested text. That was okay: He was doing fine without me. And then he said it: "There's going to be people who say, we can't have the tax cut go through anymore. That's a tax raise. And I challenge their economics, when they say raising taxes will help the country recover. *Not over my dead body will they raise your taxes."* I almost hit a lamppost.

The push and shove of normal politics had returned. I suppose this should not have surprised anybody, least of all Bush. He himself had said repeatedly, "It is my hope that in the months and years ahead, life will return almost to normal. We'll go back to our lives and routines, and that is good." But as John McCain sardonically cracked, Bush probably never anticipated *how* normal things would become—and how fast. The push and shove of politics could not be restricted only to issues of taxing and spending. They became personal, as they always do.

Early in January, *The New York Times* ran a little item reporting that some Daschle aides were complaining that Bush seemed "disengaged" and "uninformed" at the breakfasts with congressional leaders. Soon afterward, I attended a meeting at which Bush issued stern orders: Nobody in the White House was to reply to this story. There must be no criticism of Daschle, not a single word. It was a magnanimous order, but it was delivered in a more embittered tone than I had ever heard from him. He sounded as if he felt not merely angry, but surprised—and betrayed.

I talked it over later with some of the people in the meeting.

They theorized that Bush did not believe his own light words about life returning "to normal." Bush believed that September 11 was an event as historically profound as the beginning of the cold war. And on the cold war model, Bush had hoped that Daschle would grow into the Arthur Vandenberg of his administration, Vandenberg being the formerly isolationist Republican senator from Michigan who put aside his differences with President Truman on domestic policy to help pass the Marshall Plan and military aid to Greece and Turkey in 1947. Instead, Daschle was proving himself Bush's Robert Taft, another senator (and would-be president) who could not let go of the partisan animosities of the past—or curb a sharp and spiteful tongue.

I don't know whether Daschle ever offered any personal apology for the secondhand insult. But the more important mystery is the motive of the person who repeated Daschle's contemptuous words to the *Times*. Was it pure Washington blabbermouthery? Or was it more deliberate? The purpose of the breakfast meetings was to draw the leaders of Congress closer to Bush. Did Daschle fear being pulled *too* close? Was he looking for some way to break Bush's embrace? Did he hope by offending Bush to be disinvited from the breakfasts—and thus (in his own mind, at least) be relieved from any duty to support the president in time of war? A friend of mine put this last question to Daschle directly—and the only reply the majority leader made was an enigmatic smile. Whether Daschle intended it or not, relations between the men never recovered. The leadership breakfasts dwindled away. The five men met at the end of February—then not again until the middle of April and hardly at all after that.

Bush had hoped for too much. He had expected the war to trump politics. But for his opponents, the question of whether the nation really was "at war" was rapidly becoming the central issue *in* politics. *New York Times* columnist Paul Krugman pungently summed up the emerging point of view of the Democratic Party, or at least its liberal wing. "I predict," he wrote in a January 29, 2002, column, "that in the years ahead Enron, not September 11, will come to be seen as the greater turning point in U.S. society." Daschle never denied the significance of the war quite so boldly. But from the January 5 speech onward, he and the Senate Democrats certainly *acted* as if they agreed with Krugman that the war was really a distraction from more important domestic issues. There would be no more sinking of old differences for the common cause. To win his war on terror, Bush would first have to win the right to keep fighting it.

B EFORE SEPTEMBER 11, the administration had begun to hope that the 2001 recession might end before Christmas.

Nobody could ever accuse the president's economic adviser Larry Lindsey of undue optimism. He had been predicting since 1997 that the U.S. economy was heading for a crash at least as bad as that which hit Japan in 1989. So it was big news when Lindsey peered up from his crystal ball in late summer 2001, took off his high cone hat with the moon and stars on it, and announced that the economy seemed to be rebounding. The rebound might not be felt in time to save the Republican majority in the House of Representatives. But there was every reason to hope that strong employment growth would resume by 2003.

Lindsey's conversion to the Bright Side startled some members of the senior staff—and worried some others. After all, his gloom-and-doom predictions had been all wrong. Why should his optimistic predictions be any more reliable? The general re-action to Lindsey's prognostications, however, was relief.

Tragically, some disasters do not reveal themselves to the economist's wizardry. September 11 rendered all previous fore-casts instantly obsolete. The terror attacks devastated Manhat-tan physically—and cast a frightening pall over the future of the whole world economy. The exciting Internet future we had been promised just a couple of years ago—the one in the dot.com commercial where little Ming in Shanghai e-mails the answers to math problems to young Estella in Montevideo—vanished in an instant. The vision of a future with no barriers had sent the Nasdaq rocketing up past 5000. Now the barriers were rising all over the United States.

The immediate cost of those barriers was very large. If secu-rity measures require airline passengers to arrive at the airport as little as thirty minutes earlier than they otherwise would have, then each two-hundred-passenger flight deducts one hun-dred hours of productive labor from the U.S. economy. If we es-timate the average value of an air traveler's time at $50 an hour, then the people on that one flight will produce $5,000 less wealth that day than they would have before September 11. And there are as many as eighty thousand commercial flights a day.

The indirect cost of the anxiety that erected the barriers was even larger. The stock market rose so high in the 1990s less be-cause corporate profits rose substantially, although they did, than because people became willing to pay higher prices to ac-quire a share of those profits. Historically, a company that earned $10 a share could expect to see those shares trade for anywhere between $100 and $150. At the top of the bull market of the 1990s, investors valued shares that earned $10 at an average of $320. People agreed to pay more not only because they were greedy and gullible, although greed and gullibility certainly played their part, but because the future looked so rosy then. The world was at peace, and seemed likely to remain at peace. Hundreds of millions of Chinese and Indians and Latin Americans and Southeast Asians whose governments had locked them out of the world market were reentering it. The United States cut its military budget to the lowest share of its economy since before 1940 and was using the savings to repay its public debt. To many, it seemed as if the world were returning at last to the path of freedom and development from which it had detoured so disastrously in 1914. I once worked as a teaching assistant to a professor who would begin his course by sternly informing his students, "You are living in a terrible century." By 1998, my former students were saving for college for their own children. And as they tucked those children in at night, they had good reason to hope that the professors would tell the class of 2018, "You are living in a wonderful century." Those hopes for a wonderful new century had burned with the World Trade Center towers.

Between September 11 and the end of the year, close to one million Americans lost their jobs. At the beginning of October, Bush outlined a set of proposals for cushioning the economy's plunge. Despite his amazing popularity, the proposals represented his best assessment of the halfway point between the Democrats' wish list and his own. If there was ever a moment at which a president might get carried away with his own power, the first week in October was it. But Bush restrained himself and suggested:

1. *A package of emergency aid to displaced workers.*
2. *Changes in the tax laws to get companies investing again.*
3. *Acceleration of already enacted income tax reductions.*
4. *$300 checks for lower-income workers who did not pay enough income tax to qualify for a rebate in the spring.*

It might not have been the most elegant package, but combined with the $60 billion in emergency spending already committed, Bush's October proposals would have administered a good old-fashioned Keynesian jolt to the slumping U.S. economy.

The House quickly approved a plan resembling Bush's. The Senate spurned him.

So Bush tried again. In late October, Republican and some conservative Democratic senators negotiated a less generous stimulus plan. Treasury Secretary Paul O'Neill gave it the nod on Bush's behalf—and again Daschle rejected it.

Now there were only a few weeks left before Congress's Christmas recess. The odds of getting anything from Congress were lengthening by the day. Glenn Hubbard, the chairman of Bush's Council of Economic Advisers, joked to Budget Director Mitch Daniels, "Looks like your spending is the only thing holding this economy up." Daniels accepted the tribute gloomily.

Only a man equipped with Daniels's sense of the ridiculous could have appreciated the turn of fate that had assigned him, the first truly conservative budget director in fifteen years, the task of overseeing the biggest federal spending binge since the Johnson administration. In a speech to the National Press Club, he said that the famous "lockbox" should really have been called a "lockdown"—and that after September 11, the budget debate looked like a "jailbreak. . . . And I might hasten to add that the first escapees that I observed were representatives of our own administration. . . ."

Daniels wrote a memo in December pointing out that when Franklin Roosevelt mobilized the nation to fight World War II, he ordered that all expenditures be "held at the present level and below if possible, and all new work projects trimmed out." Between 1939 and 1942, federal social spending was cut by 22 percent. Famous New Deal programs like the Civilian Conservation Corps, the Works Progress Administration, and the National Youth Administration were abolished outright.

Daniels was not suggesting—not seriously, anyway—that we attempt to emulate FDR's draconian fiscal discipline. He understood the limits of his position: From time to time, he would indicate the wall of photographs in the suite at the Office of Management and Budget, a line that began with black-and-white pictures of men in celluloid collars and pince-nez, moved through black-and-white pictures of men in herringbone double-breasted suits and horn-rims, and culminated with a black-and-white row of men (and a woman) in contemporary clothing and contact lenses. "My predecessors," he would explain, and then add with mock mournfulness that it was the destiny of budget directors to be "anonymous, forgotten, and unlamented." But he did try to remind Congress that the year in which the federal government had to rebuild New York, save the airline industry, help modernize the nation's emergency forces, and fight a war on the other side of the planet against all the governments implicated in terrorism was not the ideal time to raise domestic spending. The senators blew right past him. As they saw it, a year when all these commitments had to be paid for was a *perfect* time to spend more on their pet projects—with everybody so distracted, people were unlikely to notice the pilfering of a few hundred million dollars here and the misdirection of a billion over there.

The new leadership of the Senate hardly bothered to tabulate this spending. Daschle's January 5 "fiscal deterioration" speech listed three causes for the country's move from large projected budget surpluses to large projected budget deficits: the war, the recession, and the Bush tax cut. He did not even mention domestic social spending. And of course Daschle attributed "most" of the fiscal deterioration—54 percent, to be exact—to the tax cut.

This was misleading, seriously misleading.

In the fiscal year that ended on September 30, 2001, the U.S. government had posted a budget surplus of $127 billion. At the time of Daschle's speech, January 2002, the Congressional Budget Office was projecting a deficit of $21 billion for fiscal 2002. It would ultimately weigh in at more than $106 billion. Almost all of this hard, hold-it-in-your-hand swing from surplus to deficit can be attributed to war and recession: the tax cut accounted for only about 15 percent of it.

What Daschle was lamenting on January 5 was the drastic shrinkage in the surpluses *projected* for the decade from 2002 to 2011. In January 2001, these were estimated to total $5.6 trillion. By January 2002, they had shrunk to $1.6 trillion.

Daschle was right that the Bush tax cut was the single most important cause of *this* shrinkage. Over the next ten years, the federal government would have $4 trillion less to play with than Daschle hoped, and of this $4 trillion close to one-third had been sent home by the Bush tax cut.* No surprise there: Returning the surplus to the taxpayers before Congress could spend it had been one of the tax cut's principal objectives, as Bush had consistently said. But what had happened to the other *two-thirds* of the surplus?

The short answer is that, by Daschle's own accounting, it was the slowdown in economic growth after September 11 that ate most deeply into this spendable $4.3 trillion. Congress's endless demands for more money for domestic programs, war or no war, did not help, either.

Daschle saw the "who lost the surplus" argument as a devastating weapon against Bush. But Bush was a third-generation Republican politician, whose ancestors had lost elections since the 1920s on the fiscal responsibility issue. Let Daschle have it, was his view, and good health to him. Bush was only too delighted to play Roosevelt to Daschle's Hoover. As he said in a radio broadcast the day after Daschle's "fiscal deterioration" speech, "Some in the Senate seem to think we can afford to do nothing, that the economy will get better on its own, sooner or later. I say that if your job is in danger or you have a loved one out of work, you want that recovery sooner, not later." Headline: BUSH LEADS.

So, at the beginning of December, Bush fired up Air Force

---

* You can get the figure closer to 40 percent if you attribute to the tax cut some of the higher-interest costs caused by the bigger deficit.

One to campaign for his second round of antirecession tax cuts. His first stop was Orlando, Florida, a city hit hard by the collapse in the travel business. Bush would visit a job training center and then lead a Town Hall meeting at the Orange County Convention Center. I wangled a place on the manifest. Except for a short excursion to New York in October, I had been trapped in Washington since September 11. I was eager to see and hear firsthand how Americans responded to their wartime president.

Presidential travel was another of the things that had changed since September 11. When the shuttle buses from the White House arrived at the gate of Andrews Air Force Base, our way was blocked by military policemen in combat fatigues, assault rifles at the ready. A big board displayed that day's alert status: It was red, the very highest. I was alarmed for a second, then relaxed—of course it was red, the president was flying today. The MP inside the guardhouse scrutinized each of our badges and then carefully compared them to our faces. He waved us on—and we were allowed to proceed only twenty feet before we were halted again and inspected again. Cleared at last, we drove onto the tarmac, gave our names one last time to the air force officer on duty at the rear jetway, and walked up the steps into the aft of the big plane.

The only thing unchanged was the plane itself. Even the food was the same. The menu on Air Force One was a throwback to the days when American food meant eggs, and cream, and processed meats. The meals all blur together in my memory, but if I remember right, a typical day would feature selections like these:

BREAKFAST
*Cheese Omelette*
*Ham Slice*
*Blueberry Muffin*

LUNCH
*Hot Dog*
*Potato Chips*
*Creamy Coleslaw*
*Fudge Brownie*

DINNER
*Fried Chicken in a Basket*
*French Fries*
*Creamed Corn*
*Deep Dish Apple Pie à la Mode*

I walked over to the baskets at the side and grabbed a plate of fruit and a bag of nuts to see me through the trip.

But if the plane was unchanged, the country onto which we disembarked two and a half hours later was transformed. Normally, about the very last place you would send a sitting president—especially a sitting Republican president—would be an unemployment center, even one filled with carefully screened unemployed. Who can predict how people who have been laid off will react? What if they cry? What if they jeer? What if they say nasty things to the television reporters afterward? Those worries belonged to a different world. The unemployed workers at the center greeted Bush with the dignified friendliness with which a wounded soldier greets a popular commanding officer.

"Just a scratch, sir! I'm almost embarrassed to be taking the day off." They sat at little desks in classroom-style rows, carefully roped off from both the press and the staff. But I was able to buttonhole a couple of them and ask what they thought of the president's coming here—and they cheerfully said they were very glad he came, and that although they had not voted for him last time, they certainly would next time.

This is weird, I thought—heartening, but weird. And it was soon to get much weirder.

Our motorcade raced off to the nearby convention center. For security reasons, local officials had been given only forty-eight hours' notice of the presidential visit rather than the customary two weeks. That's not much time to fill a six-thousand-seat hall at three o'clock on a workday. Yet every seat in the joint was taken, all the way to the back of the room.

The Town Hall was not one of Bush's favorite formats. The question-and-answer format was too unpredictable and presented too many opportunities for mistakes. Bush was not skilled at evasive maneuvers—he had never mastered the politician's trick of sounding forthright while in fact dodging and weaving to avoid being trapped by nightmarish questions.

Yet here Bush was—ready to take an hour's worth of questions from a crowd too big to screen. And every single question was a big, fat softball:

Q: "What are some of the things you are doing to help people like me, who have been out of work for the past few months?"

Q: "I'm a seventh-grader at Shelley Boon Middle School. I'd like to know [how] children and young people can help the economy."

Q: "Is the government planning to offer assistance to the self-employed?"

Q: "Mr. President, I'm an educator for the Orange County Public School System. I'd like to thank you very much for your ethics and integrity. I would like to hear from you where you are with education."

And even Q: "Our family wants to help out our country, and we think that making families strong will make our country strong. My parents believe that eating meals together will do that. Is it something that you did when you were a kid and that you and Mrs. Bush believe in?"

(That last got Bush his biggest laugh of the afternoon. A: "I did eat with my family, so long as my mother wasn't cooking.")*

At any other time, these deferential—even worshipful—questions would have irked a big crowd. Not today. These people were happy just to see their president's face and hear his voice. They had pulled their children out of school. They had sat patiently through endless introductions and warm-up events. And when Bush stepped onto the stage—in front of a giant banner that read "Fighting for American Workers"—they cheered and waved and cheered some more. These were not the dedicated partisans of the Republican National Convention. They were a cross section of central Florida—white, black, and Hispanic; young, middle-aged, and old; Christian, Jewish, and Muslim—and they were cheering so loud that I worried they would hurt themselves. So this, I thought, is what a 90 percent presidency looks like.

* I've abridged and neatened the transcript. Original is available at www. whitehouse.gov/news/releases/2001/12/20011204-17.html.

Back on the plane, Bush passed through the rear, still flushed with exhilaration.

"Well, who do I blame for that fiasco?" he demanded mock angrily. He pointed a finger at Karl Rove. "You?"

"Yes, sir."

"See me up front."

As the plane headed north, I caught a glimpse of a pair of fighter jets off our portside wing.

S O HOW COULD this revered national figure fail to pass an acceleration of his tax plan through a Senate that had passed the original plan in record time only six months before? One theory blamed his Treasury secretary, Paul O'Neill. O'Neill had supposedly failed to impress the New York financial community, and that in turn had supposedly undercut his clout with Congress.

This theory was popular with the capital's media elites, who regretted the loss of Clinton's courtly and seductive second Treasury secretary, Robert Rubin. No question, O'Neill could sometimes be ham-handed. One former Treasury staffer offered a charitable explanation of O'Neill's troubles: "They put the poor man in the wrong slot. Give him a job where the raw material goes in over here and the finished product comes out over there, and he will get the job done better, faster, and cheaper than anyone else could. O'Neill could have been the greatest undersecretary of defense for procurement in American history: He could cut a billion dollars out of the cost of building an aircraft carrier—and save eight months and a dozen industrial accidents along the way. But ask him to go talk to a bunch of New

York bankers and brokers, and the guy simply has no clue what to say. He doesn't understand them, he doesn't like them, and he doesn't believe their opinions matter." But whatever O'Neill's sins and vagaries, the failure to sell the stimulus package cannot be laid at his door. Treasury secretaries do not sell economic programs. Presidents do.

Or presidents don't. And Bush didn't. When Daschle assumed full control of the Senate on June 7, 2001, Karl Rove's ground game ceased to work so well. Bush claimed in mid-December that he had the votes to pass the stimulus package if it came to a vote. I'm sure that was true. But it's the Senate majority leader who decides what comes to a vote and what does not. And the only way to change the mind of an unwilling majority leader is by bringing immense public pressure to bear on him—in other words, to switch to a genuine passing game, as opposed to the diversionary passing game of the spring. And such a game would require Bush to play rougher than he had ever willingly played before.

Daschle was too cool a customer to be frightened by the mere fact of Bush's popularity. He knew that a 90 percent approval rating is like the million-dollar banknote in the Mark Twain story: too big to be easily cashed.

To have forced his tax cut past Daschle, Bush would have had to threaten him with a direct leader-to-leader clash on fiscal issues. He would have had to stop being president of all the people and resume his former identity as a Republican president with a Republican agenda. Bush would probably have won that clash, but Daschle would have achieved his larger aim: shattering the mood of national unity and returning the country to politics-as-usual—or rather, politics-uglier-than-ever.

For in the first week of December 2001, American financial markets were rocked by appalling news: The Enron Corporation, the world's largest energy trader, confessed that it had been guilty of the biggest fraud in American financial history and was about to go bankrupt.

The Enron news hit the Bush White House like a death in the family. Enron had been to Texas what Microsoft was to Washington State: the leader of the local New Economy, a focus of hometown pride. Texans had taken pride in Enron's success. They bought stock in the company. Their political leaders competed for Enron's support. And now they all suffered in its fall.

The tone of much of the reporting on Enron insinuated that the Bush team were somehow complicit in the Enron debacle or, at any rate, had benefited from Enron's fraud. Enron was often described as Bush's "biggest supporter." This was crazy. Different sources add up the money in different ways, but if you total every dollar that Enron, its affiliates, and its executives and their families gave to Bush's two gubernatorial campaigns, his run for president, the recount fight, the Republican convention in 2000, and the Bush inaugural in 2001, you would arrive at a figure of at most $1 million. That's a figure that would impress Bush's favorite movie villain, Dr. Evil. But considering that Bush raised $190 million for his presidential run *alone,* it's fair to say that Enron's financial contribution to Bush's political career amounted to little more than a rounding error.

The only election in which Enron and its CEO, Ken Lay, may have made a difference to the outcome was 1994, when Bush ran for the first time for Texas governor. And what Lay offered candidate Bush in 1994 was glamour more than money: Lay's backing would prove that Bush was supported not just by the old Texas of cotton bales and oil rigs, but also by the new Texas of glass towers and high technology. Back then, Enron was one of the most admired companies in the United States, and the incumbent governor, Ann Richards, effectively used her association with futuristic businessmen like Lay and Michael Dell to immunize herself against the fatal charge of being "antibusiness." Bush was telling the truth when he told a reporter that Lay had originally been a supporter of his opponent in 1994. Detaching Lay from Richards had been a crucial early victory for the Bush gubernatorial campaign. Now that victory returned to afflict his presidency.

The shock to the Bush staff from the Enron collapse, and especially to the more junior staffers who had not been forced to sell their shares to meet government ethics rules, was direct and painful. Their retirement plans and personal portfolios tumbled in value, a painful loss for people in government, who often supplement their salaries by drawing on their savings. The Enron bust depressed real estate values in Austin and Houston, another painful loss for those Bush staffers who had not yet sold their former homes. Even the president's mother-in-law lost money on Enron.

The Bushies' loss was the Democrats' opportunity. You almost have to admire the audacity of the Democrats' maneuver. In one breath, they took credit for the booming stock market of the 1990s; in the next, they blamed Bush for the fraud and corruption of the individual companies that made up the stock market. Had the situation been reversed—had a *Democratic* administration come to power just as eight years of corporate excess and wrongdoing under a Republican president came to light—nobody would think to blame the new administration for the crimes committed during the old administration's tenure. And just to make sure of that, the new guys would have hauled the old guys' Treasury secretary and Securities and Exchange Commission chief in front of a Senate investigating committee and tortured them for days on national television.

"And what were you doing, Mr. Secretary, while these tycoons were robbing their shareholders?"

Dick Morris was right: Republicans are not so nimble.

Enron finished off Bush's hopes for Social Security reform. Reformers wanted to turn Social Security into three hundred million 401(k) plans. With Enron employees weeping on television about their now worthless 401(k)s, reform suddenly looked scary rather than exciting.

For Bush's speech on the forming of his Social Security reform commission in April 2001, I had unearthed a nicely apposite quote from Franklin Roosevelt. In a fireside chat of 1934, FDR warned that there will always be those "frightened by boldness and cowed by the necessity for making decisions." They will complain, he said, "that all we have done is unnecessary and subject to great risks." Such people were still lurking about—only now they were Republican congressmen terrified of Democratic attack ads linking Enron to Social Security reform. In December 2001, the reform commission met for the last time, and the whole project faded out of view.

Early in January, the president summoned his writers into the Oval Office for a preview of the coming year. His message boiled down to this: We're finished on the home front until November, boys. We're finished on taxes, except maybe for capital gains—if we win the war, we'll get our recovery. We're finished on education, too—we have three years to see how the new reforms work. In fact, the only domestic issue that seemed to engage him at all was pension reform. He spent a quarter of an hour angrily denouncing the Enron executives who had sold their stock while their workers' accounts were frozen. He said over and over: "How could they do it? I don't understand it." One idea after another for a major domestic or economic speech was thrown at him: Health care? Trade? He shot them all down.

It took us a while to get the message, but get it we eventually did. There was no more domestic agenda. The domestic agenda was the same as the foreign agenda: Win the war—then we'll see.

# 12

## AXIS OF EVIL

Here's an assignment. Can you sum up in a sentence or two our best case for going after Iraq?"

It was late December 2001, and Mike Gerson was parceling out the components of the forthcoming State of the Union speech. His request to me could not have been simpler: I was to provide a justification for a war.

"Um, sure. Would after lunch be okay?"

"Very funny. Take two days."

Gerson's request did not mean that the decision for war had yet been made. At the same time as I was writing a hawkish draft, others were working on completely different versions of the speech. The 2001 joint session speech was produced by a handful of people. The 2002 State of the Union was a vast task that pulled together the labor of dozens of people across the government. 2001 was the oratorical equivalent of the Wright brothers at Kitty Hawk; 2002 was the moon launch by comparison—and the launchpads were already crowded with abandoned prototypes.

In one of the very first State of the Union meetings, Bush had speculated aloud that perhaps the theme of the speech should be the need for democracy and women's rights in the Muslim world. He had been very impressed by Bernard Lewis's argument that the economic and social backwardness against which Muslims raged could be traced to the Muslim world's failure to tap the potential of all its people to meet the needs of all its people. The Muslim world was governed by what Lewis called a "culture of command." And this "culture of command" ultimately rested on the subordination of their women. Even a landless peasant bullied and oppressed by everyone in his village could domineer at least over his wife and children.

I outlined Lewis's theory one day to a liberal friend of mine outside government. He laughed at me. "Since when did you and that gang of abortion banners you work with get sold on feminist social analysis?"

That hurt. "We're not talking about feminism," I replied. "We're talking about not being sold like chattel, and being taught to read, and the right to step outdoors without being wrapped in a decontamination suit."

I added, only half-jokingly, "I don't think you cease to be a conservative because you think that women in the Muslim world are entitled to the same rights as Harriet Nelson and June Cleaver."

He laughed again. "You're on a dangerous path, my friend. So when does the United States stop working with Muslim states at the United Nations to stop all those international treaties on women's and children's rights?"

Well, it was a fair gibe. Condoleezza Rice had warned before the election that "American foreign policy cannot be all things to all people—or rather, to all interest groups," and she had criticized the Clinton administration for confusing foreign policy with random do-goodery. Bush, she promised, would "refocus the United States on the national interest and the pursuit of key priorities." She listed five of them. The rights of women in the Islamic world did not make the cut.*

But here is what did make the cut: Rice's fifth priority was "to deal decisively with the threat of rogue regimes and hostile powers." To deal decisively with Nazi Germany and the Soviet Union, the United States had to discredit the ideologies that sustained them. To deal decisively with militant Islam, would the United States not have to do the same? Back in September and October, we had denounced Islamic extremism in the name of a mainstream Islam whose teachings were "good and peaceful." But a Protestant evangelical president of the United States is not ideally positioned to declare what is and what is not orthodox Islam. To defeat bin Laden, Americans would have to counter his Islamist ideology not with the barely comprehended values of some hypothetical Islam, but with America's own values of liberty and equality.

There are two basic approaches to foreign policy: the so-called realist, which is concerned with security and stability; and the so-called idealist, which is concerned with liberty and

* Condoleezza Rice, "Campaign 2000—Promoting the National Interest," *Foreign Affairs,* January–February 2000, www.foreignpolicy2000.org/library/issuebriefs/readingnotes/fa__rice.html.

justice. People who study foreign policy talk about these two approaches as if they were opposite poles of the compass. In practice, they function more like two halves of a single dial. Foreign policy is made where the two halves meet. American presidents are not elected to perfect the world. But it is also true that the freest countries make the trustiest friends, while bad regimes make bad allies. Americans shed blood for Saudi Arabia in 1991, but after September 11, Saudi Arabia shut down the American air base on its territory and refused to cooperate in tracking down terrorists. Who was there for America when America needed help? The countries where people can speak freely, and elect and unelect their leaders, and where the law applies equally to all. You cannot build such countries on the labor of slaves, not even if those slaves are called "wives."

News that the president's mind was evolving away from the canons of "realism"—and, more appalling still, that he was considering talking about democracy and Islam in the State of the Union—raced through the foreign-policy bureaucracy like Paul Revere on a motorbike. The possibility of such a speech drove the McClellan "small war" faction inside the administration absolutely wild.

Democracy in the Muslim world? asked the realists sarcastically. Well, that's just great. The Algerians tried it in 1991, and it would have brought the Islamic fundamentalists to power if the army had not intervened in time. Who do you think would win an unrigged election in Egypt? In Jordan? In Pakistan? *In Saudi Arabia?* Not the social democrats, and for sure not the compassionate conservatives.

What the foreign-policy bureaucracy believed in was not democracy, but *modernization*. They were transfixed by the example of Kemal Atatürk, the great Turkish modernizer of the 1920s and 1930s, who abolished Turkey's theocracy, liberated Turkey's women, introduced Western customs and Western law—and helped Turkey to evolve into America's most reliable ally in the Islamic world. For half a century, the State Department had been searching for the next Atatürk, and at one point or another its fancy had lighted on Egypt's Nasser, Suharto in Indonesia, the shah of Iran, even (we must admit the horrible truth) Saddam Hussein in Iraq. All these bets had turned up snake-eyes, but State kept returning to the craps table. Now it was promoting Pervez Musharraf, the dictator of Pakistan.

Bush had at first been enthusiastically convinced. People who visited Bush in October and November would hear ardent praise for Musharraf's promises of cooperation. "You know," they would report, "the president was saying just the other day that he thinks Musharraf could turn out to be the Atatürk of the twenty-first century."

But by late December, Musharraf was looking like another of those doubtful State Department bets. He had not been able to prevent his intelligence service from helping Pakistani supporters of the Taliban escape Afghanistan in November—that is, assuming he had even tried. Nor was he able to stop Muslim extremists on his own soil from waging war on India. On October 1, Pakistani-based militants detonated a suicide truck bomb in front of the state legislature in Indian Kashmir, murdering thirty-eight people. On December 13, Muslim extremists attacked the Indian Parliament. In mid-December, Musharraf released, "for the best interests of the nation," two Pakistani nuclear scientists who had been detained in October for providing Osama bin Laden with information about building weapons of mass destruction. There was evidence that the "shoe bomber," Richard Reid, who tried to blow up a transatlantic jet on December 22, had received his "go" order from inside Pakistan. A month later, Pakistani extremists kidnapped *Wall Street Journal* reporter Danny Pearl and videotaped his grisly murder. And as the world now knows, all the while Pakistan was secretly aiding North Korea's clandestine nuclear program.

The Indians showed amazing restraint in the face of Pakistani-based terror, and they deserved better thanks from the United States than they got. I drafted the statement Bush gave after the attack on the Indian Parliament and lavished all the compliments I could think of on Indian democracy. But I was not able to get the word *friend* past the editors at the National Security Council. I could see their point—India had never been much of a friend to the United States—but under the circumstances, the NSC's exactitude seemed rather stingy.

America's relationship with Musharraf had not been a satisfactory one. Yet something valuable had come of it. It had widened Bush's eyes and broadened his thinking. His modernizing strongman had proven to be neither very strong nor much of a modernizer. Atatürks are not found so easily.

There's a story told about Georges Clemenceau, France's leader during World War I. When a Paris wit said cynically, "I think there's a lot of money to be made from religion. I'd like to start one of my own," Clemenceau is supposed to have replied, "It's not so difficult. All you need do is be crucified and rise from the dead."

In the same spirit: All you need to do to become Atatürk is

to lead the only Muslim army in 250 years to defeat a non-Muslim force in open combat. After Atatürk drove the invading Greeks out of Anatolia in 1922, no imam dared question him. Had not the Koran itself prophesied that God would award victory to the truest believer? And after Atatürk forced the all-powerful British to evacuate Constantinople, nobody could possibly call him a stooge of the West, not even if he spoke French and wore a derby hat, not even if he banned the Arabic alphabet in favor of the Roman one, not even when he announced—like some Middle Eastern William Bennett—that there is no such thing as Western civilization, but only civilization period, and that the Muslim world must either sign up for that civilization or be considered uncivilized.

Musharraf lacked Atatürk's prestige and power—and he therefore failed to replicate his success. By February, praise for Musharraf was heard much less frequently from Bush's lips, although as long as the United States needed bases in Pakistan, the praise could never be entirely omitted. Bush was disencumbering himself piece by piece of half a century's worth of conventional wisdom about the Middle East and the world. This was not an easy thing for him to do. Bush trusted his subordinates, and he expected them to trust theirs—but in the U.S. government, new ideas flow from the top down, very seldom from the bottom up. Bush valued steady, sensible, solid people and distrusted abstract thinkers—but the way one gets a reputation for being steady, sensible, and solid is by repeating in a grave tone of voice exactly what everybody else thinks; it is from the thinkers that one gets new ideas, whether bad or good.

Yet despite these handicaps, Bush was working his way to something new. A president may run the country, but he cannot run it any way he likes. If enough of the bureaucracy opposes a presidential brain wave, the presidential brain wave must at least be postponed. Bush abandoned his plan to discuss democracy and women's rights in the 2002 State of the Union.

The squelching of this presidential idea was a victory for the McClellan faction, but a very incomplete one. They had convinced Bush that talking about democracy was going too far for the time being, but they could not convince him that "stability" ought to be his supreme goal in the Middle East. The pursuit of stability in the Middle East had brought chaos and slaughter to New York and Washington. Bush decided that the United States was no longer a status-quo power in the Middle East. He wanted to see plans for overthrowing Saddam, and he wanted a speech that explained to the world why Iraq's dictator must go.

And from that presidential decision, bump, bump, bump down the hierarchy, tumbled Gerson's request to . . . me.

Now where was I to start?

Saddam Hussein was as nasty a piece of fruit as you could find in the whole stinking bowl from Algiers to Kabul—a tyrant to his own people, a menace to his neighbors, and an implacable enemy of the United States. The problem in writing about him was that there was too much to say, and too much of it was unsayable on national television. There might be children watching the State of the Union. Did we really want the president describing how Saddam murdered his enemies by burning them alive in acid baths? Or broke their nerve by forcing them to watch as his soldiers raped their daughters and wives? Or cut off the hands and ears or gouged out the eyes of soldiers he suspected of lack of courage—or of too much?

We had to be careful too about seeming to criticize our

predecessors. Saddam Hussein had persistently, willfully violated the terms of his Gulf War armistice. In 1996, he had overrun the Kurdish safe haven in the north of Iraq. But if we complained about Saddam's depredations over the past decade, our friends and allies—and enemies, too—would demand to know, "So why didn't the United States retaliate at the time?" A good question—but the answer to it would spoil the bipartisan mood of the moment.

Nor did it seem wise to mention Saddam's most extreme offense: the attempted assassination of former President Bush during a visit to Kuwait in 1993. I knew that if we so much as adverted to that fact, the nation's airwaves, newspapers, and web pages would fill up with snippy commentators opining that a battle against the world's most nightmarish dictator was nothing more than a matter of Bush family *omerta*.

So: no, no, and no. What instead?

Sometimes when you are trying to decide what to say, it is best to begin by analyzing the position you oppose. I knew that opponents of action against Iraq relied on two main points. First, they said, there was no direct, conclusive proof that Saddam Hussein aided the September 11 terrorists. Then they added that while Saddam Hussein was certainly a very bad man, so was Josef Stalin. We had relied on deterrence, not war, to contain him—why should we not do so with Saddam, who after all controlled a much weaker state than the old Soviet Union?

I had my private doubts about the sincerity of these two often heard arguments. My own suspicion was that the opponents of action against Iraq in this country and overseas were *really* motivated by quite other concerns. An American-led overthrow of Saddam Hussein—and a replacement of the radical Baathist dictatorship with a new government more closely aligned with the United States—would put America more wholly in charge of the region than any power since the Ottomans, or maybe the Romans. People who resent American power, not all of them non-Americans, very understandably dreaded such an outcome.

But suspicions remained only suspicions. It was the two explicit arguments that would have to be dealt with—but indirectly. Presidents do not bandy words back and forth. They do not debate, they do not rebut—after all, they're the *president*.

Bush needed something to assert, something that made clear that September 11 and Saddam Hussein were linked after all and that for the safety of the world, Saddam Hussein must be defeated rather than deterred.

I began pulling books off the shelves. I reread a speech that I had last read on September 11 itself: Roosevelt's "date that will live in infamy" speech. On December 8, 1941, Roosevelt had exactly the same problem we had. The United States had been attacked by Japan, but the greater threat came from Nazi Germany. Hitler solved Roosevelt's problem for him by declaring war on the United States on December 11. But on the day after Pearl Harbor, Roosevelt could not be certain that Hitler would do so foolish a thing. That left Roosevelt with a very tough political problem: While even the blindest isolationists now accepted that the United States must fight Japan, many of them still hoped to avoid a clash with Germany. Roosevelt had to explain to the country why it could not afford to fight only a one-ocean war. So he added one cryptic and now little-considered sentence to his speech to Congress on December 8. "I believe I interpret the will of the Congress and of the people when I assert that we will not only defend ourselves to the uttermost *but will make very certain that this form of treachery shall never endanger us again"* (my italics).

For FDR, Pearl Harbor was not only an attack—it was a warning of future and worse attacks from another, even more dangerous, enemy. The soft-on-Iraq lobby promised that Saddam Hussein could be deterred forever. But if deterrence always worked, there would never have been a Pearl Harbor. Japan was insane to attack the United States: It had barely one-tenth America's industrial capacity, it depended on imports for all its food, fuel, and metals, and it was already bogged down in a huge war in China. Hitler was likewise crazy to declare war. He was fighting the British Commonwealth and Russia already; if he had professed peace, more than a few Americans would have eagerly taken him at his word. But unlike Stalin, Hitler was reckless, and the Japanese even more so—and it was this recklessness that made the Axis such a menace to world peace.

Hold that thought.

Saddam was as reckless as the Japanese had been. He had started two mad wars already—one against Iran, one against Kuwait. During the Gulf War, not content with fighting the United States, Britain, France, Canada, Australia, Turkey, and all the Arab states except Jordan, he had also tried to provoke an air attack from Israel. No country on earth more closely resembled one of the old Axis powers than present-day Iraq. And just as FDR saw in Pearl Harbor a premonition of even more terrible attacks from Nazi Germany, so September 11 had delivered an urgent warning of what Saddam Hussein could and almost certainly would do with nuclear and biological weapons.

The more I thought about it, the more the relationship between the terror organizations and the terror states resembled the Tokyo-Rome-Berlin Axis. The Axis was not a union of head and heart like the Atlantic Alliance between the United States and the British Commonwealth. The Axis powers disliked and distrusted one another. There was no Nazi lend-lease. Nor did the Axis powers have much in common ideologically: Nazi Germany was a revolutionary dictatorship. Italy was a reactionary regime like interwar Hungary or Spain. Japan was governed by bureaucrats who answered to a hereditary monarch. According to Nazi racial ideology, the Japanese were subhumans and the Italians barely better. Had the Axis somehow won the war, its members would quickly have turned on one another. They shared only one thing: resentment of the power of the West and contempt for democracy.

Was not the same now true of the terror organizations and the terror states? Saddam Hussein had fought Iran for a decade in the 1980s, in a war that inflicted more than a million casualties. Yet when the United States came for him in 1991, he flew his air force to Iran for safekeeping. Osama bin Laden's Sunni Islamic extremists despised Shi'ites: Their allies in Pakistan in fact specialized in the random murder of educated Shi'ites, especially physicians. Yet when al-Qaeda was driven out of Afghanistan, many of its leaders took refuge with the Shi'ite ayatollahs of Iran. Saddam Hussein was supposedly an extreme secularist. Yet he offered rewards of $25,000 to the families of the Islamic extremist suicide bombers of Hamas.

Much as they quarreled with each other, Iraq, Iran, Hezbollah, and al-Qaeda shared beliefs that harked back to European fascism: disdain for free inquiry and rational thought, a celebration of death and murder, and obsessive anti-Semitism. They all resented the power of the West, and they all despised the humane values of democracy. Indeed, Saddam Hussein's Baathist ideology was cobbled together in the 1940s by Arab admirers of Hitler and Mussolini. So there was our link—and our explanation of why we must act: Together, the terror states and the terror organizations formed an axis of hatred against the United States. The United States could not wait for these dangerous regimes to get deadly weapons and attack us; the United States must strike first and protect the world from them.

I wrote up these thoughts in a memo to Gerson and included with it a short description of some of Saddam Hussein's cruelties. I had just become a father for the third time a few days before, and perhaps for that reason one thing I had read had made an especially vivid impression on me—Jeffrey Goldberg's description in the *New Yorker* of the fallen bodies of the Kurdish women gassed by Saddam in 1988. They had been found wrapped around their babies, trying desperately to shield their children with their own bodies from the poison in the air.

I sent my memo off with a pang. The large majority of the work any speechwriter does for a president—including much of the best work—vanishes unnoticed, and I expected that my radical memo would almost certainly meet that fate. I never doubted that Bush would deal with Saddam Hussein sooner or later. But I did doubt that he would announce his intentions in the ringing language that I hoped to hear.

I returned to my normal work, trying to vacuum and polish the Bush administration's second-year domestic agenda into something that gleamed a little in the showroom window. The

New Year came, and work on the State of the Union intensified. Gerson, the rocketmaster of this moon launch, was arriving at work earlier and earlier: seven in the morning, six, five, four. He looked ill with exhaustion: His eloquent words cost him dearly.

But this speech would be remembered for more than eloquence. I could see it growing in vigor and clarity. My strong language had concerned only Iraq. Now, Condoleezza Rice and Steve Hadley at the NSC wanted to go further: They wanted to take on Iran as well. Through the fall and winter, protests against the mullahs' rule had become bigger and bolder. Against the wishes of the regime, crowds had gathered to mourn America's loss on September 11. There were riots at football stadiums; resignations of top ayatollahs; chants in the streets of "Death to the Taliban in Kabul and Tehran"—a slogan that apparently rhymes even better in Farsi than in English. The economic situation in Iran was desperate. So many women were selling their bodies to support their families that the mullahs proposed to organize Islamic brothels for them. Michael Ledeen, a former National Security Council staffer who followed events in Iran closely, had been arguing for months that Iran was moving toward revolution—and that a signal of support from the United States could hurry things up.

The notion that the United States might ever support a popular uprising in the Middle East horrified the custodians of stability. In fact, when a reporter asked State Department spokesman Richard Boucher in July 2002 whether the United States had anything to say to the people of Iran, Boucher replied curtly, "No."

But if Boucher had nothing to say, Rice did. Iran had waged terror war against Americans and American interests since

1979. Now, the mullahs were granting refuge to many of the top leaders of al-Qaeda, while attempting to subvert the Hamid karzai government in Afghanistan. The Iranian regime had willfully flunked the test that Bush had set in his speeches to Congress and the United Nations. It harbored terrorists. It had revealed itself as a flagrantly hostile regime. Four years of attempted conciliation of the Iranian regime had abjectly failed.

The Iranians' own actions had proven the need for a new policy. So out of the careful word factory at NSC came a sentence to be inserted into the State of the Union announcing the end of America's four-year courtship of the supposed moderates around President Khatami. "Iran aggressively pursues these weapons [of mass destruction] and exports terror, while an unelected few repress the Iranian people's hope for freedom." The United States no longer sought change from *within* Iran's terrorist theocracy; it sought the theocracy's overthrow.

The speech was now nearing completion. To my amazement, my Iraq memo was incorporated almost verbatim. Gerson wanted to use the theological language that Bush had made his own since September 11—so "axis of hatred" became "axis of evil." North Korea was added to the axis last: It was attempting to develop nuclear weapons, it had a history of reckless aggression, and it too had been cosseted by the United States in the recent past and needed to feel a stronger hand.

Bush read the speech closely. He edited it in his own bold hand. He understood all its implications. He backed them with all the power of his presidency.

Bush delivered his State of the Union speech with force and confidence—and this time, nobody was surprised by his success.

"The Iraqi regime has plotted to develop anthrax, and nerve

gas, and nuclear weapons for over a decade. This is a regime that has already used poison gas to murder thousands of its own citizens—leaving the bodies of mothers huddled over their dead children. This is a regime that agreed to international inspections—then kicked out the inspectors. This is a regime that has something to hide from the civilized world.

"States like these, and their terrorist allies, constitute an axis of evil, arming to threaten the peace of the world. By seeking weapons of mass destruction, these regimes pose a grave and growing danger. They could provide these arms to terrorists, giving them the means to match their hatred. They could attack our allies or attempt to blackmail the United States. In any of these cases, the price of indifference would be catastrophic. . . .

"We'll be deliberate, yet time is not on our side. I will not wait on events, while dangers gather. I will not stand by, as peril draws closer and closer. The United States of America will not permit the world's most dangerous regimes to threaten us with the world's most destructive weapons."

The next day, the headlines of every paper on the planet echoed and amplified Bush's warning of the emergence of an "axis of evil." The phrase was of course instantly controversial. The axis powers themselves responded indignantly. My own favorite was this comment from the North Korean press agency: "The war maniacs of the United States' Bush administration continue to spew out vicious remarks against us, despite the strong protest and denunciation of people around the world. . . ." When I later left the White House, the North Koreans had a few choice words for me personally as well. "[Frum] inevitably had to leave the White House, driven out by the anti-Bush hot winds from around the world. . . ."

Neo-isolationists in Congress, the universities, and the press liked the speech little better. A surprising number of people were prepared to make excuses for Iraq, and they hated the phrase for identifying too clearly the kind of regime Iraq was—and its implications about the character of the people who spoke up for it.

The controversy did not daunt Bush. Bush was extraordinarily responsive to international criticism—but his response was to tuck back his ears and repeat his offense. Once he uttered it, "axis of evil" ceased to be a speechwriter's phrase and became his own, and he defiantly repeated it over and over again. The president's firmness compelled even the most truculent members of his administration to follow him. At the State Department's senior staff meeting the morning after the "axis of evil" speech, Colin Powell sternly informed the undersecretaries and assistant secretaries that there would be no criticism of the president's remarks by anyone in his department—and to their credit, there was none.

Much of the criticism in the press was merely pedantic. Any number of talking heads and op-ed columnists dusted off their *World Book Encyclopedia*s to explain the numerous ways in which the relationship between the terror states and terror groups of the twenty-first century differed from that of the Axis powers of the 1940s.

A more serious line of criticism was articulated by many in Europe. Why did the president use such moralistic language? By comparing Iraq and Iran to the Axis, Bush implicitly analogized those who advocated compromise and negotiation with Saddam and the mullahs to the now condemned souls who appeased Hitler—and that was highly insulting to (just to name a few) French president Jacques Chirac, German chancellor Gerhard Schröder, the editors of the continent's leading left-of-center newspapers, and so on. I found this objection very strange. European political and opinion leaders are at least as moralistic as their American counterparts. When Colin Powell toured Europe at the beginning of the Bush administration, he was scolded by French foreign minister Hubert Vedrine about America's retention of the death penalty; it would never have occurred to Powell to reply by scolding the Dutch for the prevalence of euthanasia in their hospitals. ("In America," he could have said, "we kill murderers, not grandmothers.") On issues from land mines to genetically modified foods, European leaders cheerfully use the language of blame and condemnation. It sometimes seems that the only thing these European leaders are loath to call evil is . . . evil.

The criticism most frequently heard in America and Great Britain was more pragmatic: By criticizing Iran, Bush had supposedly weakened the moderates around President Khatami and strengthened the hard-liners around the Ayatollah Khameini. These critics reasoned that much as the Iranian people might dislike the tyrannical mullahs, they resented Western interference in their affairs even more. By denouncing the mullahs' rule, Bush enabled them to present themselves as the guardians of national independence. Much of the U.S. media parroted this line of objection, without troubling themselves to verify the assumptions on which it rested. *Did* the Iranians *really* dislike hearing their rulers insulted? *Could* the mullahs *in fact* tap nationalist sentiment after two decades of oppression and horrific war? *The New York Times* credulously repeated Iranian television's claim on February 11, 2002, the regime's

Revolution Day, that "millions of Iranians galvanized by President Bush's branding of their nation as part of an 'axis of evil' marched in a nationwide pep rally today. . . ."* Even if that claim were true, it proved no more than the turnout at May Day parades in the old Soviet Union showed the popularity of that regime: The government produced the crowds by ordering government employees and military personnel to attend, busing in schoolchildren, and threatening poor people with a loss of their benefits. But the claim was false. Nongovernment sources and Western media other than the *Times* put the turnout at about three hundred thousand, or less than one-third the level of Revolution Days past. In fact, as Michael Ledeen tartly observed, "The last time a million people demonstrated in Tehran was to demand an end to the regime, just a few months ago."†

The critics who argued that we ought to keep mum about the mullahs were often the very same people who had argued in the 1980s that we ought to accommodate ourselves to the Soviet Union, lest we "strengthen the hard-liners in the Kremlin." But the hard-liners in the Kremlin were already fully as strong as they needed to be, and the same was true in Iran. The Iranian theocrats distracted their people with presidential and legislative elections. But no candidate could run for any office unless the mullahs approved him. The mullahs, not Iran's president, controlled the army and the security services. They named all

---

* Neil McFarquhar, "Millions in Iran Rally Against U.S.," *New York Times,* February 12, 2002, www.nytimes.com/2002/02/12/international/middleeast/12IRAN.html.

† Michael Ledeen, "The Great Iranian Hoax," *National Review Online,* February 12, 2002, www.nationalreview.com/contributors/ledeen021202.shtml.

the judges. They owned many of Iran's productive assets through their religious foundations. They appointed the upper house of the Iranian legislature, a body with the power to veto any act of the lower house. Oh—and they could fire the president at any time.

In the 1980s, Ronald Reagan's campaign of truth telling about the Soviets accelerated the delegitimization of Soviet rule. Two decades later, George Bush's words had the same effect in Iran, only faster. Not only did antiregime demonstrations and protests in Iran spread after Bush's speech, but the regime's ability to repress them deteriorated. By July 2002, Iranian dissidents observed that the authorities were no longer employing Iranian-speaking police to attack protesters but were instead importing Palestinians, Afghans, and Chechens.

I have my own theories as to why the "axis of evil" phrase provoked so much resentment at home and abroad. In the long period of years in which the United States shied away from confronting the terror regimes of the Middle East, nations that were not as strong as the United States had reached accommodations and understandings of one kind or another with Iraq and Iran. Iran in particular is a very frightening country. It respects none of the rules of the international system. It has sponsored terrorism from Buenos Aires to Ankara. It possesses vast oil wealth and it is developing nuclear weapons and ballistic missles. People who are not strong enough to topple a dangerous regime like that must appease it—and if those people possess a conscience, they must then work out some rationalization to justify what might otherwise feel like cowardice. The rationalization on which the appeasers had agreed was the fiction that the mullahs were "liberalizing." The "axis of evil" speech directly challenged this fiction. By identifying the Iraqi and Iranian regimes with the Axis of the 1940s, Bush was challenging all those European governments that had denounced the rather pallid menace of Jörg Haider in Austria to join him in confronting the transplanted fascism of the Islamic world. By naming this fascism for what it was, Bush shamed those who had done business with it—and their shame expressed itself as indignation against the shamer.

In some cases, that indignation was inflamed by an extra resentment. There are many people in the world, and even many inside the United States, who dislike American culture and oppose American power. In the 1970s and 1980s, those people consoled themselves with the thought that American culture and power were declining. There were limits to American growth, Japan would become number one, the United States was just another great power fated to rise and fall. When the Soviet Union fell instead, those same ill-wishers hastened to bind the United States within a new network of international agreements and treaties: the international convention on land mines, the Kyoto Accords, the International Criminal Court. These agreements cost the United States much and offered it very little, but out of a combination of guilt and self-doubt and the urge to be seen as good fellows, much of the American elite was willing to see their country's freedom of action constrained. With his "axis of evil" speech, President Bush served notice to the world: *He* felt no guilt and no self-doubt, and he was a lot less eager to be perceived as a good fellow than he was to stand up to the bad fellows. In Afghanistan, the United

States had discovered its true strength. Now, to the cheers of the assembled Congress, Bush was announcing that this strength would be used without remorse. No wonder the speech dismayed America's enemies and its detractors—both overt and concealed.

# 13

## PROMISED LAND

THE MIDDLE EAST was not going to be George Bush's problem. He had watched Bill Clinton pour himself heart and soul into brokering a deal between the Israelis and the Palestinians, only to have Yasser Arafat reward him with a new war. Bush seems to have believed that Clinton inadvertently helped to cause the war by pursuing peace too avidly. Ari Fleischer indiscreetly expressed this opinion in March 2002: "[By] push[ing] the parties beyond where they were willing to go . . . it led to expectations that were raised to such a high level that it turned to violence."

Bush was not much tempted to repeat that error. Clinton was lured into the Middle East morass by two concerns. One was the need to protect America's oil supplies. By settling the Palestinian issue, Clinton hoped to reduce political radicalism in the Arab world and thus enhance the security of America's non-democratic allies in Saudi Arabia, Kuwait, and the other Gulf states. The second motive was more personal. Clinton can fairly be called the most philo-Semitic president in U.S. history. His closest friends and most trusted aides were Jewish, his administration was crammed with Jewish appointees, both his nominees to the Supreme Court were Jewish—even his most famous girlfriend was Jewish. And Jews liked Clinton as much as he liked them. They appreciated his intellectuality and his social tolerance, his liberated wife, and his moderate liberalism. Jewish donors contributed generously to Clinton's election campaigns; after he left office, some of those former donors helped him to grow very rich very rapidly.

Bush was governed by neither of these motives. Bush's favored response to America's dependence on imported oil was not a Palestinian state, but a shift to Mexican and Russian sources of supply—and, ultimately, to electric cars that plugged into sockets powered by nuclear energy. As for Clinton's obsessive interest in Israel and Jews, Bush did not share it. It would be almost impossible to invent a candidate less likely to appeal to Jewish voters than George W. Bush. His personality seemed to fuse together in one body the three personality types most calculated to frighten and annoy Jews: the redneck, the Bible-thumper, and the upper-class frat boy. His social conservatism worried Jews, his apparent anti-intellectualism offended them, and above all, they mistrusted his "born on third base" background. American Jews regard themselves as a self-made immigrant community, and when they looked at Bush, many of them thought: If *he* had been *my* father's son, he'd be working in retail, not running for president.

So Bush entered office with fewer Jewish friends and supporters than any president since perhaps Dwight Eisenhower. There were no Jews in his cabinet and few on his staff. The scarcity of Jewish staff was never an awkward or uncomfortable fact, but it was a fact all the same. Bush made a series of friendly, generous gestures to the Jewish community, culminating in an especially nice ceremony at Hanukkah 2001. The White House borrowed an immense antique silver menorah from the Jewish Museum in New York and invited Jewish staffers to bring their children to light candles with the president and Mrs. Bush in the foyer near Jackie Kennedy's garden. The event drove home how few of us there were: By my count, there were more press covering the event than there were Jewish staffers participating in it—and had Diana Furchtgott-Roth of the Council of Economic Advisers not arrived minutes before the president with five of her six children, the number of children at the candlelighting would not have broken out of the single digits.

It is, then, really quite a stunning turnabout of history that George W. Bush should have emerged as one of the staunchest friends of Israel ever to occupy the Oval Office—not (as the paranoiacs of Europe and the Middle East believe) because of the Jews, but almost entirely despite them.

O NE OF BUSH'S few prominent supporters in the Jewish community was a Los Angeles lawyer named Bruce Ramer, who happened to be president of the American Jewish Committee, one of the country's most venerable Jewish organizations. Ramer invited Bush to address the group's annual convention in May 2001. Bush accepted, and for obvious reasons, the speech was assigned to me.

The AJC had a distinguished record of defending religious

minorities around the world, non-Jewish as well as Jewish, so I proposed as the speech's main theme a restatement of Bush's commitment to religious freedom in China and a denunciation of the persecution of the African Christians in the south of Sudan by the country's Arab Muslim overlords. China had released America's detained air crew only a couple of weeks before, and they amply deserved a presidential scolding.

Of course, Bush would also have to address more specifically Jewish concerns. I proposed two: first, the Jewish community's apprehensions about Bush's religious tolerance; and, second, Israel's security.

The widespread view that Bush's intense Christianity somehow biased him against non-Christians was both unjust and unintelligent. It was precisely the most religious members of the Bush administration who tended to be the friendliest to Jews as individuals and most sympathetic to the state of Israel as a Jewish state. This was not, as some liberal Jews insisted, an untrustworthy friendship. Those who believed most strongly in the Bible naturally felt the strongest affinity to the people of the Bible—and it seemed to me that American Jews were making a catastrophic political error by refusing to acknowledge and absorb this truth.

The community would want and need to hear Bush's views about Israel. Yasser Arafat had launched his newest terror war in September 2000, and so far Bush's statements on the conflict had been studiously vague. By May 2001, the fighting that Arafat called the "al-Aqsa *intifada*" had already claimed dozens of Jewish lives, including a ten-month-old girl targeted by a Palestinian sniper and two army reservists who were stabbed to death by a Palestinian mob that then dipped its hands in the blood and danced for the television cameras. Close to four hundred Palestinians had also been killed by then, either in clashes with Israeli forces or in Israeli reprisals. (Unlike the Israeli casualties, however, the majority of the Palestinian dead were men of military age.) Few American Jews had any clear idea of what they wished Bush to do, but almost all of them wished he would do *something*.

The portion of the speech about China and Sudan was easy enough to write. Not so the portion on Israel. All presidential remarks on foreign affairs had to be cleared by the relevant regional director at the National Security Council. As late as May, astonishingly, Clinton's regional director for the Middle East had yet to be replaced. The day of the AJC speech happened to be the day that Clinton's Middle East envoy, former senator George Mitchell, was due to present his report on the origins of the al-Aqsa war and the resumption of Israeli-Palestinian negotiations. The peace processors attached great, even absurd, importance to the Mitchell report and were adamant that Bush not say or do anything that might contradict it. And since the Mitchell report blamed the war on Israel for not offering even more concessions than it did, a ban on contradicting Mitchell was a ban on expressing any meaningful support for Israel.

Still, I tried my best to produce something zesty. Working within the NSC's strict rules, I imagined I had found a way to send a strong message of empathy and support to the Jewish community at a time when it yearned for hopeful news. I secured tickets for my wife and me to the AJC dinner at the National Building Museum, a vast nineteenth-century redbrick pile where in former times they had processed the pensions of Union veterans of the Civil War. Ramer had assembled a glittering roster of speakers: first, Israeli foreign minister Shimon Peres; then German foreign minister Joschka Fischer; after him, Mexican president Vicente Fox; and Bush last. I sat at my table listening to the first three speeches with growing smugness. They were adequate, but no more. Fox's in particular struck me as ill judged. Its theme, as I recall, went something like this: It's a pleasure to visit the capital of the United States. And speaking of capital, I understand you Jewish people have a lot of it, so I hope you will consider investing some in the new, democratic Mexico.

Yet the audience vigorously applauded all three men. So I concluded happily that we had a really lively crowd here. If they liked those lame speeches, I told myself, they will *love* Bush's.

After the opening compliments, Bush began:

"I took a look at this weekend's program before coming here. I was flattered to read that 'understanding the new administration' is called a 'central feature' of this year's meeting. I may be able to save you a little time.

"I believe in equal opportunity for all, without discrimination or prejudice of any kind. I believe that tolerance and respect must be taught to all our children, because too many young minds and souls are lost to hate. I believe that government should support the works of charity that are motivated by faith—but our government should never fund the teaching of faith itself.

"I am a Christian. But I believe with the Psalmist that the Lord God of Israel neither slumbers nor sleeps."

As Bush built to that climactic line, I braced myself for the expected torrent of applause. There was nothing. Not a clap, not a cheer. Silence. Maybe even a rather disapproving silence.

Then he came to the portion of his speech dealing with Israel. Bush had visited the country for the first time in 1998 and had been startled by Israel's smallness and vulnerability. The speech built on his experience: "For a Texan, a first visit to Israel is an eye-opener. At the narrowest point, it's only eight miles from the Mediterranean to the old armistice line: That's less than from the top to the bottom of Dallas–Fort Worth Airport. The whole of pre-1967 Israel is only about six times the size of the King Ranch. It's a small country that has lived under threat throughout its existence. At my first meeting of my National Security Council, I told them that a top foreign-policy priority of my administration is the safety and security of Israel. My administration will be steadfast in supporting Israel against terrorism and violence, and in seeking the peace for which all Israelis pray."

The official transcript of the event is kind enough to note "(Laughter)" and "(Applause)" in a couple of places during that long paragraph. All I can say to that is that the laughter, if any, occurred beyond my earshot and that the applause was of the kind that is described as "polite" by friendly reporters and "scattered" by hostile ones.

I was surprised and downcast. My first impulse was to ask my tablemates what was wrong, but they were all connected to the Turkish embassy and so in no position to enlighten me. But thinking the speech over that night, I came to understand what had gone wrong. Bush always took exquisite pains to avoid sectarianism when he talked about God. It was not by accident that he spoke of his "faith" rather than his "Christianity." He hoped and trusted that American Jews would feel included by such language: After all, isn't Judaism a "faith" too? But the

American Jewish community is so terrified of non-Jewish religiosity that *any* reference to God by a non-Jew, no matter how friendly its intent, unnerved them. They do not trust people who talk too much about the "Lord God," and they do not like it any better when such people remind them that the Lord God in question is their Lord God, too. The intense, devout secularism of the American Jewish community baffled Bush. And in the end, he could not allay fears he did not understand.

The cool reception of the Israeli portion of the speech was a rather more complicated matter. By early May, the American Jewish community was in the midst of something like a collective nervous breakdown over the failure of the peace process. They recognized that it had brought war, not the promised peace: Polls showed that a majority of them supported Ariel Sharon and his tough policy of reprisals and border closures. Yet at the same time they were not prepared to admit that the policy was a mistake: Those same polls showed broad support in the American Jewish community for an independent Palestinian state. Bush's vague words of support for Israel's security satisfied neither of these conflicting emotions. He offered neither hope that America would intervene to bring a negotiated solution nor an endorsement of Sharon's attempts to win a military victory. Although his description of the inadequacy of Israel's old borders suggested that he recognized Israel's security needs, the vagueness of his commitment to "support" Israel implied that this recognition would not be translated into positive action. And as for the final hint that peace was something to be prayed for—rather than won on the battlefield or negotiated at a peace conference—that could easily be interpreted as indifference to Israel's fate, or worse than indifference.

With each passing month, that unbenign interpretation of Bush's policy took on greater plausibility. Bush's decision to pass responsibility for the Middle East to the State Department and the Central Intelligence Agency empowered those foreign-policy bureaucrats most eager to appease the Arab oil states. All through the month of August, Colin Powell's staff worked on a big speech announcing a three-year timetable for the creation of a Palestinian state defended by an international military force. When a suicide bomber blew up a Sbarro's pizzeria in central Jerusalem, killing fifteen people, including six children and three Americans, the State Department's spokesman condemned Israel for retaliating. On August 28 came another condemnation of Israel, this one coordinated with Great Britain. Arafat's war seemed to be succeeding. Terror was winning the Palestinian Authority a better offer than the deal it had snubbed in December. The United States and Britain seemed to be working together to offer Arafat a state guarded by an international protective force to guarantee its borders. Once he was protected by his international bodyguards, Arafat could instigate terror against Israel, safe from Israeli retaliation. So while the deal Arafat had rejected in December had put peace first and statehood second, the offer that seemed to be coming his way in August was statehood first and peace later, if ever.

You might think that September 11 would have discredited the old terror master. Bush said that if you fed, sheltered, clothed, or armed a terrorist, you were a terrorist. The Palestinian Authority consistently did all those things. But as Bush focused on danger at home and the war in Afghanistan, his State Department reverted to its old Gulf War theory that the United

States could earn the right to defend its interests in the Middle East only by first ostentatiously whacking Israel.

On October 2, 2001, the same day that Palestinian gunmen burst into a settlement in the Gaza Strip, randomly shooting civilian residents and killing a young courting couple, President Bush announced his personal support for a Palestinian state. "The idea of a Palestinian state has always been a part of a vision so long as the right to an Israeli state is respected. . . . I fully understand that progress is made in centimeters in the Middle East. And I believe we're making some progress." Two weeks later, Tony Blair invited Yasser Arafat to 10 Downing Street, and stepped out to announce that Britain too now supported the prompt creation of a state for Arafat.

It seemed as if September 11 had changed nothing about the peace process. But it had—it had changed everything.

On October 17, four members of Arafat's personal entourage entered a Jerusalem hotel and assassinated an Israeli cabinet minister after breakfast. Israel demanded that Arafat surrender the killers. When he did not, Israel accused the Palestinian Authority of being a "state that supports terror" and rolled out its troops in the largest military operation in two decades. Now Bush had to decide: Could he condemn Israel for doing in the West Bank exactly what he was doing in Afghanistan? Every Middle East expert around him, beginning with his own national security staffers, argued that the two operations were completely different. But the line between the two terror wars could not honestly be drawn, and if something could not be done honestly, Bush could not do it.

Bush began to speak more frequently with Ariel Sharon—

but he absolutely refused to see or even speak on the telephone
with Arafat. Bush's disdain so maddened the Palestinian leader
that Arafat actually tried to shove himself into the president's
presence at the United Nations meeting in November and had to
be physically blocked by the Secret Service. August's "state first,
peace later" policy was definitively repudiated. By November,
when Powell at last delivered his big Middle East speech, all the
deadlines and time lines and talk of international protection for
Arafat had been deleted.

Then Arafat made what may someday be reckoned as the
most fateful miscalculation of his career. On January 5, 2002,
Israeli naval forces intercepted a Gaza-bound merchant ship
loaded with fifty tonnes of arms from Iran. Arafat hastily sent
Bush a letter denying any involvement in the shipment. Probably Arafat did not even intend his denial to be interpreted literally; he may have written it as a social form, like the phrase *I
regret* in a letter declining an invitation to a wedding or a dinner
party. If so, Arafat sorely misunderstood his man. Bush does not
lie to you. You had better not lie to him.

The *Karine A.* incident finished off Arafat in Bush's eyes. In
conversation, Bush ceased to conceal either his contempt for the
thuggish Palestinian or his irritation with the thug's European
protectors. "They just luuuuuve Arafat," he would say with
elongated wonder.

It's an extraordinary thing about appeasement. As Bush became firmer and stronger, all those Arab despots who had for
years appeased their radicals suddenly began to try to appease
him. At the end of February, Crown Prince Abdullah of Saudi
Arabia stepped forward with an extraordinary initiative: He of-

fered Israel full normalization of relations in exchange for a Palestinian state on the West Bank and in Gaza with Jerusalem as its capital. What was extraordinary was not the content of the offer—it followed the main lineaments of every peace plan proposed since 1974. What was extraordinary, rather, was the man who proposed it. The Saudis had always made clear that they would be the very last Arab country ever to make peace with Israel. Their sudden proposal to lead the way was an indication of just how nervous they had become.

They had reason to be nervous. Americans were learning just how up-to-the-eyeballs went the Saudi complicity with terror in Afghanistan and the West Bank. President Bush visited the 101st Airborne at Fort Campbell, Kentucky, at Thanksgiving. He told the troops: "If you train or arm a terrorist, you are a terrorist. If you feed a terrorist or fund a terrorist, you're a terrorist." By that standard, the flow of money and support from Saudi Arabia to al-Qaeda, Hamas, Hezbollah, and the terrorists of Kashmir and Southeast Asia damned the Saudi monarchy as the world's outstanding terrorists.

If the Saudis were nervous, however, they were not quite nervous enough to offer the United States cooperation in the fight either against al-Qaeda or against Iraq. Perhaps they feared that cooperation against al-Qaeda might expose disturbing connections between bin Laden and the House of Saud. As for Iraq, the Saudis seem to have decided that bad as Saddam was, he was still to be preferred to the risks of a democratic regime in a major Arab state. Unwilling to cooperate against terror, the Saudis desperately needed to produce something to distract and placate the Americans. The Abdullah peace plan was it.

Bush was certainly eager to accept it. But he was not willing to be distracted, nor was he willing to collar Sharon and protect Arafat.

The pressures now gathering on Bush were immense. By the spring of 2002, the governments of almost every American ally were clamoring for some kind of pressure on Israel. The European Parliament was debating anti-Israel sanctions, left-wing protesters were flying to Ramallah to insert their bodies between Arafat and the Israeli army, the governments of Britain, Canada, and Australia were casting increasingly ominous anti-Israel votes at the United Nations. Yet in a rocking chair news conference in Crawford, Texas, on March 30, 2002, Bush bluntly refused to rescue Arafat from defeat.

"I fully understand Israel's need to defend herself; I respect that. It's a country that has seen a wave of suicide bombers coming into the hearts of their cities and killing innocent people. That country has a right to defend herself."

Had the president of the United States been even marginally less firm, Israel would have found itself in the same predicament as it did when it confronted Arafat in 1982: utterly alone. Many remember Ronald Reagan as a great friend of Israel, and so he was, but in 1982 he buckled under the pressure to rescue Arafat. Twenty years later, Bush sometimes bent a little—but he never broke.

He had seen the evidence. Arafat was a liar, a thief, a killer, and a protector of killers. By Bush's own rules, Arafat was an enemy of civilization in general and the United States in particular. As Bush himself said in a speech in the Rose Garden on April 4, 2002, "Since September the eleventh, I've delivered this message: Everyone must choose; you're either with the civilized world, or you're with the terrorists. All in the Middle East also must choose and must move decisively in word and deed against terrorist acts.

"The chairman of the Palestinian Authority has not consistently opposed or confronted terrorists. At Oslo and elsewhere, Chairman Arafat renounced terror as an instrument of his cause, and he agreed to control it. He's not done so."

Yet even at this late date, Bush could not bring himself to accept all the logical implications of his own words. Having condemned Arafat for using terror, Bush limited himself to one final appeal to the Palestinian Authority—that is to say, to Arafat himself—to cut it out. "I call on the Palestinian people, the Palestinian Authority, and our friends in the Arab world to join us in a clear message to terrorists: Blowing yourself up does not help the Palestinian cause. On the contrary, suicide bombing missions could well blow up the best and only hope for a Palestinian state."

Why did Bush take the stance he did? Not—as the European press insinuated—because of the "Jewish lobby." That lobby exists, but what did Bush care for it? He would not need Jewish votes in 2004, and he certainly would not need Jewish political donations. As a challenger in 2000, Bush had raised nearly $200 million; as an incumbent, he needed only to raise a finger and the skies would shower gold wherever he directed. If Bush had a political worry, it was his own political base: conservatives, both religious and secular.

"What do you think our folks think of the Israeli-Palestinian conflict?" Bush asked Rove one spring day.

Rove answered, "They think it's part of your war on terror."

That's certainly what the polls showed. A Gallup poll

conducted in April 2002 found that Republicans overwhelmingly took Israel's side: 67 percent of Republicans said they supported Israel, as against only 8 percent who supported the Palestinians. Although close to 90 percent of Jewish voters are Democrats, the Democratic poll was much less lopsided: 45 percent of Democrats supported Israel, 21 percent favored the Palestinians.*

Why did the Republican Party become so Zionist? Certainly the influence of evangelical Christians has a lot to do with it. Many evangelicals identify the return of the Jews to Israel as a sign of the imminence of the Second Coming—and see the attacks on Israel as portending the Antichrist. But important as evangelicals are, they do not constitute 67 percent of the party. Republicans supported Israel because they intuitively sensed that the people who hated Israel, the only democracy ever to exist in the Middle East, were people who hated America. All the criticisms of Israel levied at the European Union and the United Nations ("How dare you live on ground once occupied by other people? Why must you use force to defend yourself? Why must you be so offensively sure of yourselves?") could be, and usually were, directed at the United States as well. Republicans supported Israel so militantly, and so much more militantly than Democrats, not because of Israel, and certainly not because of Jewish influence, but because of their own principles and beliefs. Here is a striking fact: While almost two thirds of American Jews favored the creation of a Palestinian state by the summer of 2002, fewer than half of Americans in general did so.† And of

* www.jpost.com/editions/2002/04/18/LatestNews.47184.html.
† http://abcnews.go.com/sections/us/DailyNews/palestine_poll020624.html; http//www.ajc.org/InTheMedia/RelatedArticles.asp?did=601.

all Americans, it was conservatives who most opposed a Palestinian state. They remembered the images of gleeful Palestinians celebrating on September 11—and the conservative impulse, when confronted by an enemy, is not to mollify him but to resist him. "Those who choose America for an enemy choose their own destruction" was a great phrase that never made it into a presidential speech: too bellicose. But it aptly described how right-of-center Americans felt, both about the leaders of the Palestinian movement and about their Saudi sponsers and paymasters.

These feelings ran especially strong across the Potomac, over in the Pentagon. The leaders of the Department of Defense felt horribly betrayed by the Saudis. The United States had saved the Saudi monarchy in 1990–1991, and done so with rare deference. When Saudi troops fled the town of Khafji, General Norman Schwarzkopf saved the Saudi army's face by issuing predated orders ordering a withdrawal from the town.[*] And when the coalition forces advanced, U.S. forces would identify surrounded and demoralized Iraqi units for the Saudis to attack—rather like the Edwardian gamekeepers who placed fat, helpless partridges in bushes for the inept gentry to shoot. Now, eleven years after this rescue, the Saudis denied the United States access to the Prince Bandar air base that American forces had constructed for use in a future war against Iraq—and American engineers had to build a whole new air base in the Qatari desert in less than ten months. Even the most pro-Saudi officials at Defense could offer no better excuse than "The Saudis have done everything we asked them to do."

But do not believe for a minute that the Saudi attitude in

[*] Norvell B. De Atkine, "Why Arabs Lose Wars," *American Diplomacy,* www.unc.edu/depts/diplomat/AD__Issues/amdipl__17/articles/deatkine__arabs2.html.

America's hour of need went unnoticed or forgotten. The Palestinian enthusiasm for Osama bin Laden and Saddam Hussein was registered as well. In one of his many astonishingly candid moments, Donald Rumsfeld expressed in the summer of 2002 the view of many Republicans about all the various peace plans that would require Israel to surrender the West Bank to Arafat's rule: "If you have a country that's a sliver and you can see three sides of it from a high hotel building, you've got to be careful what you give away and to whom you give it."

*To whom you give it*—that summed the issue up for Rumsfeld, and it came to sum it up for Bush. It summed up the issue in Iraq, where America's Arab allies urged the United States not to try to create a representative regime, but to replace Saddam Hussein with a more rational strongman. It was the issue in all those Arab countries where rage boiled against the United States because the United States was seen to prop up unresponsive and corrupt kings and presidents-for-life. It was the issue in Saudi Arabia, the homeland of bin Ladenism, where hundreds of billions of dollars from Western oil consumers had vanished who knew where.

And it summed up the issue on the West Bank. Could we really suppose that we could begin the war against terror by creating an Arafatistan on the West Bank? That would be like Churchill starting the war against Nazism by ceding Northern Ireland to the British Union of Fascists or Truman opening the cold war by inviting the Communist Party to seize power in New York City. In his speech to the joint session of Congress, Bush had explained that freedom was now at war with fear. Was this mere rhetoric? If we were fighting for freedom in the war against terror, as we had fought for freedom against Nazism and against communism and the other evil ideologies of the twentieth century, then we had to speak up for our ideals. Yes, war is an ugly business that sometimes requires ugly compromises. To defeat communism, America had sometimes allied itself with Islamic fanaticism; to defeat Nazism, America allied itself with communism. But despite these bad associations, Americans did not lose sight of what they were fighting for then. During World War II, Americans came to understand that the fight for freedom was not just America's fight, it was also Germany's fight, and that the war against Nazism would not be truly won until Germany rejoined the democratic world. During the cold war, a succession of American presidents took care to describe the fight for freedom as not just America's fight, but also Russia's and Ukraine's and Poland's and Hungary's fight—and that the war against communism would not be won until the communist countries were liberated from the criminal elite that misruled them.

The radical idea that had been growing in Bush's mind since December 2001 expressed itself the following June. As Israeli troops battled in some of the fiercest fighting of the entire al-Aqsa war—and the United Nations and European Union hurled false charges of massacre and genocide against Israel—pressure intensified on Bush to give the big speech that the international community had sought for a year: the speech that would at last smack down Israel and announce the date by which Arafat would get his state. All through the month of June, Bush thought and thought. There would be a story that tomorrow would be the day—and then the Palestinians would commit an atrocity, and the speech would be postponed. There would be another leak that the speech was now coming at last—and then another cancellation as Bush threw away the latest draft in exasperation.

At last, on June 24, 2002, at a little before four in the afternoon, with just a few hours' warning, he stepped into the Rose Garden with Colin Powell and Condoleezza Rice at his side to announce that the United States would support the creation of a Palestinian state only if that state were democratic, tolerant, and liberal.

"I call on the Palestinian people to elect new leaders, leaders not compromised by terror. I call upon them to build a practicing democracy, based on tolerance and liberty. If the Palestinian people actively pursue these goals, America and the world will actively support their efforts. If the Palestinian people meet these goals, they will be able to reach agreements with Israel and Egypt and Jordan on security and other arrangements for independence."

He continued: "Today, Palestinian authorities are encouraging, not opposing, terrorism. This is unacceptable. And the United States will not support the establishment of a Palestinian state until its leaders engage in a sustained fight against the terrorists and dismantle their infrastructure." There would be no more exemptions and exceptions for Palestinian terror. One month later, on July 26, Bush's ambassador to the United Nations, John Negroponte, told a closed session of the Security Council that from now on the United States would veto any resolution on Israel that did not also condemn Hamas, Islamic Jihad, and Arafat's al-Aqsa brigades by name.

This was not a message of threat. It was a message of hope: Democracy for the Palestinians could be the beginning of democracy for the whole Arab world. But for Palestinian democracy to prevail, Palestinian terror would have to cease.

"If liberty can blossom in the rocky soil of the West Bank and Gaza, it will inspire men and women around the globe who are equally weary of poverty and oppression, and equally entitled to the benefits of democratic government."

It was a breathtakingly ambitious message, and one much more likely to end in heartbreak than success. But if Palestinian democracy was improbable, the old goal—a Palestinian dictatorship at peace with Israel—had shown itself to be utterly impossible. The cold realists who had promised that only a thug like Arafat could control the real Palestinian crazies had been exposed as the goggly-eyed romantics.

Bush had found what all the great American presidents have believed: America's principles are as real and necessary and powerful as oil reserves, aircraft carriers, and spy satellites. War had made him, as it had made Roosevelt and Reagan, a crusader after all.

# 14

# THE RIGHT MAN

T HE BIG OAK doors closed behind me, and I paused at the head of the great flight of stone steps to admire the view one last time: the White House, flag snapping, shining bright against the cool winter night. I heard the big doors push open again, and a woman stepped out. She looked at me—a box of photographs in my arms, a briefcase perched on top of the box—and instantly understood. She smiled. "Ah," she said, "having your moment, are you?"

So I was. But it wasn't the moment that she might have supposed. I was not musing wistfully about leaving behind the glamour and excitement of the White House. I was calculating how I would spend the money I would get by suing the syndicated columnist Robert Novak for libel.

It was February 25, 2002—my last day in government. I had handed in my resignation a month earlier, after finishing work on the State of the Union. It had grieved me to do it. I was proud to have served here, and sorry to say good-bye to my colleagues.

But a war presidency had decreasing need for the services of an economic speechwriter. After the petering out of the stimulus package in December, I found myself wandering about the Executive Office Building volunteering to help other people with their projects. I worked on the Social Security commission reports and the 2003 budget. I began to wonder whether I would not soon be writing ergonomic regulations for the Department of Labor. I could not deny it any longer: My work here was done. I had contributed what I had to contribute, and I had seen what I had wanted to see—more, in fact, than I had ever imagined I would see. Now it was time to heed Andy Card's admonition: to remember that a White House job was an honor, not a career.

As I was packing my things, one of my speechwriting colleagues stuck his head in the door.

"Turn on CNN!"

"Why? Is something happening?"

"Robert Novak said the president fired you."

"*What?*"

But before I could dial CNN to find out, my phone had already lit up with my first three phone calls from curious reporters. Novak's brief item had just pitched me into a Washington media sandstorm. They're a strange part of the local climate. One minute you're walking through the desert, minding your business, and the next, everything is howling around your ears, and your skin is being sheared off by *swoosh-ing* grains of dirt. The phone never stops ringing, and photographers show up on your front steps, and your children's teachers cluck at you sympathetically, and you get weary of your own voice saying over and over again, "I'm sorry, I have nothing more to say about this matter, I have nothing more to say about this matter." But maybe I had better start from the beginning.

A couple of days after the 2002 State of the Union, my wife had written an e-mail to some family and some of her friends about the speech crediting me with writing "the 'axis of evil' segment" of the State of the Union. There was nothing very unusual in this. The Bush speechwriting department was discreet, but hardly anonymous: Karen Hughes talked to *The New York Times Magazine* and *The Wall Street Journal* about the September 20 speech, pointing out the individual lines that were her handiwork. Mike Gerson had spoken with Bob Woodward and Dan Balz of *The Washington Post* about his contributions to the National Cathedral and joint session speeches. From time to time, other colleagues would e-mail friends the texts of speeches on which they had worked.

But e-mail is a treacherous medium. The on-line magazine *Slate* got hold of my wife's e-mail and gleefully published it. *The Washington Post* followed up with a short item in its gossip column—and suddenly the whole thing was a real news story. Journalists and television pundits who had disliked the "axis of evil" formulation suddenly had a way to complain about it without tangling with a 90 percent president. Rather than dangerously alienating their viewers by criticizing the president, they could denounce the sinister cabal of hawkish neoconservatives who had supposedly led Bush astray.

But the e-mail story was a one-week wonder. Even for my wife and me, irritated as we were at the interception of personal letters, the story was beginning to seem more funny than nasty. When *The Washington Post* gossip columnist asked her for a comment, she quipped that she had no comment: "I feel enough like Lucy Ricardo already."

But Novak was not bored with the story. Novak was a hard-working and able reporter, but a dangerous character, famous for his witticism that he knew only two kinds of people in Washington: "sources and targets." Shortly after September 11, Novak invited me to lunch. I declined, citing the then prevailing ban on contacts with the press. Two months later, the ban had been retracted, and Novak invited me once more, rather more menacingly this time. I cleared the lunch with Gerson—"Be careful," he warned—and ended up listening attentively as Novak warned that the war in Afghanistan was likely to end in disaster and that any war in Iraq was certain to end that way. I walked away from the lunch feeling that I had executed an especially deft evasive maneuver: I had avoided becoming a source, and I believed I had convinced him that I was not interesting enough to be a target.

I was wrong. Which is how it happened that Novak had me for target practice on my last day at work.

"You remember two weeks ago . . . that . . . we reported that . . . speechwriter David Frum's wife had sent out an e-mail to friends saying that her husband was the author of President Bush's famous axis of evil speech in the State of the Union address. People at the White House said that didn't bother them. But, in fact, today is Mr. Frum's last day on the job—very hush-hush. Nobody but his closest friends knew about it until last week. There had been no plans for him to leave. He is telling friends that he is leaving on his own volition. The White House aides I talked to say the same thing. But there's a lot of suspicion that nobody does that with George W. Bush and stays very long in the White House. There's suspicion he's been kicked out."

Now *there's* a memorable send-off. I walked over to the press office and asked them to issue some kind of statement that Novak's story was fabricated, that I had not in fact been fired. "This makes me look kind of bad, you know?"

"You?" the press officer said scornfully. "It makes the *president* look bad—petty and vindictive."

"Oh, yes, well, I hadn't thought of that," I said.

"You're not even out the building yet," she said with ironic mock regret, "and you're already forgetting what's important." But she obliged, issuing a statement that pointed out I had resigned in writing a month before. CNN quashed my hopes of using the Novak story to finance my children's college education by running a correction of Novak's story the next evening. (Judy Woodruff, the host of the program on which Novak appeared, asked me: "Well, what about this point that nobody but your closest friends knew you were leaving?" I answered: "Who else would care?")

But the correction came too late. For the next two weeks, I could not read the newspaper, could not finish a cup of coffee, could not walk the dog in the park without being interrupted by the ring of the telephone or the chirrup of the cell phone. There was hardly an hour from dawn till midnight when I was not on the phone telling a reporter that no, I was not fired, and that if they wanted a quote, they should use the White House statement. The *New York Post* sent a photographer to my house. Hong Kong television woke me up in the middle of the night. My hometown newspaper, the Toronto *Globe and Mail,* ran an article speculating whether I would now divorce my wife. *The New York*

*Times* quizzed me about my vacation plans: The White House had said I was leaving for a holiday in Mexico, but here it was, a week later, and I was still at home—would I care to explain this glaring contradiction? The British newspaper the *Guardian*, without a hint of humor, dubbed the affair "Frumgate."

About five days into the story, I got a call from a reporter I particularly respected. After repeating my standard line, "No, I was not fired; if you want to quote anything, I refer you to the White House statement," I asked her if she would answer a question for me: "Would you mind telling me why this ridiculous story is supposed to be news? I mean, suppose I *had* been fired? So what? Why am I getting twenty calls a day?"

"You don't understand," she said, "how frozen out from this administration the press feels. They don't tell us *anything*—and so when we got something that seems to lift the curtain a little, we go kind of crazy. The idea that this administration is so paranoid that it would fire somebody for an e-mail fits all our prejudices. And the possibility that there might be a disgruntled former employee eager to dish the dirt . . . well, we've been waiting for that for more than a year."

So I should not have been surprised when the NBC tabloid program *Inside Edition* called the next day. They wanted to send a camera crew around to the house, to give my wife and me an opportunity "to tell your side of the story—and what you *really* think of President Bush."

The sheer weirdness of the situation hit me all at once. "You want to know what I *really* think of the president?"

"Oh yes—I mean, you worked with him, you know the secrets, the dark side, oh yes, we'd love to hear it."

"Okay," I said, casting my voice into the best imitation I

could of Karen Hughes, "I think President Bush has an exciting agenda for America that's both compassionate *and* conservative . . ." I went on in this vein for about three-quarters of a minute, feeling the booker's enthusiasm dropping a degree per second, like a thermometer during one of Washington's savage summer rainstorms. "Above all, though," I concluded my little speech, "I think he's got a vision for the future, a vision for *all* our children."

"Oh," the booker said with audible disappointment. "Say: Can we get back to you later?"

I never did get to give my candid opinion of President Bush.

GEORGE W. BUSH is a very unusual person: a good man who is not a weak man. He has many faults. He is impatient and quick to anger; sometimes glib, even dogmatic; often uncurious and as a result ill informed; more conventional in his thinking than a leader probably should be. But outweighing the faults are his virtues: decency, honesty, rectitude, courage, and tenacity.

Despite these virtues, on September 10, 2001, George Bush was not on his way to a very successful presidency.

First, he was unlucky in his timing: He arrived in office to a recession, a stock market slump, and a wave of corporate scandals. Since the mid-1990s, America's political center of gravity had been shifting leftward. Polls showed rising confidence in government and dwindling support for the death penalty, and the election returns confirmed the polls. The corporate scandals of 2001 and 2002 amplified the trend toward activist government and away from free-market solutions. Had 9/11 not occurred, Bush would probably have had to choose between compromising with an ascendant liberalism like Richard Nixon or fighting desperate veto battles against it like Gerald Ford—neither of them a strategy for a presidency of conservative achievement.

Second, Bush was unsuccessful in his political strategy. He had sought to build a new political coalition to replace the fading Nixon-Reagan "silent majority" of white, married, middle-class voters. He had hoped to appeal to minorities and women with his "compassionate" appeals on education and immigration reform and to affluent professionals with his proposals for Social Security reform. That strategy earned him 538,000 fewer votes than his opponent in November 2000 and crippled his presidency from the start. The fight to enact his first big initiative, his tax cut, depleted the strength of his weak administration. As a result, from May 2001 onward, his domestic policy consisted of a series of increasingly desperate concessions to his opponents (on education, on spending) and to small interest groups within his own ranks (on steel, on farm subsidies). These concessions won him the occasional cosmetic victory: Steel protection, for example, bought him the authority to try to negotiate new trade deals. But the concessions gained him little with the general electorate and alienated him from his own supporters. He was in danger of becoming his father: a candidate elected by the dwindling conservative coalition, who generated less and less enthusiasm within that coalition.

Third, Bush's political vision was unclear. He was a politician of conservative instincts rather than conservative principles. He knew in a general way what he believed and what he did not. But on any specific issue, nobody could ever be sure where the line was beyond which he could not be pushed. This pragmatic vagueness tempted members of Congress to test him—by spending more, mucking up his education bill, or bloating up his farm bill. When Bush drew a line in the sand, he could not be budged—as Tom Daschle discovered when he suggested in January 2002 canceling Bush's tax cut. Bush, however, seldom drew those lines: Congress could send him legislation he believed to be flagrantly unconstitutional, like the McCain-Feingold campaign finance reform, and he would shrug and sign it and leave it to the courts to sort out.

Above all, Bush lacked a big organizing idea. A veteran of the first Bush White House has commented astutely that the Democrats are a party with a lot of little ideas, the Republicans the party with a few big ideas. Ronald Reagan: "Government is the problem." Richard Nixon: "Law and order." Dwight Eisenhower: "Peace and prosperity." But with every passing week in the first half of 2001, it got harder and harder to sum up who George Bush was. "Compassionate conservatism" turned out in practice not to be a big idea at all, but a whole agglomeration of little ideas—government funding for religious organizations, school testing, a higher minimum wage, tax credits for young children—wrapped together to look like a big idea. I think it was the randomness and unrelatedness of George Bush's policies, much more than his relative newness on the national political scene, that explains why so many Americans felt in September 2001 that they did not know this new president of theirs.

Well, they know him now.

George Bush, the uncertain peacetime president, has been nothing short of superb as a wartime leader.

His success can be summed up in three words: moderation, persistence, and boldness.

*Moderation.* On September 11, the country was ready to hate, smash, and kill. Those are powerful emotions, easily exploited. Bush set himself instead to quiet and calm them. With his insistence upon tolerance for Arab and Muslim Americans, his program of swift and massive aid for the oppressed people of Afghanistan, and his generous reconstruction program for New York, Bush waged war in a way in which the whole country could take pride.

You will sometimes hear it said that Bush abridged civil liberties or failed to pay due respect to the opinions of America's allies. Neither charge can be sustained.

Consider Bush's record on civil liberties. The list of all the things he decided *not* to propose—no national ID card, no central registry for foreign students, no military tribunal for Zacarias Moussaoui—suggests that the question about Bush ought not to be "Has he gone too far?" but "Has he gone anything like far enough?"

As for the charge of disrespect for allies, who really is disrespecting whom? The Bush administration laboriously consulted with America's friends and treaty partners—who returned the favor in many cases with scandalous indifference and ill will. What is one to say, for example, about Gerhard Schröder's anti-American reelection campaign in Germany? Or Saudi Arabia's sullen noncooperation against al-Qaeda and Iraq? Or Mexico's abrogation of the Rio defense pact in the middle of the war on terror? Well, Bush said nothing at all for the record except endlessly to praise allies and friends whose leaders insulted him to their local press. And in the end, those allies—even the French, even the duplicitous Saudis—fell into line behind Bush's leadership.

*Persistence*. American troops had been in Afghanistan for less than five months when Senator Robert Byrd complained that "no end was in sight" to the war. When Bush insisted that the war had not finished with the fall of the Taliban, Democrats accused him of plotting to win reelection with "a state of war until zero four." The war on terror, by its very nature, yielded few spectacular victories. For the most part it looked like a combination of police work and counterinsurgency in remote corners of the earth: Mindanao, Yemen, Kurdistan. Yet Bush kept at it. As he promised in his September 20 speech to Congress, he did not relent—and neither did he succumb to the temptation to lunge into rash adventures in pursuit of a triumph for the cameras. His strategy in Iraq and Iran was judicious, deliberate, unhasty—and certain. He made the big decisions on the war in the first forty-eight hours after September 11, and he adhered to those decisions to the end.

*Boldness*. A president's natural inclination is to take the middle way. Bush certainly shared that bias toward caution. But at every important juncture of the war on terror, he nonetheless opted for the high-risk option: sending a small force to Afghanistan rapidly rather than waiting to build up a big one, continuing the war as a war after the fall of the Taliban, turning his back on the State Department's advice about the calamity that must befall the United States if it fought Osama bin Laden without first placating Yasser Arafat, and on and on.

At West Point in June 2002, Bush unveiled the most ambitious rethink of American strategic doctrine since the beginning of the cold war. In the past, the United States had always let the other guy throw the first punch: the Confederacy at Fort Sumter, the kaiser with his subs, the Japanese at Pearl Harbor. No more. "[I]f we wait for threats to fully materialize," Bush said, "we will have waited too long." From now on, there would be no more free punches for America's enemies. It was a bold policy—and it rested on a bold new moral confidence. "We are in a conflict between good and evil, and America will call evil by its name." How could Bush be so sure what was evil and what was not? For him, it was not a difficult question. "Moral truth is the same in every culture, in every time, and in every place."

... The longer the war on terror lasts, the more criticism one hears of Bush. This is natural and maybe even healthy. But there are two big complaints one hears, one from the political Left, the other from the political Right, that seem to me especially wrong and unfair and that demand reply.

The Left cannot seem to rid itself of its image of Bush as a giddy, reckless boob ready to plunge the world into war out of ignorance and pique. A small sampler of examples: Democratic congressman Jim Moran of Virginia accused Bush of "reckless rhetoric" after the "axis of evil" speech.* Maureen Dowd of *The New York Times* sniffed at Bush's mix of "insecurity and hauteur."† In November 2001, the civil libertarian Nat Hentoff charged that Bush, "dangerously ignorant of the Constitution" and "terrorized by the terrorists, . . . is abandoning more and

---

* Morton Kondracke, "Bush Was Right to Declare War on 'Axis of Evil,' " *Roll Call*, February 7, 2002, www.rollcall.com/pages/columns/kondracke/00/2002/kond0207.html.

† Maureen Dowd, "Treadmills of His Mind," *New York Times*, August 25, 2002, www.nytimes.com/2002/08/25/opinion/25DOWD.html.

more of the fundamental rights and liberties that he—and his unquestioning subordinates—assured us they were fighting to preserve."* The cartoonist Tom Tomorrow, in drawings reproduced in the *American Prospect* and the *New Yorker,* draws Bush as the befuddled underling of men he calls "Mr. Cheney" and "Mr. Rove."

Similar things are said even less delicately abroad. Gerald Kaufman, a venerable leader of the British Labour Party, grumbled that "Bush, himself the most intellectually backward American president of my political lifetime, is surrounded by advisers whose bellicosity is exceeded only by their political, military and diplomatic illiteracy."† In May, the British newspaper the *Guardian,* though not normally admiring of the Saudi royal family, gleefully quoted remarks of Crown Prince Abdullah in the Saudi press: "[Bush] is the type of person who sleeps at 9:30 P.M. after watching the domestic news. In the morning, he only reads a few lines about what is written on the Middle East and the world due to his huge responsibilities."‡

Yet the record shows that at every turn Bush has behaved with remarkable caution, circumspection, and deliberation. Using only conventional weapons, the armed forces of the United States could have obliterated in any single afternoon after the fall of Kabul not merely Iraqi military power, but Iraq's

---

* Nat Hentoff, "Abandoning the Constitution to Military Tribunals," *Village Voice,* November 21, 2001, www.villagevoice.com/issues/0147/hentoff.php.

† Gerald Kaufman, "Why I Oppose an Attack on Iraq," *Spectator,* August 31, 2002, www.spectator.co.uk.

‡ Matthew Engel, "Bush? He's Nice but Dim, Says Crown Prince," *Guardian,* May 15, 2002, www.guardian.co.uk/bush/story/0,7369,715714,00.html. One cannot help thinking that if more Saudi princes went to bed at 9:30, that monarchy would be in a lot less trouble with its people.

existence as an organized society. But Bush waited and waited and waited. He took time to listen to his allies' views. He developed a war plan that minimized civilian casualties and maximized the odds of incapacitating Saddam's arsenal before it could be used. He built support for the United States among Iraq's opposition groups and took time to build facilities in the region to replace the bases closed to him by the Saudis. He sought and obtained support from Congress and presented his case to the United Nations. To be "reckless" is to refuse to calculate risks rationally. Really, it's an adjective better applied to those who wish to leave Saddam Hussein in place than to George W. Bush.

The complaints of my friends on the Right also must be answered. Given Bush's weak record on the home front, conservatives keep expecting him to "go wobbly" abroad. Actually, they continually suspect that he *has already* gone wobbly.

Many conservatives convinced themselves in the fall of 2001 that Bush did not really mean to fight the Taliban. "There has been at times an eerie lack of urgency in Washington about the Afghan war. . . . A chance to show awe-inspiring, sudden force and joltingly mighty resolution has probably already been lost." So complained the editors of the *Weekly Standard* only days before the fall of Mazar-i-Sharif.*

In the spring of 2002, conservatives spooked themselves that Bush had secretly given up on Iraq. "The blogosphere is in revolt," observed the conservative journalist John O'Sullivan in *National Review Online* on May 28. "The conservative webzines are seething. The cry of 'sell-out' rends the air. And a

---

* Robert Kagan, "Fighting to Win," *Weekly Standard,* November 12, 2001, www.ceip.org/files/publications/standard11-12-01.asp.

dreadful fear spreads among his conservative and neoconservative supporters that George W. Bush may have shrunk back hesitantly from the historical imperative of invading Iraq and replacing Saddam Hussein in Baghdad. The war on terrorism, they lament, just ended—and with a whimper too."*

In the summer of 2002, conservatives complained that Bush deferred too much to the Saudis. "If sucking up to the House of Saud were an Olympic event," wrote *Boston Globe*'s conservative columnist Jeff Jacoby on September 1, "George W. Bush would be a contender for the gold."†

No matter how many times Bush did the brave thing, his conservative supporters inexplicably continued to expect that next time, he would do the weak thing.

. Some of this persistent mistrust can perhaps be blamed on Bush's style of leadership. Bush allowed his cabinet officers wide latitude, and some of them abused that latitude to wage internal war against the president's policies. As late as the end of August 2002, by which time hundreds of American airplanes and thousands of American troops had taken up positions around the Persian Gulf, State Department sources were telling journalists that "it was too early to start enlisting foreign support for an attack on Iraq because President Bush had not yet decided on a course of action."‡ From time to time, the White House would gently remind the secretary of state that he was supposed to execute the president's policies rather than his own—and Colin Powell would rush to complain to his friends in the press that he

* www.nationalreview.com/jos/jos052802.asp.
† Reproduced at www.jewishworldreview.com/jeff/jacoby.html.
‡ Reuters, "State Department in No Hurry to Sell Iraq Campaign," August 27, 2002, www.miami.com/mld/miami/news/politics/3948838.htm.

had been affronted and insulted. All through the month of April, for example, Powell endeavored to persuade Bush to halt Israel's security operations in the West Bank. Bush refused. In Powell's eyes, this refusal could be explained only by crass political imperatives, and somebody close to him shared this unpleasant theory with *The New York Times:* "Karl Rove, President Bush's top political adviser, is expanding his White House portfolio by inserting himself into . . . foreign policy matters, say outside advisers and administration officials, including some who are rankled by his growing involvement. . . . Increasingly, administration officials say, Mr. Rove's involvement has put off Secretary of State Colin L. Powell, who is described by associates as questioning why someone with a background in domestic politics should be an important voice in foreign policy."* Since Bush himself was someone whose background lay also exclusively in domestic politics, Powell's question drew blood. And since everybody in Washington thought they knew that Bush did not tolerate insubordination, the only explanation conservatives could imagine for Powell's survival was that he was *not* insubordinate—that Bush remained genuinely open to the soft-line policies Powell recommended.

Bush exacerbated those bitter doubts by his own disinclination to communicate his thoughts to the public. In his big prepared speeches, Bush exerts himself, often with tremendous success, to explain his plans and intentions to the public. Read George Bush's major speeches—*and nothing else*—and nothing he does will come as a surprise to you. Like Babe Ruth pointing

---

* Richard L. Berke and David E. Sanger, "Some in Administration Grumble as Aide's Role Seems to Expand," *New York Times*, May 13, 2002, www.nytimes.com/2002/05/13/politics/13ROVE.html.

to the stands before hitting his home run, Bush clearly indicates in advance exactly what he will do.

But Bush's more informal remarks can be cryptic, if not unintelligible. When Bush responded to questions about the whereabouts of Osama bin Laden or the administration's plans for Iraq with "I'm a patient man," he was in his own mind reaffirming his intention to take action in a considered, deliberate way. But that sentence could easily be interpreted as a prelude to a wimp-out.

And so many anxious conservatives did interpret it, again and again and again.

THE TERROR AND burden of war were thrust on George W. Bush. To defeat that terror, the United States has been drawn into an ambitious campaign to undo and re-create the repressive and intolerant Middle Eastern status quo. If successful, this campaign will bring new freedom and new stability to the most vicious and violent quadrant of the earth—and new prosperity to us all, by securing the world's largest pool of oil. Successful or not, it is the issue that will define this presidency and this era.

On this issue, Bush's record has been dauntless, far-seeing, and consistent. He announced his war aims at the very beginning, and he has adhered to them steadfastly. He said the United States would fight terrorist groups of international reach with all its power—and it has. He said that any state complicit with terrorism would be regarded as a hostile regime—and so it has been. Afghanistan was first. The others will follow each in its turn.

President Bush immediately understood the war's meaning; recognized how it must be fought; and refused to be satisfied with anything less than victory. He quelled the country's fears, hushed the country's anger, summoned the country's strength, and held the country to its course. He was ambitious in his vision, but careful in his methods; flexible in his relations with Congress, determined in his conduct of the war; stern when sternness was called for, humane when humanity was needed.

I N SEPTEMBER 2002, Bush invited five religious leaders—three Christian, one Jewish, one Muslim—to meet with him in the Oval Office. He wanted them to know that the war on terror had not ended and that some of its hardest battles still lay ahead. Then he asked them to pray for him.

"You know," he said, "I had a drinking problem. Right now I should be in a bar in Texas, not the Oval Office. There is only one reason that I am in the Oval Office and not in a bar. I found faith. I found God. I am here because of the power of prayer."

It was an astonishing moment, more astonishing than the clergymen perhaps appreciated. Bush seldom refers to his drinking days, and almost never acknowledges how close he came to wasting his life altogether. Although he was born to wealth and privilege, up until 1992 his career was, as a biographer said of Winston Churchill's first fifty years, a study in failure. George W. Bush was named for a father who excelled at everything he did: war, athletics, scholastics, business, politics. He tried everything his father had tried—and, well into his forties, succeeded at almost nothing. The younger Bush scraped through Andover and Yale academically, never made a varsity team, earned no distinction in the Air National Guard, and was defeated in a run for Congress in 1978. He lost millions in the oil business and had to be rescued by his father's friends in 1983. It was after that last humiliation that he began drinking hard.

Two of Bush's critics wrote a book that described his life as "short but happy." It was their theory, apparently, that failure stings less if one comes from a family in which everybody else has prospered—or perhaps that only the children of the poor can know bitterness and shame and despair. But in that confessional conversation, Bush told the clergymen that his favorite psalm was Psalm 27, one of the Bible's most searing statements of loneliness and remorse.

> *Hide not thy face from me. Turn not thy servant away in anger, thou who hast been my help. Cast me not off, forsake me not, O God of my salvation! For my father and my mother have forsaken me, but the Lord will take me up.*

The psalms are of course attributed to David, and if you know your Bible, you will remember David's story. The prophet Samuel was ordered to Bethlehem to find a new ruler for Israel from the sons of a farmer named Jesse. Jesse produced seven young men, all of them tall and handsome and strong. Each one passed before Samuel, and each time a voice inside Samuel said no. Puzzled, Samuel asked Jesse, "Are all your sons here?" Jesse acknowledged that there was one more—but he was not of much account, he was small and weak, they used him to tend the goats. "Send and fetch him," the prophet said, and when Samuel saw him, he heard a voice say, "This is he."

There is nothing divine about American political process. Yet leadership remains the greatest mystery in politics. George W. Bush was hardly the obvious man for the job. But by a very strange fate, he turned out to be, of all unlikely things, the right man.

# ACKNOWLEDGMENTS

In February 2000, my two older children, Miranda and Nathaniel, then ages eight and six, happened to see George Bush give a speech on television. One of the Bush's sentences began with the phrase "No school across America . . . "—and that was all they needed to hear. With that promise to abolish school, candidate Bush won himself Miranda's and Nathaniel's absolute endorsement. When I was invited to come work for their hero, they were adamant: I *must* do it. And even as it dawned on them that Bush might not after all keep the vow that originally won their support, that support never wavered—not during the long hours he kept their father at the office, not during the longer hours I spent writing this book. I thank them for their cheerfulness and patience—and their determination to raise their new sister, Beatrice, as a Republican too.

I thank my wise and unflappable editor, Jonathan Karp, and my all-powerful literary agent, Jennifer Rudolph Walsh, for their guidance and their commitment. I am keenly grateful to my conscientious and astute copy editors, Sona Vogel and Steve Messina, and I am honored to have worked with the legendary Ann Godoff.

I have been honored by the friendship of my colleagues in the White House speechwriting department: Michael Gerson, Pete Wehner, Matthew Scully, John McConnell, John Gibson, Charlene Fern, Krista Ritacco, Ed Walsh, Michelle Brawer, and Jen Reilly—altogether the finest presidential writing team since Alexander Hamilton and James Madison collaborated on Washington's Farewell Address. On September 11 and then again after I left the White House, the American Enterprise Institute's president and vice president, Chris DeMuth and David Gerson, gave me the most generous of welcomes. I thank them both. Adam Daifallah of *The New York Sun* surrendered the last week of summer to help me fact-check my final draft; any mistakes that have crept past him are my fault entirely.

My father, Murray Frum, was an enthusiastic early reader, supporter, and confidant. This book is dedicated to him for all that—and a lifetime more besides.

Between us, my wife and I have now written three books in her parents' barn in Prince Edward County, Ontario. Someday, Peter and Yvonne Worthington should open a writers' colony. In the meantime, I thank them for their astounding hospitality, their critical judgment, and their bottomless bottles of gin.

Finally, my wife, Danielle Crittenden Frum: Without her strength and endurance, this book would never have been written. Without her editorial pencil, it would not have been worth reading. Without her, nothing would be worth anything.

# INDEX